The Leadership Walk
by John W. Stanko
Copyright © 2015 John W. Stanko

All rights reserved. This book is protected under the copyright laws of the United States of America. This book may not be copied or reprinted for commercial gain or profit.

Unless otherwise identified, Scripture taken from the HOLY BIBLE, NEW INTERNATIONAL VERSION®. Copyright © 1973, 1978, 1984 by International Bible Society. Used by permission of Zondervan Publishing House. All rights reserved.

ISBN 978-1-63360-017-1
For Worldwide Distribution
Printed in the U.S.A.

PurposeQuest Ink
P.O. Box 8882
Pittsburgh, PA 15221-0882
412.646.2780

Table of Contents

Introduction	v
January	3
February	24
March	45
April	67
May	89
June	111
July	134
August	159
September	183
October	207
November	231
December	255
Appendices	281
End Notes	314
Scripture References	315

INTRODUCTION

The content in this daily devotional represents the fifth consecutive year in which I have written and published a daily devotional. I am not sure how I got so addicted to writing, but I am hooked (in a good way I think) and there is no end in sight. Almost more difficult than writing the devotional is deciding the theme of what to write and then choosing the verses or passages to include. This year's theme actually wasn't difficult to choose, for the work you hold in your hands is actually the culmination of a long-standing desire to write something about leadership because of what I consider a crisis in modern leadership. Let me explain.

There is no lack of leaders, but a biblical philosophy of leadership is often lacking even in the most committed of believers. I have often told audiences at leadership seminars that at one time, leaders were made and formed in the church and then went on into the world. I highlighted many of those leaders in my book The Price of Leadership. Leaders like Florence Nightingale, Booker T. Washington, Sojourner Truth, Martin Luther King and John Wesley had a call to do something that was nurtured and cultivated in the community of faith. When they stepped out to lead, they changed the world in their particular sphere of influence.

I am not sure that same dynamic is present today for it seems that leaders are being made and shaped in the world and then they come to church before or during their leadership development. These leaders already have their leadership philosophy well in place before they begin to consider leadership from a biblical or faith perspective. This has led to a crisis of leadership ethics and faith that has led to the leadership crisis I mentioned earlier.

This devotional is my attempt to equip leaders and potential leaders to consider carefully what the Bible says about leadership. First, I identified 26 areas that I felt were key to being an effective leader from a biblical perspective. That list includes the following: humility, decision making, spiritual growth, personal development, team building, strategy, change people skills, purpose, goals, organization, service, motivation, self-awareness, knowledge, wisdom, influence, power, persuasion, values, ethics, collaboration, relationships, emotional intelligence, coaching, attitude, productivity, finances, time management and rest.

This list was not meant to be exhaustive, but certainly would be the most important from my vantage point. As I was seeking the Lord about this new devotional, I agonized a bit over the title. Should it be *Leadership Talk, Your Leadership Walk, Leadership Wisdom* - but I finally decided on *The Leadership Walk*. I think this title represents what I want to convey - every leader has a unique walk, but there are many principles and lessons that are the same for all leaders. What's more, leaders are always learning and growing, so the walk never ends. And the work can be demanding, so there must be rest along the way.

Every week this past year I wrote six days of devotionals, each one concluding with a *Leadership Step* - some practical action based on the devotional thoughts I wrote. Then on the seventh day, I wrote a post called a *Rest Stop*, which was some thought or concept to consider after six days of leadership work. Obviously

I am following the biblical pattern of work for six days and one day of rest. When I first wrote this devotional and posted it online, I started on Sunday, January 4, so that each Rest Stop was posted on a Saturday. For this printed version, I have started the study on January 1, so obviously your Rest Stop entry may or may not fall on a Saturday or Sunday. I trust you will adapt and apply the rest principles to whatever day you choose to rest.

I must warn you that I did not approach the Rest Stop from the vantage point of a strict observance of the Sabbath day or Sunday. In fact, the most meaningful insight for me in this year-long study has been additional insight into the concept of rest and how it relates to the issue of work and creativity. A day of rest is not to be legalistically observed, but rather used to stimulate creativity and actually perform other acts of kindness or ministry that some may categorize as work not to be done. I disagree. I hope you find my entries as helpful as I found them when I researched and wrote them.

As has become my custom, I included at least one verse from each book of the Bible in this devotional and a summary index is found at the end of this book in case you are looking for what I wrote on a particular verse or passage. I also include in the Appendix some articles that I referenced in the online version of this devotional. By the way, you can still access the online version of this book at www.johnstanko.us

There you have the rationale behind and structure of this devotional called The Leadership Walk. I hope you find it helpful as you develop into the leader that God wants you to be. The Lord has a keen interest in what you do as a leader; may He use this book for His glory to shape you into a world-changer as your partner with God to do great things. Thank you and enjoy the journey as you read through *The Leadership Walk*.

John W. Stanko
Pittsburgh, PA
January 1, 2015

The Leadership Walk

Humility — January 1

"I hope in the Lord Jesus to send Timothy to you soon, that I also may be cheered when I receive news about you. I have no one else like him, who will show genuine concern for your welfare. For everyone looks out for their own interests, not those of Jesus Christ. But you know that Timothy has proved himself, because as a son with his father he has served with me in the work of the gospel. I hope, therefore, to send him as soon as I see how things go with me" - Philippians 2:19-23.

Paul had many who were part of his team, but only one like Timothy. This indicates that great leaders are rare. Look at the things that set Timothy apart and helped make him a good follower *and* leader in Paul's eyes. Timothy learned to humble himself and put others' interests ahead of his own. What's more, his concern for others was genuine - it was not fake or self-serving. Leaders who want to be truly great must learn to emulate Timothy, while realizing the journey away from self-interest to care for others is a difficult one.

LEADERSHIP STEP: *Your Step today is to take 10 minutes to reflect on today's passage. What leadership traits from Timothy's life do you see mentioned in this passage? How do you see humility working in Timothy's life? What part of Paul's description do you want to make part of your own leadership style? Paul only saw one such leader in his lifetime; what will it take for you be the one that others meet who fits this description?*

Decision Making — January 2

"When I heard these things, I sat down and wept. For some days I mourned and fasted and prayed before the God of heaven" - Nehemiah 1:4.

One of the key roles for leaders is to make decisions or to help others makes decisions. One leadership expert stated that leaders make 'life and death' decisions, for often those decisions affect people, whether they stay or go, are successful or not, or have the resources or work with little. Even family leaders make decisions that affect not just this generation but also the ones following. Nehemiah had a decision to make, and started the process by intensely seeking the Lord through prayer and fasting.

LEADERSHIP STEP: *As you begin the New Year, your Step today is to set aside some time this month to fast and pray. When you fast, first seek some information on how to do it properly (assuming your medical condition permits). If you can't fast from food, perhaps you can from television or newspapers and use that time to pray and read God's word, specifically about some decisions you have to make.*

Communication   January 3

"I, Paul, write this greeting in my own hand"
- 1 Corinthians 16:21.

Communication is important for any leader, and personalizing communication can be special to those who receive it. A handwritten note, personal email, greeting card or even a personal visit from a busy leader can make a deep and lasting impact. With today's social media options, the opportunities to do what Paul did - include his own mark and energy into his letter - are endless. Yet if you are going to use social media, do not have someone do it for you! Take the time to create and send your own posts, letters or emails.

LEADERSHIP STEP: *Your Step today is to write someone and encourage them. Then make it part of your weekly ritual to communicate personally with someone important* in your world. What's more, you need to establish a social media philosophy for how you will use that media to improve your communication. Use it for more than trivial personal updates, but to share important information about who you are and what you do.

Spiritual Growth   January 4

"This day I call the heavens and the earth as witnesses against you that I have set before you life and death, blessings and curses. Now choose life, so that you and your children may live and that you may love the Lord your God, listen to his voice, and hold fast to him . . . ."
- Deuteronomy 31:19-20a.

Leaders are not in a special class all by themselves. The Lord expects them to follow Him and His ways no matter what or whom they are leading, regardless of how small or large the enterprise is. The first priority of leaders is to serve Him and His purposes, keeping in mind that they will be held accountable and will reap what they sow. If they don't heed this warning, there are not only repercussions for them and their organization, but for their families as well.

LEADERSHIP STEP: *Your Step today is to reflect on your leadership world, whether it is business, ministry, or family. Are you being true to the Lord in what you do, following the precepts in His Word? Are you reflecting His love in your actions and words? Has an attitude crept into your thinking that, because you are the 'boss,' you can lord it over others? Are you choosing life and blessings in every situation?*

Personal Development   January 5

"For this very reason, make every effort to add to your faith goodness; and to goodness, knowledge; and to

knowledge, self-control; and to self-control, perseverance; and to perseverance, godliness; and to godliness, mutual affection; and to mutual affection, love. For if you possess these qualities in increasing measure, they will keep you from being ineffective and unproductive in your knowledge of our Lord Jesus Christ" - 2 Peter 1:5-8.

When a leader stops growing, a leader stops leading. At that point, leaders start to rely on their past accomplishments or job title to establish leadership. The four key words in this passage are 'effort,' 'increasing,' 'ineffective,' and 'unproductive.' Leaders must make a sustained effort to grow, which means that personal development must be their top priority. Done properly, that effort will help them be both effective and productive as a leader - they will do right things and do them well.

LEADERSHIP STEP: *Your Step today is map out your plan for personal and professional development. What classes are you taking? What books are you reading? What seminars do you plan to attend? What new skills are you developing? Give some thought to these questions today and then map out a plan for the coming year that will enable you to grow with a view toward being effective and productive.*

Team Building   January 6

"Now in the church at Antioch there were prophets and teachers: Barnabas, Simeon called Niger, Lucius of Cyrene, Manaen (who had been brought up with Herod the tetrarch) and Saul. While they were worshiping the Lord and fasting, the Holy Spirit said, 'Set apart for me Barnabas and Saul for the work to which I have called them.' So after they had fasted and prayed, they placed their hands on them and sent them off" - Acts 13:1-3.

After Jesus, no one impacted the New Testament church

more significantly than Paul. Paul was a great leader, but he never functioned alone. He always traveled and worked with a team. In this passage, one sees that Paul was with a team in Antioch when the Holy Spirit spoke and established a new team made up of him and Barnabas to do missions work. That team emerged from a team, for truly all are smarter than one and that holds true for the family, business, or ministry.

LEADERSHIP STEP: *Your Step today is to take a moment to assess your teamwork. First, if you are leading a team or teams, how healthy are they? Do you have the correct people on them? Are you carrying or covering for dead weight? As a member of a team, are you being a good and effective team member? Finally, if you are not building or part of a team, are you being most effective by going solo? Why are you working alone?*

Rest Stop 1   January 7

"Then he said to them, 'The Sabbath was made for man, not man for the Sabbath'" - Mark 2:27.

God rested on the seventh day, not because He was tired, but because He was establishing a pattern for man to work hard, stop to replenish and refresh to enjoy what has been done and then to begin again. The principle was not to establish a holy day, but to establish a holy cycle of work and rest, work and rest, rest and work. The Sabbath day was made for man to enjoy and worship and not for man to slavishly observe legalistic rituals or work stoppages.

LEADERSHIP STEP: *There is a saying, "Word hard, play hard, rest hard." Your Step today is to ask yourself some questions. Are you earning your rest times through diligent work? When you shut down, are you doing things that refresh and strengthen you? Do you feel refreshed after your* down time? What can you do to establish a cycle in your life of work and rest, work and rest? Is the Lord included in those rest times as you worship and are immersed in His Word?

Strategy   January 8

"As soon as you hear the sound of marching in the tops of the poplar trees, move out to battle, because that will mean God has gone out in front of you to strike the Philistine army" - 1 Chronicles 14:15.

Leaders must help develop and implement strategies for any decision an organization makes, whether it is family, ministry or business. In today's verse, the Lord gave David a strategy for battle and it was supernatural. David prayed for it, God gave it and then expected David to follow it if he wanted and expected success. That strategy was clear and simple, but unlike any other strategy David had received.

LEADERSHIP STEP: *Your goals and plans are useless without strategies for how to accomplish them. These strategies must be as simple or complex as the task requires, and should be clearly communicated and understood by your teammates, members or family. Today's Step is to ask yourself the following questions: In what area of your leadership direction is the strategy unclear or insufficient? Whom do you need to convene to develop a new strategy or better communicate the old one?*

Change   January 9

"He who was seated on the throne said, 'I am making everything new!' Then he said, 'Write this down, for these words are trustworthy and true'" - Revelation 21:5.

Change and progress are God's plan for mankind. Man often perverts the purpose for the change toward selfish reasons, but change is to be a positive, God-inspired part of life. Leaders lead change initiatives, first providing a vivid picture or vision of the new reality and the reasons for pursuing it. Then they help equip people to be successful in the changes. Leaders who have a godly perspective on change can count on His help in the process.

LEADERSHIP STEP: *The next Step in your leadership walk is to consider a change initiative in your family or organization. Are you prepared to lead that change? Before you do, make sure you are clear about what kind of change you want. Take some time today to write out the change. What will it look like when it's done? Be specific, so then you can graphically explain the end you have in mind to those who will be most impacted and affected.*

People Skills   January 10

> *"His name was Nabal and his wife's name was Abigail. She was an intelligent and beautiful woman, but her husband was surly and mean in his dealings—he was a Calebite"* - 1 Samuel 25:3.

Abigail was intelligent and knew how to work with people. Her husband had terrible people skills and almost brought calamity down on himself and his family if his wife had not intervened. No matter what entity leaders lead, they are leading people. Therefore people skills are perhaps the most critical leaders can develop and hone. Those people skills start with leaders understanding themselves and their own heart, which gives them a foundation and perspective from which they can begin to understand others.

LEADERSHIP STEP: *There are many personality assessment tools available, like Myers Briggs, DISC, Enneagram and a host of variations. It should not be too hard to find someone who can administer one of these to you, or perhaps you can* even do it online. Your Step is to start amassing information about who you are and how you relate to other personalities and life situations. This will help you skillfully deal with the people issues that come your way as a leader.

Purpose   January 11

"Moses thought that his own people would realize that God was using him to rescue them, but they did not" - Acts 7:25.

Moses knew his purpose and that was the foundation or basis for his leadership. He realized what God had called him to do and he began to do it, albeit in the wrong manner - his first strategy was to kill an Egyptian. Perhaps he thought he could wipe out the whole Egyptian army singlehandedly! When leaders know their God-given purpose, they will still need God-given strength and strategies to fulfill it. Yet purpose is the starting point for meaningful and godly leadership. Moses had it and went on to change history as God's purpose partner.

LEADERSHIP STEP: *Your Step today in your leadership walk is to take some time to reflect on your purpose. Are you clear as to what it is? Purpose requires different thinking than career, so you will need to approach it with a different mindset. Identify a book, website, article or a seminar that can help you clarity purpose, and then order or register for it. You may want to obtain a purpose journal so you can record your purpose thoughts as you seek to clarify what it is.*

Goals   January 12

"I press on toward the goal to win the prize for which God has called me heavenward in Christ Jesus" - Philippians 3:14.

This verse describes the anatomy of a goal. The first concept is that a goal helps leaders to press on. That means there is something pressing against the organization - resistance to change, economic concerns, uncertainty - and the goal helps leaders and their teams press back with greater force and energy so progress can be made. Goals harness energy, and that energy can be used to overcome the inertia and obstacles that oppose change and achievement.

*LEADERSHIP STEP: Today's Step is to think about your organization's goals? Is your team clear on the goals you are pursuing? Are **you** clear and precise? Do you have goals to help you 'press on'? Meet with your team, your family or maybe just spend some time alone and determine if you have the kind of clarity of goals that has everyone pulling in the same direction. If not, then it's time to go back to the vision and set goals to help achieve that end.*

Organization   January 13

"Not only was the Teacher wise, but he also imparted knowledge to the people. He pondered and searched out and set in order many proverbs" - Ecclesiastes 12:9.

The Teacher in this verse was not only a wise teacher, but he was also a good researcher and skilled organizer. God wants to expand every leader's sphere of influence, but their lack of organization where time and things are concerned can hinder their growth, and even cause their influence to shrink and be less than it can be. If they are spending large amounts of time going through work to get to work, if they are resisting new opportunities because they don't know how to organize their world, then they are thwarting God's plan for their lives - all because they can't or won't organize.

LEADERSHIP STEP: The next Step on your leadership journey is to consider organization. Is your inability to organize the 'more' God sends you costing you your leadership effectiveness? If the answer is 'yes,' then it's time to change or you will continue to miss opportunities for growth and promotion. Find someone in your world and get their input on what you can do to better organize your time, work tools or work schedule. Once you have talked to that person, repeat that process again and again.

Rest Stop 2   January 14

"Then Jesus asked them, 'Which is lawful on the Sabbath: to do good or to do evil, to save life or to kill?' But they remained silent" - Mark 3:4.

Jesus challenged the Jews to think about how they were approaching their Sabbath day of rest. They had defined it as a day to do nothing much but maintain the basic functions like eating or worship. Jesus was trying to expand their thinking that it was permissible to do good deeds on the Sabbath, for in doing good deeds, they would be doing what God Himself does, not just on the Sabbath, but every day. Leaders should also take your times of rest to consider how to meet the needs of others and to address those needs where they have the opportunity and authority to do so.

LEADERSHIP STEP: *Rather than focusing on your own needs as you rest this week, consider the needs of someone else. Visit someone in the hospital, write them a get well card, sit down and write a check to an organization helping those in need, or spend some time praying for those in your world who could use God's touch or care. Perhaps even visit an elderly family member who would be blessed by your presence.*

Service   January 15

"... just as the Son of Man did not come to be served, but to serve, and to give his life as a ransom for many" - Matthew 20:28.

Jesus was the consummate leader, yet He did not come to do anything but to serve both His Father and His people. You are called to follow Him, so that means if you are to lead, you must learn how to serve. That service must be more than being polite. On the contrary, you must learn how to use your power to empower others rather to build a kingdom for yourself or your cause. What's more, Jesus did not serve a few but many and you too must be willing to serve many people according to the call that God has bestowed on you.

LEADERSHIP STEP: *It is easy for a leader to be served, for the leader can expect it and the people can hope to garner the leader's favor. Don't allow that to happen! Instead of being served, make your Step today that you will serve others with the power you have as a leader (or the power you will have when you become one). Develop and write out a servant strategy for how you can serve others effectively and in ways that will please God.*

Motivation   January 16

"Do all that you have in mind," his armor-bearer said. "Go ahead; I am with you heart and soul"
- 1 Samuel 14:7.

Jonathan set a daring goal of scaling the cliffs to attack the Philistines, and it inspired his armor-bearer to follow. Note that the armor-bearer did not have to go; he enthusiastically chose to risk his life to follow Jonathan. The results were astonishing, for those two did what the entire army of Israel was unable to do. Leaders motivate people through their example, and then they harness the energy to go in a direction that is best for the organization and ultimately in the best interests of the followers as well.

LEADERSHIP STEP: *Today's Step is look at your team's'*

motivation. First of all, do you have any followers? If so, how would you assess their level of motivation - high, medium or low? There is no better way to know than to ask them point blank. Then determine if you are doing what you can as a leader to direct their energy into projects and goals to which they willingly devote themselves. Then check your own heart to see just how motivated you are for the tasks at hand.

Self-Awareness   January 17

"But Peter declared, 'Even if I have to die with you, I will never disown you.' And all the other disciples said the same" - Matthew 26:35.

Peter was convinced of his own loyalty and commitment, and so were the other disciples. They were sincere, but sincerely wrong! Where did they go wrong? Those men were not in touch with the true state of their hearts, their inner being, and it caused them to make statements they could not back up in reality. Leaders must do necessary internal work to be in touch with their heart condition and take steps to address whatever is found there. This is part of a process called personal or leadership development.

LEADERSHIP STEP: *Are you walking in self-awareness? There is a process called a 360-degree profile that gathers information from a number of people close to you and then gives you feedback about your current state of leadership skills and heart matters. Today's Step is to find someone to administer this for you. But watch out! It is like taking a spiritual x-ray and will show you the reality that others see every day, but you may not.*

Knowledge   January 18

"The discerning heart seeks knowledge, but the mouth of a fool feeds on folly" - Proverbs 15:14.

When a leader stops learning, that leader stops growing, and eventually stops leading. When that happens, leaders begin to rely on their authority-power - the "I-am-in-charge" mentality - or their history – "I have done so much for this organization that you owe me" - or deception - avoiding tough decisions under the guise of gathering more information or "waiting on the Lord." There is only one way to seek knowledge and that is to study and learn, especially learning from mistakes - your own or those made by others. Knowledge without effort to pay the price is impossible.

LEADERSHIP STEP: What are you doing to seek knowledge? There are obviously many paths that include classes, a new degree, a reading program, seminars, a mentor, travel to see another company's operations, and sabbatical leaves specifically to gather new knowledge. Which one of these do you have or engage in regularly? Today's Step is to make a plan to engage one of those paths that will be new for you (like going back to school) and then do it.

Wisdom   January 19

". . . let the wise listen and add to their learning, and let the discerning get guidance" - Proverbs 1:5.

Yesterday we discussed knowledge and today we look at wisdom. Leaders must amass and develop wisdom, which is knowledge practically applied to life situations, usually situations that leaders have never faced before. Today's verse indicates one way to get wisdom and that is to "listen." To what do leaders listen? First, they listen to other people, especially those who have done something similar to what leaders are attempting to do. Then they listen to their heart, for if they have developed their heart, it will speak to them. Finally, and most importantly, they listen to the Lord, who will speak through His still small voice and His word.

LEADERSHIP STEP: Have you ever gone to a party or

meeting, been introduced to people and immediately forget their names. Your Step today is to make an effort from this day forward to listen to, use and remember people's names. Why is it important to do this? Because it is a practical way to help you sharpen and develop your listening skills. Work on names and hearing wisdom will not be far behind!

Influence   January 20

"Therefore, although in Christ I could be bold and order you to do what you ought to do, yet I prefer to appeal to you on the basis of love" - Philemon 8.

There is no question that at times a leader must tell, even order, others to do something. Yet when possible, there is a better way, and it is described in today's verse. Leaders can take the time and make the effort to *influence* others to do the correct thing. The problem for some leaders who are addicted to action is that influence can take time and it requires effort to fashion the most effective appeal possible. Yet people who have some say in the decision are much more likely to commit all their intellectual and creative capabilities when they do so willingly.

LEADERSHIP STEP: *Are you relying too much on your authority and ordering people under you to do this and that? Today's Step is to borrow a page from Paul's book and begin to find ways to influence people to decide for themselves to take the right course of action. Yet this requires that you know your team and learn what motivates them to action. Your step today is to schedule some team-building time where you can learn more about what motivates and demotivates the people who report to you.*

Rest Stop 3   January 21

"He went to Nazareth, where he had been brought up, and

on the Sabbath day he went into the synagogue, as was his custom. He stood up to read, . . ." - Luke 4:16.

Jesus had a custom, as did all Jews, of going to the synagogue on the Sabbath day. For them, it was a day, not just to hang around or do nothing, but a day to break from their regular routine to worship God and focus on Him. While they broke from their regular daily routine, they had another routine for the Sabbath day. This gave them a rhythm to their lives that enabled them to work hard and worship regularly. Added to that were the regular holidays and holy days that provided some customs passed down from generation to generation that also helped shape their rest and work lives.

LEADERSHIP STEP: *Is there a rhythm to your life? Is every week different, or do you have a pattern you don't have to think about that you can just flow? Does that rhythm include worship and family time? Your Step today is to* **commit** *to a church or, if you must work on Sunday, to find some acceptable worship alternative on your day off, and maintain that commitment to develop your own rest/work rhythm.*

Power   January 22

"So even if I boast somewhat freely about the authority the Lord gave us for building you up rather than tearing you down, I will not be ashamed of it" - 2 Corinthians 10:8.

Authority is another word for power, and there is no question that leaders have some measure of power. Leaders cannot be ambivalent about this power or try to avoid it. What they can do is learn how to use that power in the correct way, and that is to build up and empower other people around them. In other words, their job is to give their power away, and then watch the Lord replenish it with even more power - but only if they use it for the good of others and their organization. One leadership author has stated that leaders are 'ridiculously in charge.' That means they have the authority to promote change, help people and launch initiatives - not build a personal kingdom.

LEADERSHIP STEP: *Are you fearful or ashamed of your position, power and authority? Don't be! Are you using your power for all God intended? In the Appendix you will find my leadership philosophy. Read it and write your guidelines for how you will use the power of your position for the good of others and the organization. Once you have it, live by it and refer back to it regularly to evaluate how you are doing.*

Persuasion   January 23

"Then Agrippa said to Paul, 'Do you think that in such a short time you can persuade me to be a Christian?' Paul replied, 'Short time or long—I pray to God that not only you but all who are listening to me today may become what I am, except for these chains'" - Acts 26:28-29.

Paul was in chains, but he was making a strong case that almost persuaded Agrippa to become a believer. On occasions, leaders issue orders. It is much more effective, however, if people buy in to the idea, decision or concept. That requires the leader to paint a vivid picture of the need for or benefit of a new reality. To do that, leaders must have credibility, good communication skills, and understand the people with whom they are working. That requires work, which is why some leaders just fall back on a command-and-control style of leadership - it takes less time and the leader is sure to gain compliance, at least temporarily.

LEADERSHIP STEP: *The Bible has much to say about the tongue, especially the book of Proverbs. Your Step today is to do a quick study of the words 'lips' and 'speech' in Proverbs. You can use the online program BibleGateway.com to* conduct this search. Just put those words in the search box and print the results. Take this list with you this week and study what it says about effective and influential speech.

Values   January 24

"Surely you remember, brothers and sisters, our toil and hardship; we worked night and day in order not to be a burden to anyone while we preached the gospel of God to you" - 1 Thessalonians 2:9.

Paul worked a full-time job whenever he went into a new place to spread the gospel so he would not be a financial burden to his new converts, and also so he would not be confused with teachers who traveled the Greek world teaching secular subjects for pay. He wanted people to know he was on a different mission than those other teachers. He did this because it was part of a personal values system that guided his daily decisions on ministry, finances, learning and work. All leaders also have a values system, and those values will make them productive servants, overbearing tyrants or a leader someplace between those two possibilities.

LEADERSHIP STEP: *To ensure that your values are taking you in the correct leadership direction toward service and team building, your Step today is to sketch out your values and put them in order of priority. You can start this today and then revisit and refine this list the next time values are discussed in this devotional. Visit the Appendix to view a sample list of values to help you get started that explains how to produce them. Don't put this off!*

Ethics   January 25

"Like a muddied spring or a polluted well are the righteous who give way to the wicked" - Proverbs 25:26.

The Leadership Walk

From time to time, the media focus on ethical lapses in business or government. Usually a leader has succumbed to temptation and perpetrated some scheme that costs taxpayers, employees or customers millions of dollars. At other times, followers suffer under the oppressive hand of a despotic government, cruel supervisor or dictatorial pastor. In every case, it is faulty ethics that causes the leader to go awry and the people to suffer loss or pain. Leaders must have an ethical code that is constantly maturing to meet the temptations the Internet age presents.

LEADERSHIP STEP: *Who or what is influencing your ethical concepts and approach to leadership? Yesterday's Step was to identify values you will follow in your leadership and life roles. Continue working on those values today, and then do a self-assessment of how faithfully you are applying those values. Talk is cheap where ethics are concerned; right action is what matters most, so choose one area from your list and ask, "How am I doing?"*

Collaboration   January 26

"Jonathan climbed up, using his hands and feet, with his armor-bearer right behind him. The Philistines fell before Jonathan, and his armor-bearer followed and killed behind him" - 1 Samuel 14:13.

Jonathan had a bold plan to attack the Philistines, but he needed help from his assistant to carry it out. No matter how bold leadership's vision is, they need others to help make the vision a reality. Thus leaders need to learn how to collaborate with others - to be open to the input, assistance and expertise of others. This may require that leaders adjust their original vision as others contribute their own perspective. This is one sure way for leaders to secure buy-in from others so that the work will truly be a team effort.

LEADERSHIP STEP: *How well do you collaborate with others? Your Step today is to make a list of all those who are part of a team you lead. Then journal your thoughts as to how well you are involving others in your leadership vision. Next, ask them point blank how involved they feel, and compare their evaluation with yours to see how accurate you were. Finally, make adjustments to bring the two perspectives together to ensure you are maximizing your collaboration.*

Relationships   January 27

"When Jesus came to the region of Caesarea Philippi, he asked his disciples, 'Who do people say the Son of Man is?'" - Matthew 16:13.

Jesus took his disciples off on a retreat to a remote area and there he asked them a question about His true identity. The answers ranged from the absurd to the recognition that He was the Messiah. The point is that the disciples were free enough in their relationship with Jesus to tell Him anything and not be rejected. What's more, in the midst of the silly answers came true insight and revelation. Leaders must develop that kind of relationship with their peers, followers and their oversight so that honest communication can benefit the team and the organization.

LEADERSHIP STEP: *Your next Step is to consider an off-site meeting with your family, staff or leadership team. Perhaps you can set up a special outing, such as a sports event or concert. The goal is not only to have fun, but also to build trusting relationships that can engage in honest and open communication from which people and the organization can grow and flourish.*

Rest Stop 4   January 28

"How much more valuable is a person than a sheep!

The Leadership Walk

Therefore it is lawful to do good on the Sabbath"
- Matthew 12:12.

The Jews had an elaborate system that described and limited what anyone could do on the Sabbath day. That led them to actually limit or restrict the good deeds anyone could consider doing on the Sabbath. Jesus confronted their system to set the day free from the legalism that had become attached to it. In setting the day free, He really wanted to set the people free from the false interpretations of what that day meant and why it existed. Leaders must always work to set people free from the limiting thoughts and beliefs that bind their behavior and practice.

LEADERSHIP STEP: *Take some time today to reflect on and evaluate your work world, whether it is in school, ministry, business or family. Are there any beliefs or customs that are actually limiting the freedom, joy and creativity of those closest to you? What can you do to change that and set them free? Where do **you** need to be set free where your work and play habits are concerned?*

Emotional Intelligence   January 29

"Some men brought to him a paralyzed man, lying on a mat. When Jesus saw their faith, he said to the man, 'Take heart, son; your sins are forgiven'" - Matthew 9:2.

Jesus always paid attention, especially to people and their condition or emotional state. In the case in today's verse, He was teaching but he "saw" the faith of those who brought the man to be healed. It is easy to get so immersed in the things of leadership that the people in the leader's world can become a means to an end. In leadership circles, this is called 'emotional intelligence,' which is awareness of what is going on in the leader's heart as well as in the minds and hearts of those around the leader.

LEADERSHIP STEP: *If you have never encountered the term 'emotional intelligence,' there is a large body of work done on the subject. If you are familiar, perhaps it's time for a refresher. Either way, your Step today is to read any of the introductory articles that can be found online. Another possibility is to re-read a book or article you already have on the subject. The important thing, however, is that you begin to apply the principles to your own life today.*

Coaching   January 30

"The way of fools seems right to them, but the wise listen to advice" - Proverbs 12:15.

Leaders are not islands who have everything they need to be effective. Even the best leaders have advisers and counselors - those who help them frame their thinking and decisions in the best possible terms. These coaches also help leaders personally develop their leadership, business and people skills. Once they appreciate the role of coaches, these leaders who were coached become coaches themselves, looking to reproduce their own effectiveness in others.

LEADERSHIP STEP: *Make a list of all the coaches and mentors in your leadership life right now - even if your leadership is currently limited to your own home as the next Step in your Leadership Walk. Are you making optimal use of those people at this point in time? What can you do to maximize their impact on your leadership? In what areas of personal development do you need some new coaching expertise? Can this be done through a reading program?*

Attitude   January 31

"In your relationships with one another, have the same mindset as Christ Jesus . . ." - Philippians 2:5.

An attitude, like that of an airplane, is the direction someone is leaning when compared to a fixed point, like the horizon. Leaders have attitudes toward people, projects or duties, either leaning into them with a positive or away from with a negative attitude. Leaders must work to develop and maintain a positive attitude, just like Jesus, toward service, humility and team relationships. Thus the directive in this verse is not just for church leaders. It is for **all** leaders, who should ask God's help to have the correct attitude in every situation, including a negative attitude toward bad leadership behavior.

LEADERSHIP STEP: *Today's Step is to assess your attitude toward the various aspects of your leadership walk. On a scale of 1 to 5 (with 5 being the highest), rate your attitude in the following areas: team relationships, humility, service, learning new things, encouraging others, honesty and integrity, and exercise (feel free to add others). What are the areas in which ranked lowest? What are you going to do to improve your attitude in those areas of life and work?*

Productivity   February 1

"... so that you may live a life worthy of the Lord and please him in every way: bearing fruit in every good work, growing in the knowledge of God, ..." - Colossians 1:10.

Leaders should keep growing and developing in three areas: in their ability to bear fruit as defined by their role; in their knowledge of their line of work; and in the practice of leadership. When leaders stop being fruitful, they begin to rely on their history, their title, where they are in the organizational hierarchy, their charisma, or their ability to manipulate and control the system or their followers. This is never a healthy situation, whether in the church or in business. It is obvious from today's verse that ongoing growth and fruitfulness are pleasing to God, who is the ultimate Director and Evaluator of any leader's development and work.

LEADERSHIP STEP: Your Step today is to inspect your fruit and the 'vine' on which it is produced. Read John 15:1-8 and then examine your fruit, both internally and externally. Are you growing in patience and kindness? Are you being fruitful recently in new projects, creativity and the ability to lead your team or family? Are you growing in the knowledge of who God is and what He wants from you in your leadership role?

Finances — February 2

"Be shepherds of God's flock that is under your care, watching over them—not because you must, but because you are willing, as God wants you to be; not pursuing dishonest gain, but eager to serve;" - 1 Peter 5:2.

This verse obviously addresses church leaders, but there are principles that apply to any godly leader, whether in or out of church. One of the principles is how a leader relates to money and compensation. Leaders who do what they are hired to do solely for money are called hirelings in biblical terms, no matter how noble the work. Leadership should be compensated fairly and well for expertise and experience they bring, but must be motivated first and foremost by a desire to serve - money should not be the top priority.

LEADERSHIP STEP: *What would you do if you had all the money you needed to survive? If you answer that you would do what you are doing right now, then you are in the right place, and money is not your motivator. If you answer that you would do something else, then you must ask yourself if you are doing what you do now strictly for the money. If that's the case, your Step today is to meditate on whether or not it's time to find something else to do.*

Time Management — February 3

> *"But do not forget this one thing, dear friends: With the Lord a day is like a thousand years, and a thousand years are like a day" - 2 Peter 3:8.*

If a day is like a 1,000 years, then an hour would be like 46 years and a minute like nine months. Therefore, if the Lord says He will be there in just a minute, it may take longer than expected! Yet the opposite is also true; something that one thought would take nine months can happen or require much less time than anticipated. Leaders know how to have faith for time. They don't procrastinate for fear they don't have enough time to do something well or at all. Leaders also know how to invest time in a long-range goal, putting off immediate gratification for long-term gain.

LEADERSHIP STEP: *Time is the most precious possession for any leader. Therefore, it is important to know where your time is going, just like your money. In the Appendix is a time inventory sheet for you to copy. Your Step today is to choose three days next week (or you can start today) to keep track of your time in half-hour segments. At the end of the three days, add it all up to see where you can adjust how you are spending your time. You can do it for more than three days but make sure you don't procrastinate!*

Rest Stop 5 — February 4

> *"For the Son of Man is Lord of the Sabbath" - Matthew 12:8.*

Leaderships' rest days do not belong to the leader. It is not their day to do only what they want, but is rather another day under the Lordship of Christ. He has the right to guide and direct it, just like He does the other days. The beauty of the day, however, is that God has 'programmed' leaders to do what He wants by giving them joy in the doing, so the Sabbath rest can be one where leaders pursue their joy in hobbies, travel, sporting events or family visits. Yet His Lordship will almost always direct leaders toward a worship expression during their rest times as well.

LEADERSHIP STEP: *As today's Step, pursue something joyful without guilt. Do you have a hobby? Maybe this is time to start one. Is there a family member you can visit today, establishing a tradition to visit them regularly on your day of rest? Don't forget worship; even if your day of rest is not on a Sunday, what can do you refresh yourself in the Lord? Remember, this day is not exclusively "yours" to do nothing, but to pursue meaningful activity that is restful for you.*

Humility — February 5

"The Lord detests all the proud of heart. Be sure of this: They will not go unpunished" - Proverbs 16:5.

Pride in leadership is a blinding force, causing them to believe anything good that's happened is because of them and their ideas and behaviors. When they believe they can replicate what they have done anywhere at any time, it turns into something called *hubris*. Hubris says, "Whatever I or we want to do, it is a guaranteed success, because I am or we are special!" Pride is bad enough, but hubris sends God a special invitation to get involved to thwart any hubris-inspired project from succeeding. When that happens, the proud are often punished for their arrogance.

LEADERSHIP STEP: *Today's Step involves a pride/hubris check to ensure you have not crossed over into this dangerous territory. The antidote for pride is humility and that is an attitude you must cultivate to prevent pride from morphing into hubris. The check is simple: how often do you thank God for your success? And then, how do you express your thanks* to others, without which you would be and do nothing? Regularly saying" thank you" is a great check against pride.

Decision Making   February 6

"Suppose one of you wants to build a tower. Won't you first sit down and estimate the cost to see if you have enough money to complete it?" - Luke 14:28.

When leaders approach a decision, they must first be clear on what they want to accomplish – in today's verse, it is to build a tower. Then they need to 'sit down,' which means stepping away from the adrenaline of the day to be rational and circumspect - either alone or with trusted advisers. Then they must estimate what that decision will cost in terms of manpower and money. Finally, they need to determine where they will get the resources to complete the task. That decision-making process involves both rational and intuitive skills, both of which can be developed and honed over time.

LEADERSHIP STEP: *Today's Step requires that you examine a decision that you recently made - or didn't make. Did you walk through the five steps outlined above - vision, 'sit down,' estimate the cost, determine availability of resources, and impact of final decision? Did you walk through this alone, or did you seek out advisers and counselors to assist you in the process? Would you do anything differently if you had followed this process? On which of the steps do you need to improve?*

Communication   February 7

"A good man brings good things out of the good stored up in his heart, and an evil man brings evil things out of the evil stored up in his heart. For the mouth speaks what the heart is full of" - Luke 6:45.

Leaders can study the technical side of communications and become proficient in email, podcasting, live streaming, video conferencing and publishing. Yet the Bible is clear that proficiency in communications is a heart matter, not just a skill matter. If leaders want to produce good communication, they must have a good heart - not a perfect one, but a heart that is open, honest and aware of its condition and need for the Lord. The spoken, sung or written words that come from a leader's mouth are an expression of a leader's heart.

LEADERSHIP STEP: *What condition is your heart in these days? You can tell by the words you are uttering or writing. If you are not encouraging others, accept that it is a heart matter and ask God to show you the root cause. If you are being critical or sarcastic, it's a heart matter and not just a matter of controlling your tongue. Today's Step is to ask God to help you face and deal with your heart so that your leadership communication will improve.*

Spiritual Growth — February 8

"Now when Daniel learned that the decree had been published, he went home to his upstairs room where the windows opened toward Jerusalem. Three times a day he got down on his knees and prayed, giving thanks to his God, just as he had done before" - Daniel 6:10.

The source of Daniel's leadership skill and wisdom was obviously his prayer life. When his enemies wanted to trap him, they knew exactly where to go and what to look for - they focused on his spirituality as expressed in prayer. And Daniel did not disappoint them, leading to his arrest and overnight stay in the lion's den. The source of his persecution, however, became the source of his deliverance and God intervened in the plot to save Daniel's life and promote him yet again during his Babylonian service.

LEADERSHIP STEP: *There is no substitute for prayer. You can't read about it, get a bigger journal or attend a prayer seminar. Those things may help, but you still have to put in the time on your knees. Many people overcommit to prayer ("I am going to pray an hour a day!") and cannot maintain it, so your Step today is to start slowly. What if you commit to pray five minutes every day for the next week, with your journal open before you?*

Personal Development   February 9

"Do you see someone skilled in their work? They will serve before kings; they will not serve before officials of low rank" - Proverbs 22:29.

Success is no accident nor is promotion always a political or random act. God does not promote leaders with potential. He promotes people who have worked hard to **develop** the potential that He assigned them. That development is referred to as personal or professional growth, and takes place through practice, training, education, mistakes, learning from mistakes and more practice. This produces what's called skill and customers and companies pay good money for skill, and the leaders who develop it earn a reputation that leads to more promotion and more responsibility.

LEADERSHIP STEP: *Obtaining skill is never random. It requires focus, a plan, diligence and time. Author Malcolm Gladwell maintains that it requires 10,000 hours of effort to become an expert in anything, and "expert" is another word for skilled. Forgetting how young or old you are, your Step today is to decide what area of work (or play) you would like to invest 10,000 hours? How many years will this require? What activities will fill those 10,000 hours? What will you do when you have finished?*

Team Building — February 10

"Then Moses set out with Joshua his aide, and Moses went up on the mountain of God" - Exodus 24:13.

Moses started out alone when God called him to go back to Egypt to lead His people to the Promised Land. Before Moses left, God gave him Aaron as his spokesman. Later God assigned Joshua to be Moses' assistant. And after that, Moses team was expanded to include both faithful men who helped him administer the people and the priests who would oversee worship and the tabernacle. The point here is that Moses had a team and it was constantly expanding as his world and duties grew. Moses didn't always want a team, but he needed a team, and he submitted to the need as time went on.

LEADERSHIP STEP: *Just like Moses, you need a team, which requires you to adjust and adapt your leadership style to include team dynamics like mentoring, team building, delegation, expansion and succession planning. What are you doing to be a more effective member of a team or to help develop your team members? Your Step today is to make a list of all your team members, and spend 20 minutes praying for them. Listen and write down anything God shows you about the team.*

Rest Stop 6 — February 11

"Six days you are to gather it, but on the seventh day, the Sabbath, there will not be any" - Exodus 16:26.

God sent manna to feed His people in the wilderness, but on the seventh day or the Sabbath, He sent none. Instead He sent a double portion the day before, enough for them to feed themselves for two days. The Sabbath day was not just to be a day of rest, therefore, but also a day of faith - a day when Israel would stop and purposefully trust the Lord for their provision while they tended to other matters of worship and rest. This day set them apart from all the other nations, who feverishly tried to provide for themselves, while Israel's God provided for His own in His own way - and His people allowed Him to do so.

LEADERSHIP STEP: *Do you have a day of faith, a time when you trust the Lord for what you need? That means you stop what you normally do to earn a living, and put your provision in God's hands. That means you don't worry or work, but go about the business of resting, trusting God and worshipping Him. Your Step today is to make an offering to your church or other organization to practically express your faith in Him.*

Strategy   February 12

"Many are the plans in a person's heart, but it is the Lord's purpose that prevails" - Proverbs 19:21.

To neglect strategy and replace it with wishful thinking has been the downfall of many leaders and the people they lead. Every leader must help develop strategies to carry out changes and initiatives in businesses, families and organizations. These strategies involve plans for how to deploy people, distribute resources and spend time. Yet Joseph and Daniel showed that God also has strategies for countries and enterprises that He is willing to share with leaders who know and ask Him - and those strategies have the greatest impact and longest lasting effects.

LEADERSHIP STEP: *Do you believe that God has a strategy for the work you are doing? What's more, do you have faith that He will share it with you, and then help you carry it out? In Appendix Four is an article outlining the leadership strategy for an obscure biblical character, a leader* who you have probably never considered. Your Step today is to read the article and then reflect on how his approach can be helpful to your own leadership at this point in your career.

Change — February 13

"Moreover, I will give you a new heart and put a new spirit within you; and I will remove the heart of stone from your flesh and give you a heart of flesh" - Ezekiel 36:26.

God is in the change business, in a manner of speaking. He initiates changes in culture and history on a larger scale, but then He is also in the business of changing hearts, one person at a time. This means that people can change, learning new things that will alter their perspective and then their behavior. Leaders must have faith that people can change with God's help, and that is why leaders conduct performance reviews, send people to counseling and workshops, and assign them mentors and coaches. Of course, leaders must model this first, showing their followers they are willing to change right along with them.

LEADERSHIP STEP: *What is your attitude toward change? Do you think it's possible for people, including you, to change? If you do, then your Step today on your leadership walk is to map out a plan for change. Today you will have what may be a difficult conversation with someone in your world who needs to alter his or her attitude or actions. You may have to confront them, but then help them by mapping out a plan that will enable the change to take place. Then follow the same procedure for yourself.*

People Skills — February 14

"Nabal answered David's servants, 'Who is this David? Who is this son of Jesse? Many servants are breaking

away from their masters these days. Why should I take my bread and water, and the meat I have slaughtered for my shearers, and give it to men coming from who knows where?'" - 1 Samuel 25:10-11.

The biblical couple of Nabal and Abigail exhibited extreme examples where people skills were concerned. Nabal was boorish and rude, and it almost cost him his life at David's hand. His wife Abigail had great people skills and was able to quickly soothe David's anger after Nabal had mistreated David's men as seen in these verses. David was so impressed that he made Abigail his wife after Nabal's death and she went from a businessman's wife to the throne! People skills in today's workplace are skills that often lead to promotion, for you are in the people business no matter what business you are in.

***LEADERSHIP STEP:** There are some that are more naturally skilled at working with people, able to empathize and relate with more ease than others. Yet these skills can be learned and perfected with effort and the desire to do so. Your Step today is to follow up on the People Skills Step that was assigned on January 10. Analyze your style to see how it relates with other people in your team or family. How can you use that insight to improve your people skills?*

Purpose   February 15

"God blessed them; and God said to them, 'Be fruitful and multiply, and fill the earth, and subdue it; and rule over the fish of the sea and over the birds of the sky and over every living thing that moves on the earth'" - Genesis 1:28.

Work was and is God's idea. He blessed Adam and Eve by assigning them meaningful work that made them the rulers over creation as God's coworkers. When one rules, that indicates that one leads, so leadership was the first work God assigned to anyone. Part of their leadership was to be expressed in their fruitfulness, which was tangible productivity that would emanate from their God-assigned and God-directed work and creativity.

LEADERSHIP STEP: *Your work is a calling from God. It should be a source of joy, meaning, and fulfillment. Is that what you derive from your work? If not, it could be a season you are going through, or it could be you are bored and in the wrong business! The answer may not be to quit your job, but to find meaningful labor outside of work hours. That may start out as a hobby or ministry, but could grow into a second career. Your Step today is to come up with some ideas of what those activities may be for you.*

Goals   February 16

"Now David had said, 'Whoever strikes down a Jebusite first shall be chief and commander.' Joab the son of Zeruiah went up first, so he became chief" - 1 Chronicles 11:6.

Leaders help establish goals and rewards for the people in their organization, and promote people based on performance - realizing that different things motivate each team member. In today's verse describes the instance when David attacked Jerusalem and set a goal to see which of his fighting men would respond with faith and zeal. David made good on his promise to promote the man who led the way, and the city was taken, becoming the capital of Israel and a city that to this day is the focus of much of the world.

LEADERSHIP STEP: *Are you clear in your family or organization as to what behaviors are desired and will be rewarded? Are you consistent to follow through on the rewards when those behaviors are exhibited? While loyalty is desired, you must reward people for performance and not just staying around. Your Step today is to spend some time with your team members to see if they are clear on what they should be doing, what it is you desire from them, and what rewards are connected to those desired outcomes.*

Organization   February 17

"But when you blow an alarm, the camps that are pitched on the east side shall set out" - Numbers 10:6.

When Israel moved through the desert, Moses had to coordinate the movements of millions of people and livestock. That required structure and organization so that each start and stop had rhythm and sequence, or in other words they had to have organization. His answer for this challenge could not be to shrink Israel down to where it was small and manageable, but to learn how to organize something large and complex. There are some leaders who don't want their organization to get too big because they don't want to be bothered with the problems, but by doing so they thwart the impact God intends for them and their group to make on the world.

LEADERSHIP STEP: *Are you biased against 'big' in your organization? If so, your Step today is to identify why. Do you fear not having the ability to handle 'big's' challenges? Or is it a wrong perspective on 'big', that somehow it's not God's will? Whatever reasons you uncover, develop a plan to grow beyond that fear, whether through education, hiring people who can handle 'big,' or repenting for lack of faith. Remember: If it's too big for you to lead and manage, it's not too big for God who is willing to help!*

Rest Stop 7   February 18

"See, the Lord has given you the sabbath; therefore He gives you bread for two days on the sixth day.

Remain every man in his place; let no man go out of his place on the seventh day" - Exodus 16:29.

God gave the Sabbath Day as a gift to His people. By the time Jesus came, the Sabbath was anything but a gift. It was a day of stifling limitations, authoritatively enforced by God's "police," who were the religious leaders of Jesus' day. Notice God provided for every day, not just the Sabbath.

The Jews were to stop what they normally did on the Sabbath to commemorate and recognize their work was not the source of their provision, God was. It is also interesting that worship was not part of the original Sabbath; they were just to stay in their tents and not gather manna.

LEADERSHIP STEP: *The Leadership Walk is a tiring road with great stress, success and even failure. It can be a rewarding but frustrating road as well with turns and hills to climb. Your Step today is to step away from your normal duties - don't think about work and go have some fun. What is fun for you? A movie? A visit to your parents or children? A museum? Reading? Whatever it is, make a conscious effort to leave your work alone today (or one day soon), and that includes not even thinking about it.*

Service   February 19

"But Jehoshaphat said, 'Is there not a prophet of the Lord here, that we may inquire of the Lord by him?' And one of the king of Israel's servants answered and said, 'Elisha the son of Shaphat is here, who used to pour water on the hands of Elijah'" - 2 Kings 3:11.

Elisha was the prime prophetic leader in Israel at the time the king asked his question above. What was Elisha's preparation for leadership? First, he was chosen by God, but then he spent time "pouring water on Elijah's hands' (see 2 Kings 3:11b). As an apprentice, he served Elijah as

Elijah mentored him. Elisha went from serving one man to serving the nation, all the time serving the Lord's purpose for his life. This is the same path that David, Joseph and Moses followed: seemingly meaningless and perhaps even boring service was part of their preparation for leadership.

LEADERSHIP STEP: *If you are an emerging leader, then serving is part of your training! If it is not part of your job or degree training, then your Step today is to find a situation that will ground and humble you through service. If you are already a leader, regularly spend some time in the field - customer service, finance, maintenance - and serve the people there, staying in touch with reality and with the people who do the front-line work, while not letting leadership power go to your head.*

Motivation — February 20

"Delight yourself in the Lord; And He will give you the desires of your heart" - Psalm 37:4.

God grants the desires of the heart, not because He is some cosmic Santa Claus who gives everyone what they want, but because He put those desires there in the first place. Thus when leaders get in touch with their heart, and seek to lead God's way, those leaders can count on God's help. It is not only the leader, however, who has heart desires; the same is true for followers. So leadership expresses their heart's desires through vision, which in turn provides opportunities for followers to fulfill their heart's desires by being part of the vision's fulfillment.

LEADERSHIP STEP: *Are you "fighting" your heart, seeking only to lead through the "head" matters of finance, strategy and production? Then it's time to get in touch with your heart along with the hearts of others. Your Step today is to write down what your elegant dream is, then call together others* on your team for lunch one day this week and have them do the same. Talk about how your dreams can become a reality together. Don't be discouraged if that seems impossible at first for everyone will probably have a variety of heart's desires.

Self-Awareness   February 21

"It is a trustworthy statement, deserving full acceptance, that Christ Jesus came into the world to save sinners, among whom I am foremost of all" - 1 Timothy 1:15.

Paul was aware of his condition before the Lord. He was not being overly humble to say that he was a great sinner, for he had at one time put people in prison and to death, all the while thinking he was doing God a favor. Yet he did not allow that reality to hinder him from serving the Lord and becoming a great leader who is still impacting the world. Leaders do not have to hide from or deny their weaknesses. They simply acknowledge them while looking to operate in their God-given strengths, all the while acknowledging their propensity to "sin" and failure.

LEADERSHIP STEP: How transparent and self-aware are you as a leader? You don't have to hold a special meeting to confess your sins, but you do need to be aware when you acted inappropriately or are demotivating your team. On Week 4, Day 3 you were encouraged to have a 360-degree profile done. Did you do it? If not, your Step today is to get one completed and study the results. Then walk in a humbling but freeing awareness that you have blind spots, and they are negatively impacting your team.

Knowledge   February 22

"I have filled him with the Spirit of God in wisdom, in understanding, in knowledge, and in all kinds of craftsmanship . . . ." - Exodus 31:3.

Bezalel is the name of the man described in this verse, and he was a craftsman, chosen by God to do special work. He became a leader of the people and other craftsmen based on his skill, experience and giftedness. This is what's called expert or charismatic leadership, for the head craftsman was the best at what he did, and God gifted him to do such distinctive work. Not all leaders are equal, for there are some who are more gifted than others and have insights or gifts that are unique to them and their work.

LEADERSHIP STEP: *Do you have the desire to be the best, to be world-class at what you do? Don't dismiss that as ego, but your Step today is to accept it as a desire God gave you. Rather than fight it, go with it and lay out a plan for how you can gain knowledge, skill and insight in your chosen area of work. That may involve school, working for several companies, or an apprenticeship. Then go be the best anyone will see in their lifetime in your area of knowledge or skill.*

Wisdom   February 23

"Give me now wisdom and knowledge, that I may go out and come in before this people, for who can rule this great people of Yours?" - 2 Chronicles 1:10.

There is an aspect of wisdom that a leader earns through experience and study. Then there is wisdom that God gives leaders to help them recognize opportunities and threats for their family or organization. Wisdom also helps leaders "connect the dots," which means they recognize patterns that help them discern what is happening today based on what they have seen in the past or what God gives them special insight to see. When Solomon asked for wisdom in this verse, it enabled him to recognize the dilemma presented to him shortly thereafter when two women came, each claiming a certain baby was theirs. Solomon's God-given wisdom helped him make the right decision.

LEADERSHIP STEP: *Do you have the wisdom you need to lead effectively? Your experience will not be enough to get the job done, but will also require God's help. Your Step today is to read James 1:5-8 and pray God will open your eyes and ears to receive what you need. You must not second-guess or doubt the process, however, but trust God will give you what you need, perhaps through others, or through something you read or some thought you have about a past experience.*

Influence   February 24

"But I did not want to do anything without your consent, so that any favor you do would not seem forced but would be voluntary" - Philemon 14.

One of the key characteristics of servant leadership is influence, which is leadership's ability to direct people under their care through persuasion and patience. Paul could have ordered the man in this verse to do the right thing, but he appealed to him, wanting the man to consent from free will. Influence cannot just happen, but must stem from a credible and established relationship between the influencer and the influenced. If leaders only show up when they need something, the followers will feel manipulated and the influence process will not work.

LEADERSHIP STEP: *How are your relationships with those whom you are asking to follow you? Do you know their birthdays? What motivates them to work or minister? Your Step today is to assess and score your relationship with each follower - 1 (poor) to 5 (great). Then set dates to visit each team member twice over the next month to talk. The goal is to build a better relationship with them than you have now.*

Rest Stop 8   February 25

"But the seventh day is a sabbath to the Lord your God.

The Leadership Walk

On it you shall not do any work, neither you, nor your son or daughter, nor your male or female servant, nor your animals, nor any foreigner residing in your towns. For in six days the Lord made the heavens and the earth, the sea, and all that is in them, but he rested on the seventh day. Therefore the Lord blessed the Sabbath day and made it holy" - Exodus 20:10-11.

When the Lord rested, He did not take a nap or do nothing, putting creation on autopilot. He rested to enjoy His creation and to set a pattern for humanity that they were to step away from their God-ordained activities for one day to enjoy what they had accomplished. The Sabbath was a chance for people to refocus, realizing that it was not their efforts producing their provision, but rather that the Lord was their source. Notice also that nothing is said about worship on this 'holy' day - that custom came later. The original intent of the Sabbath was for people to refocus their reliance on, need for and appreciation of the Lord.

LEADERSHIP STEP: *How do you spend your rest day? Is it consumed in fretting and planning the next six days, or in appreciation for what you have done in the past week? Your Step today is to do some things you enjoy or that are related to your values - things you don't have time to do during the week, like visiting family or drawing or reading. Stop working and reconnect with both the Lord and your joy, however you do those two things best.*

Power   February 26

"In your relationships with one another, have the same mindset as Christ Jesus: Who, being in very nature God, did not consider equality with God something to be used to his own advantage . . . ." - Philippians 2:5-6.

Jesus had all power but He did not use that power to lord

it over others or to build His own Kingdom. He used power to do the Father's will, to set people free, and then to empower them to live abundant, productive lives. Leaders should follow Jesus' example and not use their leadership power to their own advantage. Rather leaders should use their power for the benefit of others, even those who don't agree with them or celebrate their leadership.

LEADERSHIP STEP: Are you using your power to build your organization or to build your own little kingdom? The way you know is to look at the benefits your power brings to you personally. Do you have a special parking space? Do you have the best office? Do you use your position and authority to get yourself benefits to which others don't have access? Your Step today is to add it all up and see what your power is getting you. Then decide how you are going to use your power for the benefit of others.

Persuasion   February 27

"Through patience a ruler can be persuaded, and a gentle tongue can break a bone" - Proverbs 25:15.

Persuasion is a key element of effective leadership, especially of what's known as servant leadership. Many leaders take some time to make a decision, announce the decision and don't allow followers the same amount of time to process it. That's where persuasion comes into play, for leaders must make a skilled presentation that will allow followers to be convinced in their own mind of the correctness of the decision. What's more, persuasion cannot be a manipulating sales job, but rather a sincere and patient attempt to explain the rightness of a course of action, allowing people to conclude for themselves the decision's value.

LEADERSHIP STEP: On Week 4, Day 2, you were directed

to do a study of the tongue and words as presented in the book of Proverbs. Did you do that? Let's revisit that exercise, looking up the words tongue, lips and speech in Proverbs using the online tool called Bible Gateway. Once you have your list, go over it once more to see where you can improve your speech to be more persuasive and convincing, rather than just relying on your power to order people to comply.

Values   February 28

"As was his custom, Paul went into the synagogue, and on three Sabbath days he reasoned with them from the Scriptures, . . ." - Acts 17:2.

Leaders have thought through and established personal values that guide their daily decisions. They don't have to think or pray when faced with expressing their values through their actions; they simply do them. In this verse, it is clear that Paul had a value to visit the synagogue on any Sabbath day to teach and talk about the Lord. When leaders have values, they show up in their calendars and in their checkbooks.

LEADERSHIP STEP: *On Week 4, Day 3, you were encouraged to write out your personal values. The worksheet to help you to do so is in the Appendix in case you did not finish or need to revisit that exercise. When you have identified your values, go through your calendar and your checkbook (personal or company) to see if you have consistently expressed those values. Your Step today is to set out a plan for the next month where your values can find expressions in what you do on a regular basis.*

Ethics   February 29

"The fear of the Lord is the beginning of knowledge, but fools despise wisdom and instruction" - Proverbs 1:7.

John W. Stanko

Leaders are not exempt from or beyond the authority of God's ethical requirements. This ethical awareness begins with having a teachable spirit, no matter how experienced or mature that leader is. If leaders do not have that spirit, then they despise wisdom and instruction and are missing the key component to learning, which is the fear of the Lord. Leaders must grow in their understanding of diversity, fair trade, finance, leadership styles, personality and any other knowledge that relates to their field of work and to leadership itself.

LEADERSHIP STEP: *You will not grow in your ethical awareness and wisdom where your occupation is concerned unless you acknowledge as a leader that you don't know it all and your perspective is not infallible or omniscient. Yesterday you were urged to take another look at your values. Your Step today is to assess yourself where your values are concerned, scoring 1 (poor) to 5 (great) for each value. Then have someone close to you do the same. Develop a plan for where you need to be more consistent to carry out your values, which is nothing more than ethics.*

Collaboration   March 1

"Though one may be overpowered, two can defend themselves. A cord of three strands is not quickly broken"
- Ecclesiastes 4:12.

An effective leader builds partnerships and collaborates with others on important projects. This is not just so the project can thrive, but also because the leader has a desire to see other people grow and develop. What's more, these partnerships give the leader valuable insight into how team members function best for future projects and promotions. Leaders who build a broad sense of partnership obtain their team's best creativity and total commitment to the project at hand.

LEADERSHIP STEP: *On January 26, you were urged to evaluate your team members for their level of involvement and commitment. You were to do this by doing an evaluation yourself and then asking your team members how involved and engaged they felt as part of your team. Were the two assessments close or were they far apart? If far apart, your Step today is to think about how you can you improve your team's engagement. (Here's a clue: ask them!)*

Relationships   March 2

> *"David longed for water and said, 'Oh, that someone would get me a drink of water from the well near the gate of Bethlehem!' So the three mighty warriors broke through the Philistine lines, drew water from the well near the gate of Bethlehem and carried it back to David"* - 2 Samuel 23:15-16.

Even though these men were joined together for military purposes, they still had a close personal relationship. This is evidenced through several things. First, David was free enough to express something personal that he desired. The men were close enough to David to hear it. The men wanted to please David so they risked their lives to get David his hometown water and brought it back to him. These men obviously admired and loved David and were willing to work for him even at personal risk. This speaks highly of David's leadership.

LEADERSHIP STEP: *You don't have to be close friends with your team, but you should be close enough to them to know something about their families, personal lives and professional aspirations. This takes time to discover and must be pursued with intentionality. Your Step today is to schedule time during your next meeting when everyone on your team can share something about themselves that the others may not know. The goal is to get to know one another personally.*

Rest Stop 9 — March 3

"The Lord answered him, 'You hypocrites! Doesn't each of you on the Sabbath untie your ox or donkey from the stall and lead it out to give it water?'" - Luke 13:15.

The Jews insisted no work could or should be done on the Sabbath, making a ritual out of something intended to meet people's need for a change of pace and to remind them God was their provider. Jesus pointed out things needed to be done on the Sabbath, even though they were technically considered work. In this case, it was preserving and protecting the life of an animal. The Sabbath was not to be regulated by a set of rules but by an attitude of the heart.

LEADERSHIP STEP: *Have you earned your rest this week? If so, then Step today is to take it! Do something that will refresh and strengthen you for the coming week. It may even be something you have been putting off, like cleaning out files or your car that, once complete, will bring you a great sense of relief and fulfillment. And don't forget about turning your heart toward God as part of your rest as well.*

Emotional Intelligence — March 4

"But I said, 'Should a man like me run away? Or should someone like me go into the temple to save his life? I will not go!'" - Nehemiah 6:11.

People often threaten leaders in an attempt to intimidate or control them. These threats come as possible lawsuits, questions about their performance, insubordination or disloyalty by subordinates, and criticism in general. Leaders must be confident in their ability and calling to lead, and must face their own fears in order to stand firm in the day of trouble. Nehemiah did that and was not going to run away because he was a leader!

LEADERSHIP STEP: *Are you adjusting your leadership style or decisions because others are intimidating you? Are their threats subtle or overt? Your Step today is to face your fears, but also to face the fact that "someone like you" cannot afford to allow threats to alter your course. What threat do you have to face? Clearly identify it, and then determine what is the worst that can happen if that threat comes true? Can you live with the worst? If so, then stand your ground!*

Coaching   March 5

"Of those still in the city, he took the officer in charge of the fighting men, and five royal advisers. He also took the secretary who was chief officer in charge of conscripting the people of the land and sixty of the conscripts who were found in the city" - 2 Kings 25:19.

The context of this verse is not good, for the king of Babylon identified the remaining leaders and those close to leadership and had them executed to complete his conquest of Judah. Notice, however, that the king had many servants, five of whom were his royal advisors. In other words, the king whom God appointed had advisers and people close to him who could coach him on specific decisions and even on attitudes and behaviors he should adopt. Leaders must realize that having coaches and advisers is not a sign of weakness or lack of ability. Coaches are signs that leaders are secure and committed enough to be the best leaders they can possibly be.

LEADERSHIP STEP: *Your Step today is to identify some area in which you admit you need coaching. It may be in some particular area like finance, team building or it may be around your areas of personal ineffectiveness like time management or writing. Once you have identified the area(s), then ask around and secure a coach to help you in those particular areas. That may come in the form of reading* *some expert material, going back to school or actually hiring a coach.*

Attitude — March 6

"May the God who gives endurance and encouragement give you the same attitude of mind toward each other that Christ Jesus had . . ." - Romans 15:5.

There is power when everyone in a family or organization has the same attitude of mind. Here we see in part that an attitude is a gift, just like endurance and encouragement. While God gives attitudes, it is up to the leader and the team to maintain that attitude. A positive attitude releases energy, gratitude and a can-do mindset. A negative attitude creates self-fulfilling negative scenarios that spread throughout the organization.

LEADERSHIP STEP: *If there is someone who has a negative attitude? If so, then your Step today is to confront them. The way to confront is not to hammer them with your perspective, but to open a dialog to see if you are correct in your assessment and to find out the source of the negativity, which may be you, your actions or your own attitude. A good team attitude is a blessing, but you must work to develop and maintain that good attitude in yourself and your team.*

Productivity — March 7

"Be diligent in these matters; give yourself wholly to them, so that everyone may see your progress. Watch your life and doctrine closely. Persevere in them . . ."
- 1 Timothy 4:15-16.

Leaders are expected to grow and make progress in the work they are leading. This requires them to be diligent, and to provide a role model for others to learn from and follow. When the going gets tough, leaders are expected to persevere. And all this is so that a leader can be productive, not just maintaining, but growing and expanding the work area that he or she is assigned. The key words from this verse are *diligent, wholly, progress, watch* and *persevere*.

LEADERSHIP STEP: *How do you measure growth or progress in your organization or personally? While it may be difficult to measure, you must at least try. Your Step today is to choose some metric(s) that will give you a chance to measure the job you are doing or the personal growth you are experiencing. Once you choose the metric(s), you must determine how you will measure it (them) and how often you will do so. The metrics can be financial, attendance numbers, books read or reduced costs. We will revisit this from time to time to measure your growth.*

Finances   March 8

"No one can serve two masters. Either you will hate the one and love the other, or you will be devoted to the one and despise the other. You cannot serve both God and money" - Matthew 6:24.

If leaders do what they do only for money, then they are 'hired guns,' renting their services to the highest bidder. Money is often an ineffective motivator, for to get money leaders have been known to do things they never thought they would do. What's more, the pursuit of money can take the place of God in the lives of the pursuers. This verse actually says if anyone loves money they will hate God! That is how strong the pull of money can be in a person's or leader's life.

LEADERSHIP STEP: *There is only one antidote for the love of money and that is generosity. Therefore today your Step is to be generous! Perhaps there is someone in your world* whom you can reward for a job well done by giving them an unexpected bonus, whether small or large. Or maybe you can give a personal gift out of your own funds to the poor. Finally, maybe someone in your world deserves a raise and today you will give it to him or her.

Time Management   March 9

"The Lord said to him, 'Go back the way you came, and go to the Desert of Damascus. When you get there, anoint Hazael king over Aram. Also, anoint Jehu son of Nimshi king over Israel, and anoint Elisha son of Shaphat from Abel Meholah to succeed you as prophet'" - 1 Kings 19:15-16.

In a sense, the Lord created a to-do list for Elijah, giving him things he needed to complete along with the order they needed to be done. Leaders also need this kind of list to help them focus, otherwise it is like throwing more than one ball at a time to another person. The person catching doesn't know which one is the priority to catch, so they all fall to ground. Since there are so many demands on leaders' time, it is essential they prioritize and plan their time.

LEADERSHIP STEP: *Your Step today is to actually write out a to-do list. Sit down and in five minutes list all the things would like or need to do today. Once you have that, go back and order that list in order of priority - what you want to do first make 1, second mark 2, etc. Then do your best to follow the order you have set. Do the same for tomorrow, carrying over any undone things from today to tomorrow's list. When you are interrupted, just refer back to your list to get refocused.*

Rest Stop 10   March 10

"Therefore do not let anyone judge you by what you eat or

drink, or with regard to a religious festival, a New Moon celebration or a Sabbath day." - Colossians 2:16.

Leaders are busy people and must take time to refresh. That refreshment strategy will be different for each leader according to his or her values, gifts and financial resources. Leaders can be poor, however, and still have an effective 'rest' strategy that leaves them rejuvenated and energized. Of course, worship should be part of this rest strategy, but the strategy goes beyond the weekly routine to holidays and extended periods of rest. Others should not be able to impose their expectations on any leader who needs and takes his or her rest!

LEADERSHIP STEP: *Do you have a 'rest' strategy? Are you being faithful to what energizes you, or are you succumbing to the expectations and pressure of others to work when you should rest? Your Step today is to map out your 'rest' strategy that includes a weekly day off, other days off and holiday plans for yourself or with your family. Include those things that energize you whether or not they energize anyone else and be faithful to get the 'rest' breaks you need.*

Humility   March 11

"Before a downfall the heart is haughty, but humility comes before honor" - Proverbs 18:12.

Leaders are often accorded honor, but it can be 'heady wine,' so to speak, and give them a big head. When leaders start to believe they have earned their honors, they can be upset when they don't receive the honor they think they deserve. This can cause leaders to do what they do for honor, and consequently their activities have an ulterior motive beyond serving others and their organizations. The only biblical road to honor is humility along with a proper perspective that honor can only come from the Lord.

LEADERSHIP STEP: *Your Step today is to do an 'honor check' to see if you have begun to expect honor. Do you feel slighted or hurt when bypassed for certain recognitions and awards? When is the last time you found ways to honor others? Think of ways in your organization (or your family) to honor others for their contributions, thus assuring you will stay humble and esteem others above yourself. How about a special award to recognize outstanding attitude or service?*

Decision Making   March 12

"If we say, 'We'll go into the city'—the famine is there, and we will die. And if we stay here, we will die. So let's go over to the camp of the Arameans and surrender. If they spare us, we live; if they kill us, then we die"
- 2 Kings 7:4.

Leaders have to make many decisions and, even though the choices may not be many or good, they should follow a rational approach wherever possible. Notice in this verse the lepers assessed all their options as they saw them, and three of the four outcomes involved dying. Yet they decided to go and discovered a fifth option when they arrived, for their enemies had retreated. While making rational decisions, leaders can usually never have all the information they need, so they must determine to do the best they can and then act. In today's story, a 'no-decision' would have been a bad one.

LEADERSHIP STEP: *Have you been putting off a decision because you don't have all the information you would like, or because you don't like the options or choices? Your Step today is to decide! Assemble your team, go over the information you have, and then decide, for your no-decision may be costing your organization more than making the best decision with limited information.*

Communication   March 13

"So I sent messengers to them with this reply: 'I am carrying on a great project and cannot go down. Why should the work stop while I leave it and go down to you?'"Four times they sent me the same message, and each time I gave them the same answer" - Nehemiah 6:3-4.

Leaders are pulled in many different directions by urgent voices demanding their time and energy. In these verses, Nehemiah's enemies were asking him to interrupt his work to explain himself - his work and his methods. In each case, Nehemiah turned down their request for a meeting, knowing that it would simply have been a waste of time. What's more, he did not refuse them personally, but sent emissaries to decline. The point is that Nehemiah had people with whom he had to communicate to get the work done and thus avoided meeting with those who were not in his sphere of influence or responsibility.

LEADERSHIP STEP: *It is important that you be communicating with the people who are most important to and for your work. Who are they? And how are you communicating with them? If it's only face-to-face, then you are limiting your influence and impact to a chosen few. Your Step today is to choose one means of leadership communication - training, blog, podcast, video, or book - and begin to regularly connect with as many people in your leadership world as possible through that medium.*

Spiritual Growth   March 14

"It is the glory of God to conceal a matter; to search out a matter is the glory of kings" - Proverbs 25:2.

Leadership can be hard work, especially where growth and innovation are concerned. God hides things, not to be a prankster, but so leaders will have to search out a matter of importance or innovation. It's called seeking, and it actually enhances appreciation of the final answer when it is found. If things come too easily, they can be taken for granted and not appreciated. But scaling a height that no one thought possible (or even thought to scale) can be a rewarding and memorable experience.

LEADERSHIP STEP: There is one practice that can keep you seeking and searching, and that is to set a goal. If you set a goal and know how you are going to achieve it, it's not really a goal - it's simply a forecast. Your Step today is to gather your team (or your family) and determine what you would like to be or achieve whether or not you have any idea how you will do it. Then set the goal and begin searching out the matter with God's help.

Personal Development   March 15

"You have loved righteousness and hated wickedness; therefore God, your God, has set you above your companions by anointing you with the oil of joy"
- Hebrews 1:9.

It is interesting that Jesus was anointed with oil, not of power or goodness or miracles, but of joy. It was the joy that motivated Him and directed Him to activities where He was most productive. An anointing produces noticeable even spectacular or supernatural results. Leaders are called upon to do many things, but they must and should focus as much as possible on whatever it is they do best, and that 'best' is often related to their joy - whether it is people, marketing, fundraising, innovation or team building. When leaders do this, they can then release others to do the same, thus building strong teams that all function in strengths, producing exceptional results.

The Leadership Walk

LEADERSHIP STEP: *Are you in touch with your joy? Your Step today is to carry a little notebook and keep track of what gives you joy throughout the day. It may be your staff meeting, your press conference, an interview, or an interaction with an employee or team member. When you have a few days of joys collected, study the list to see what you learn and determine how you can do more of what you truly enjoy doing and how that can help your organization.*

Team Building   March 16

"These are the names of David's mighty warriors: Josheb-Basshebeth, a Tahkemonite, was chief of the Three; he raised his spear against eight hundred men, whom he killed in one encounter" - 2 Samuel 23:8.

King David was a great leader, made great in part because of great followers. He was not threatened by, and realized his need for, followers and teammates who could produce outstanding results. What's more, they were warriors, so David provided meaningful work that gave them all opportunities to excel and do what they did best. Notice that their names were memorialized with David and their feats described for all posterity to read and admire.

LEADERSHIP STEP: *Your Step today is to give some thought to your team or family members and the work they do and roles they serve. Your Step today is to find some way to express your appreciation for their accomplishments. It doesn't have to be big, but imust be personalized. Also, ask yourself whether or not you are providing meaningful work opportunities that permit each of those members to grow and excel. If not, then use your creativity and authority to do so.*

Rest Stop 11   March 17

"As was his custom, Paul went into the synagogue,

and on three Sabbath days he reasoned with them from the Scriptures" - Acts 17:2.

Paul worked on the Sabbath! What's more he had a custom of working by going into the synagogue to reason from the Scriptures that Jesus was and is the Messiah. The point is that the Sabbath day was not a time to shut down and do nothing, but to do what God had called and appointed him to do. While not ignoring the need to rest, leaders should follow Paul's example and devote some of their down time to furthering their purpose in leadership, which may include study, reading, writing, or some other practice that will make them more effective leaders.

LEADERSHIP STEP: *Do you have any 'Sabbath customs' like Paul? Do you devote some of your rest time to activities that will pay dividends in your leadership mission and purpose? Your Step on your next rest day is to identify an existing or new habit for your rest time that includes some thing(s) that will enhance your skill and ability to lead others. Then make sure this becomes a custom and not just a wish or a one-time event.*

Strategy — March 18

"Plans fail for lack of counsel, but with many advisers they succeed" - Proverbs 15:22.

Leaders need an advisory team to help them navigate the complicated issues surrounding leadership decisions. This includes people to advise them on finances, human resources, team building, strategy, legal issues and any other area that relates to the decisions to be made. What's more, leaders need personal advisers to help them develop and grow in their leadership roles. Finally, leaders need some advisers where personal matters like family and personal finances are concerned.

The Leadership Walk

LEADERSHIP STEP: *Your Step today is to sit down and make a list of your personal advisers for business, ministry or personal matters. You can even include on this list authors, teachers and historical figures whom you have studied, listen to, learned from or read. Once you have the list, determine if it has enough people to get your job done well and to help coach you to excellence. If not, then you need to decide who needs to be added to the list.*

Change   March 19

> *". . . who despises a vile person but honors those who fear the Lord; who keeps an oath even when it hurts, and does not change their mind . . . « - Psalm 15:4.*

Leaders often lead change initiatives, which may involve changes in marketing, strategy, services, products or personnel. One thing leaders cannot and should not change is their commitment to excellence, team building and their personal values. In the midst of change, integrity, promises and commitments to customers and employees must be honored or else leaders forfeit one of their most precious and important leadership commodities, which is integrity. Today's verse stresses how important keeping one's word is to the Lord and a relationship with Him.

LEADERSHIP STEP: *As your organization navigates the seas of change, your Step today is to consider the things you will never change, which are your commitments and values. How well do you keep your word? Do you say, "I'll get back to you" and then don't? Take 15 minutes and reflect on your personal and corporate integrity, and see if there is any room for changing your follow through on commitments and vows.*

People Skills   March 20

> *"One of the servants told Abigail, Nabal's wife,*

John W. Stanko

'David sent messengers from the wilderness to give our master his greetings, but he hurled insults at them'" - 1 Samuel 25:14.

The story of Nabal and Abigail is full of insight into people skills - Nabal with poor skills and Abigail and the servant with good skills. Nabal had lived under David's protection, but treated David's men rudely when they asked for assistance. The servant recognized that David's men were angry and probably going to take revenge and Abigail understood David probably would react to her husband's boorish ways. She set out to appease David's anger, thus saving the lives of many in her household with her wisdom and soothing words. Leaders need to be more like Abigail and the servant, and much less like Nabal.

LEADERSHIP SKILLS: *This is the third time you have looked at this story in this devotional because it contains so much insight into managing and relating to people, showing the effects of good and not-so-good skills. Your Step today is to read this story in 1 Samuel 25 and journal your thoughts and insights from it, especially looking at what you can do to be more observant like the servant and conciliatory like Abigail.*

Purpose   March 21

"This is what the Lord says to his anointed, to Cyrus, whose right hand I take hold of to subdue nations before him and to strip kings of their armor, to open doors before him so that gates will not be shut" - Isaiah 45:1.

The Lord refers to Cyrus as "his anointed" even though Cyrus was a pagan king. God had chosen him to lead and do God's will where other nations were concerned. God chooses leaders, not just in the church, but also in other domains of life, and is present to guide if they choose His help. He also holds them accountable to act righteously in their positions. While most would restrict "anointing" to the church world, this verse makes it possible to have an "anointed" banker, politician, military leader, school administrator, or other position requiring a leadership role.

LEADERSHIP STEP: *Where is your anointing? In other words, where do you serve and sense God is present to help you, even if that role is outside the church? The answers to these questions should impact your prayer life, as you help direct God's involvement in your sphere of influence. Your Step today is to develop a prayer strategy that covers every aspect of your anointing, which may include things like your personnel decisions, marketing plans and innovation.*

Goals   March 22

"In the eleventh year in the month of Bul, the eighth month, the temple was finished in all its details according to its specifications. He had spent seven years building it" - 1 Kings 6:38.

Solomon built the Temple of the Lord as his father David had directed him to do. When reading the verses before this one, one sees how detailed the plans for this Temple were. When leaders set out to do something significant or great, those things don't just magically occur. They require the use of goals, plans, faith, flexibility, teamwork and vision to make it all happen. What's more, this job wasn't finished in a day, but took seven years! That's certainly a long-term goal but shows the time-tested value of goals and visions when leaders employ them in their work.

LEADERSHIP STEP: *What are your long-term goals for your organization? Where will you be organizationally or personally in five years? Ten years? Your Step today is to do some dreaming, alone or with your family or team, and write the vision down. Then spend 15 minutes setting some goals* and developing some plans to go with those dreams. Don't try to make it all 'perfect,' just let it flow for now. Later you can go back and fill in the gaps and tidy it up a bit.

Organization — March 23

"Dominion and awe belong to God; he establishes order in the heights of heaven" - Job 25:2.

When you think of it, heaven is an organized entity. There is rank among the angels, clarity of communication, assignments given, understood and carried out and punctuality (God is always on time). There is never confusion and everything is in its place and functioning properly. If God values order in heaven, He must also value it here on earth, for the Lord's prayer states, "Your will be done here as it is in heaven." Therefore leaders must spend some of their time and energy organizing their personal and professional world. When they do, they can count on God's help because He is the author of order.

LEADERSHIP STEP: *On a scale of 1 to 10, evaluate how well your various 'worlds' are organized - work, family, ministry, school, etc. (10 is excellent, 1 is poor). Which one has the lowest score? Your Step today is to devote 30 minutes to thinking through the improvements you can make. Then make a to-do list for next week of things you can do to improve (buy a planner, read a book, consult with an expert, clean off or out your desk, discard things you don't use).*

Rest Stop 12 — March 24

"Some of the Pharisees said, 'This man is not from God, for he does not keep the Sabbath.' But others asked, 'How can a sinner perform such signs?' So they were divided" - John 9:16.

If work was absolutely forbidden on the Sabbath, why was Jesus 'working' by performing miracles? The Pharisees were divided as to the interpretation of what Jesus was doing, because they had misinterpreted what Sabbath rest meant. Obviously Jesus knew best what the Sabbath meant, and He felt free to pursue His purpose of seeking and saving the lost on what the Jews considered their holy day. Paul followed Jesus' example and also performed his purpose work on the Sabbath day.

LEADERSHIP STEP: *If Jesus and Paul did it, then you can do it too. What is the 'it'? It is working in your purpose that can actually help you rest and replenish your energy and enthusiasm sapped by mundane weekly duties. What is your purpose? Is it to paint, draw, write, play sports or help the poor? Your assignment is to find a rest-day expression for your purpose on every rest day from now on.*

Service   March 25

> *"A dispute also arose among them as to which of them was considered to be greatest. Jesus said to them, 'The kings of the Gentiles lord it over them; and those who exercise authority over them call themselves Benefactors. But you are not to be like that . . . '"*
> *- Luke 22:24-26a.*

Some leaders are kind dictators. Jesus specifically forbade this benevolent dictator style, not just for church work but also for leadership in general. The word 'benefactor' is of Latin origin, the combination of two words 'doer' and 'good.' Leaders who follow Jesus are not to lord it over other people even if they consider it in the best interests of others to do so. Why is this? It is because this power, even when used to help the weak, eventually goes to the leaders' heads and they begin to believe they are actually better than others.

LEADERSHIP STEP: *There is only one antidote for leadership power and that is practical service. Your Step today is to assess your leadership style to determine if you are lording it over people, but rationalizing it by thinking you are doing it in others' best interests. Then go the Appendix to read the article there about servant leadership, and then incorporate its philosophy into your leadership style.*

Motivation — March 26

"When Haman saw that Mordecai would not kneel down or pay him honor, he was enraged. Yet having learned who Mordecai's people were, he scorned the idea of killing only Mordecai. Instead Haman looked for a way to destroy all Mordecai's people, the Jews, throughout the whole kingdom of Xerxes" - Esther 3:5-6.

Haman squandered a wonderful leadership opportunity because he was blinded by hatred. He had unlimited access to the king, authority, power and wealth. Yet he was motivated by personal gain and revenge, and those two motivators caused him to make poor decisions that eventually cost him and his family their lives. What's more, Haman used people toward his own ends and, when they could not benefit him or did not honor him, he looked to eliminate them. Leaders must confront their own heart and face what is motivating them to lead and succeed, even if it is ugly and selfish.

LEADERSHIP STEP: *What motivates you to lead or become a leader? Your Step today is to go to your journal and write out what you expect to receive as leader and what you hope to give as leader. Be honest and transparent! Then examine the list to look for patterns or hidden motivators. Is the 'receive' list longer than the 'give' list? What does this list tell you about your motivation for leadership? What can you do to improve the balance on your list?*

Self-Awareness — March 27

"I will praise the Lord, who counsels me; even at night my heart instructs me" - Psalm 16:7.

Leaders make decisions using not only their heads but also their hearts. For this to happen, however, leaders must develop their heart life and then pay attention to what their heart is telling them. When done effectively, their heart actually becomes the place where God can speak to and guide them through their desires, wishes, intuition, compassion, empathy and stored memory of positive and negative experiences. This process can go on both day and night and is not restricted by sleep or rest.

LEADERSHIP STEP: Your Step today is to take a journey into your heart. First, read Psalm 37:4. Then take out your leadership journal and write down the desires of your heart for your business, family and ministry. Don't try to figure out how any of it will happen, just listen to your heart. Once you have those things written down, examine them for insight and set goals that will help you act on your heart's desires, having faith that God is counseling you through them.

Knowledge — March 28

"Teach me knowledge and good judgment, for I trust your commands" - Psalm 119:66.

Leaders make and facilitate decisions. Notice in this verse the psalmist was praying for himself, asking God to teach and give him both knowledge and good judgment. Leaders need to be experts in the field in which their organization is involved. They also need to exercise good judgment where leadership decisions are concerned. That "good judgment" comes through learning from mistakes and learning to creatively apply specific knowledge of the business to their daily operations. Without apology, leaders must develop themselves into people of expertise and experience.

LEADERSHIP STEP: *Do you pray for yourself? If so, what do you pray? The psalmist models a prayer that you can follow as your leadership Step today. Make a personal prayer list and put on it all the things you need for your work. Ask God for financial, marketing, research, expansion or personnel knowledge, then ask God for where to get that knowledge, whether through coaches, seminars, school or reading. Get over any ambivalence you may have about praying for yourself, and then do it regularly.*

Wisdom — March 29

"Counsel and sound judgment are mine; I have insight, I have power" - Proverbs 8:14.

The personification of wisdom is speaking in this verse and claims to bring four benefits to those who utilize her: counsel, sound judgment, insight and power. Leaders need all four of these helpers as they lead their organization or family. One of the four, however, that is perhaps most discussed and coveted among leaders is power, which of course can be used to help or harm others. The power from wisdom can only help, and derives from a leader's ability to sort through various known options and chooses the one that greatly benefits the people and organization.

LEADERSHIP STEP: *It is a thought among some modern authors that you become an expert in anything if you apply yourself and invest 10,000 hours in that particular practice. This writer's choice was to put the hours into the concept of purpose and today he is known for his purpose wisdom. Your step today is to identify an area in which you are willing to invest the hours to become a source of wisdom. Then determine what you can do in those hours to make you wise.*

Influence — March 30

> *"So Elijah went from there and found Elisha son of Shaphat. He was plowing with twelve yoke of oxen, and he himself was driving the twelfth pair. Elijah went up to him and threw his cloak around him"* - 1 Kings 19:19.

Elijah had a 'word from the Lord' to go and anoint Elisha to be his successor. When he found Elisha, he did not overwhelm him by telling him that the Lord had chosen Elisha. He did not create a dramatic scene at all. Instead, Elijah just touched him with his cloak. Then he backed off and gave Elisha a lot of space to hear and figure out what God was saying to him. Leaders must learn to influence others, just like Elijah did, so followers can make their own decisions without undue pressure, manipulation or coercion from the leader. When people make decisions for themselves, they are much more apt to be convinced of the rightness of their decisions and follow through on commitments.

LEADERSHIP STEP: *If you are the 'boss,' people may be intimidated just by nature of the authority/follower relationship. Your next Step in your leadership walk is to remove any intimidation so you can truly influence others. Schedule one-on-one meetings with your direct reports and spend some time with them with no agenda other than to get to know them, and allow them to get to know you. This may take place in your office, over lunch or at a sporting event, whichever works best.*

Rest Stop 13 — March 31

> *"There remains, then, a Sabbath-rest for the people of God; for anyone who enters God's rest also rests from their works, just as God did from his"* - Hebrews 4:9-10.

Part of the Sabbath was simply a decision to put work and the things of life into God's hands and not fret or obsess over them – at least for one day. Putting things in His hands involves ceasing from trying to make it happen (whatever the 'it' is) by doing something else that is totally unrelated to the problem or work at hand. Since leaders are often under tremendous pressure to perform and succeed, it is critical that they have this ability to step away and trust God to do what the leaders cannot do.

LEADERSHIP STEP: Are you involving God in your leadership duties? One way you can do that is to go off-duty and leave Him in charge. Your Step this week is a Rest Stop with no exceptions. Plan a day off and away from work, preferably with family, but alone if need be. When you go, you must go away completely - no email, cell phone or work involvement. Specifically tell the Lord you are leaving Him in charge and then rest from your efforts for 24 hours.

Power — April 1

"God will help the king to judge the people fairly; there need be no mistakes" - Proverbs 16:10, LB.

This verse is really about power and how the leader should use it. God gives leaders power to judge and make decisions, and then He assists leaders to apply that power properly, without prejudice or self-interest. Since some decisions are complex involving many people and complicated technical issues, leaders should eagerly welcome God into the leadership process to ensure that they are not abusing their power or falling short of the lofty standard that God sets for those He has promoted to have that power.

LEADERSHIP STEP: You should have a personal leadership board of directors made of advisers and mentors who help you develop and evaluate your leadership role and progress. They can also help evaluate how effectively you are using your God-given leadership power to ensure you are accurate and without bias. Your Step today is to make a list of seven people who could function on that board. Then call or meet with them this week and ask them to serve you in this capacity.

Persuasion   April 2

"My dear brothers and sisters, take note of this: Everyone should be quick to listen, slow to speak and slow to become angry" - James 1:19.

Someone once said that we have two ears and one mouth; therefore, we should listen twice as much as we talk. That can be difficult for leaders because they are usually intelligent, quick and competitive, so they often want to overcome their opponents and win their doubters with persuasive arguments and presentations. Yet the art of persuasion that does not coerce is actually based on asking good questions and listening intently to the answers. This goes right along with Stephen Covey's second habit of effective people, which is seek first to understand others, only then attempt to be understood.

LEADERSHIP STEP: *In the first two entries on persuasion, you did a study of the tongue in Proverbs. Your Step today is to do the same but to search Proverbs for the words* **listen**, **ear** *and* **hear**. *You can expand the search to the gospels, but for now see how important this concept of listening was for the wisdom writers. Then work over the next month on asking good questions and listening intently to understand others. A good place to start this is at home or with friends.*

Values   April 3

"When all Israel heard the verdict the king had given,

they held the king in awe, because they saw that he had wisdom from God to administer justice"
- 1 Kings 3:28.

Leaders should operate with wisdom, but that wisdom must be focused and practical. In the case of Solomon, he chose to apply his wisdom from God to judge the people with justice. The people loved the king because they both 'heard' and 'saw' his values in action when he judged between the two women, each claiming a child was theirs. Values must and will be reflected in two places, the checkbook and the calendar, for them to be true values and not just talk. When people behold consistency as leaders walk out their positive values, they will tend to hold those leaders in high esteem.

LEADERSHIP STEP: *On March 17, you were given an assignment to write out your personal values. Have you completed this exercise yet? If not, you cannot put it off any longer, for you must recognize what your values are for people to 'hear' and 'see' as described in this verse. In the Appendix, you have a worksheet to guide you through the process. If you have done this, your Step today is to take the same form and develop the values, standards or norms for your organization with your work team.*

Ethics   April 4

"Differing weights and differing measures— the Lord detests them both" - Proverbs 20:10.

God is involved in every leader's business, watching to make sure that the organization is producing ethical results and following through on commitments and advertised promises. This verse refers to someone measuring out flour or some other commodity on a scale and using a false balance, pretending to sell a certain amount when it is really less. It is unethical to appear to provide one service or product, when in actuality something less or inferior is being provided. Quite simply: God hates false practices in business and it is never good to do something God hates.

LEADERSHIP STEP: *How are your ethics at work? Do you deliver on what you promise? Produce a good day's work for your pay? Pilfer company office supplies for personal use? All these things are ethical issues. Your Step today is to do an ethical review of your work attitude, habits and performance in three areas: commitment to excellence, keeping promises, treatment of others - peers and customers or clients. Score 1(poor) to 5 (excellent) for each.*

Collaboration   April 5

"Now to each one the manifestation of the Spirit is given for the common good" - 1 Corinthians 12:7.

Leaders must learn to collaborate with their team members around projects and events related to the overall mission of the organization. In order to collaborate, the leader must not try to lead every aspect of the task, for team members will have different gifts and tasks that will necessitate the leader actually following them when those team members are functioning in their strengths and expertise. Secure leaders will be happy that the job is getting done; insecure leaders will not collaborate but rather need to see themselves as the boss, with everyone else there to serve his or her whims and wishes.

LEADERSHIP STEP: *In order to collaborate, you need to know what your team members' strengths and gifts are. Therefore, you are going to ask them what they are. In the Appendix is a quote from management author Peter Drucker. Your Step today you will schedule a two-hour staff meeting this month. Circulate this quote to your team* and inform them that you will be discussing this quote to determine where their strengths and weaknesses may lie.

Relationships — April 6

> *"Perfume and incense bring joy to the heart, and the pleasantness of a friend springs from their heartfelt advice"* - Proverbs 27:9.

Leadership often rests on and stems from the relationships between leaders and followers. The strength of those relationships is bound by trust that allows a free flow of communication, which clarifies vision, produces energy and stimulates creativity. Trusting relationships stimulate open and honest dialogue that comes from the heart as well as the head, and makes everyone in the relationships more effective in what they do. It is up to leaders to establish and maintain these life-giving relationships.

LEADERSHIP STEP: *Your Step today is to institute 'ice breakers' or other exercises at the start of your staff meetings to help build trust. To start, have each person at the meeting take five minutes to share where they grew up, where they were in the birth order of their family and something about their childhood that everyone in the room probably doesn't know. If the group is large, do it over several meetings, or simply take the entire staff meeting to complete the exercise. Then identify other exercises for future meetings to keep the momentum going.*

Rest Stop 14 — April 7

> *"Now if a boy can be circumcised on the Sabbath so that the law of Moses may not be broken, why are you angry with me for healing a man's whole body on the Sabbath? Stop judging by mere appearances, but instead judge correctly"* - John 7:23-24.

The Leadership Walk

The Pharisees were the leaders in Israel and they were angry with Jesus because He was doing good deeds on the Sabbath. Their thinking was flawed and it was causing them to be agitated about something that should not have upset them. Leaders must learn how to think and frame their problems correctly so they can truly rest when they take time away from work or ministry. Otherwise, they will waste that down time because they are expending so much mind energy through anger, worry, doubt and fear.

LEADERSHIP STEP: Your Step today is a Rest Stop from anger and all other thinking practices that are draining your energy and not allowing you to rest even when you try. You will do this by controlling what's called your self talk - taking control with God's help over what you think about and how you frame your problems. No matter how often toxic, rest-robbing thoughts creep in, you simply think "No!" and focus your mind on something positive or unrelated until the negative thoughts subside.

Emotional Intelligence   April 8

"'Who touched me?' Jesus asked. When they all denied it, Peter said, 'Master, the people are crowding and pressing against you'" - Luke 8:45.

Even though He was pressed on every side, Jesus knew when someone with a special need touched Him. Leaders are usually in touch with the people around them, emotionally and physically. They are not hesitant to connect with people through appropriate physical contact like a pat on the back or a handshake, but they also 'read' people to recognize when someone is distressed, has a question, or anxious to speak. This awareness has taken on the name 'emotional intelligence,' and in many situations is considered more important than practical knowledge or skills in a particular area of business work.

LEADERSHIP STEP: *Your Step today is to practice staying in touch with people. Your assignment is to watch people this week at work or at home and try to determine what they are feeling at different times. When appropriate, tell them you noticed something and ask them to confirm what they were feeling or sensing at that moment. See how accurate you can be by reading the physical signs they are communicating.*

Coaching April 9

"Where there is strife, there is pride, but wisdom is found in those who take advice" - Proverbs 13:10.

When leaders think they know or can do it all, they are proud, and pride in a relationship or an organization eventually leads to some sort of strife. Leaders also often explore territory that others have not seen, so there are many opinions about and options for what they should and should not do. The wise leader seeks counsel not only about their business but also about their leadership style and personality traits. This is referred to as coaching, and smart leaders regularly call upon or meet with people they trust to get advice and direction.

LEADERSHIP STEP: *Where is the greatest point of tension in your organization? Your Step today is to assume you are part of the problem - whether it's true or not - and identify someone in your company, field or city who can give you input around this area of need, whether it be budgeting, staffing, production or team building. The only antidote for pride is humility and you should humble yourself and get advice from multiple sources, to help correct the problem.*

Attitude April 10

"You were taught, with regard to your former way of life, to put off your old self, which is being corrupted by its

deceitful desires; to be made new in the attitude of your minds" - Ephesians 4:23.

Leaders can transform themselves when they have a new attitude toward their supervisors, peers, customers, work, responsibilities, salary or anything else that happens to be part of their work experience. To change, they first must recognize they have a bad attitude or else that attitude deceives them either into thinking that no one notices it or causes them to do things that are not in their best interests or those of the organization. When they are deceived, they operate out of what's called a shadow side, which is often functioning without them being aware of it or its effects on those around them.

LEADERSHIP STEP: *Your Step today is to work on being aware of your attitudes at work or home. You will do this by being aware of your thought life and what makes you angry. Are you angry when you drive? Avoiding someone or something at work? Spending a lot of time dwelling on a mistake or another person? Keep a written account of all things either that cause you to be angry or consume your thoughts today; then look for clues about why you have that attitude toward those things.*

Productivity   April 11

"Remain in me, as I also remain in you. No branch can bear fruit by itself; it must remain in the vine. Neither can you bear fruit unless you remain in me" - John 15:4.

Organizations expect their leaders to be fruitful and productive on behalf of the organization. They are expected to lead new initiatives that help their teams grow, or that enhance the product line or the mission of the organization. When this doesn't happen, the organization goes into 'maintenance mode' and that is not leadership; it is management. While leaders may have to manage some things, they are paid or chosen to bear fruit as leaders and will be held accountable for that to happen.

LEADERSHIP STEP: *On March 10, you were challenged to find ways to measure productivity in your organization. Your Step today is to develop a personal scorecard for productivity in your organization (or family). Set five areas in which you would like to be productive personally for the remainder of this year. Then define what fruit you would like to bear in each area. You will review these areas for the rest of the year to be accountable to yourself not just maintain but also grow.*

Finances   April 12

"John answered, 'Anyone who has two shirts should share with the one who has none, and anyone who has food should do the same'" - Luke 3:11.

Leaders have access to resources and determine how they will be distributed, which means they must deal with greed and the desire to amass personal wealth as they serve and grow their business. While personal generosity will combat and immunize against the greed virus, leaders need to help organizations be generous in their customer service, employee compensation and community involvement. Not only is this good business but it is also a priority with the Lord for the church, business and individuals alike.

LEADERSHIP STEP: *Your Step today is to evaluate your organization's commitment to generosity. Score your group from 1(poor) to 10(exceptional) in these areas: employee compensation, bonus plan, problem solving for customers, sharing information with stakeholders, community involvement, community investment, and employee transitions out of the organization. Total your scores (70 max). Are you satisfied with the score? What can you do to improve?*

Time Management   April 13

"Then he said, 'Jesus, remember me when you come into your kingdom.' Jesus answered him, 'Truly I tell you, today you will be with me in paradise'" - Luke 23:42-43.

In these verses, Luke described what Jesus did in the last minutes before He died. Jesus was hanging on a cross, suffering one of the most agonizing deaths man has ever devised against his fellow man. When the thief hanging next to Jesus made his petition, Jesus could have said, "Excuse me, I'm a little busy dying right now." Instead Jesus granted the man's petition and proceeded to surrender His spirit to the Father, staying true to His mission, purpose and priorities up to the very end. Leaders train themselves to keep the main thing the main thing and to focus on their priorities with the limited time resources available to them.

LEADERSHIP STEP: *On March 12, you were directed to write out a to-do list and make an effort to prioritize that list. How did it go? Today's Step is to do the same but to do it for every day next week. Write out a plan of what you would like or hope to do for each day. Then establish the order in which you will do those things. That is how you prioritize your time, putting more important things ahead of other possible activities and following the plan as best you can.*

Rest Stop 15   April 14

"Hear this, you who trample the needy and do away with the poor of the land, saying, 'When will the New Moon be over that we may sell grain, and the Sabbath be ended that we may market wheat?'—skimping on the measure ,boosting the price and cheating with dishonest scales, buying the poor with silver and the needy for a pair of sandals, selling even the sweepings with the wheat" - Amos 8:4-6.

The Lord was not pleased because the people could not wait until the Sabbath was over so they could resume business, which included unethical business practices. Leadership's rest day should include time for reflection on not just what they are doing in life and work, but how they are accomplishing it. It also seems that their rest should include some thought as to what they can do for the poor in the midst of their business pursuits and how those pursuits may be negatively affecting the needy.

LEADERSHIP STEP: *Your Step is to take some time today or on your next rest day to think about four things: 1) Are you happy with the business you are in? 2) Is your business helping or hurting the poor? 3) Are you helping the poor? and 4) Are your business practices ethical and how do you measure those ethics? Obviously this will only start this assessment, and we will revisit it from time to time to see what you are learning and what changes you are making from what you learn.*

Humility   April 15

"For those who exalt themselves will be humbled, and those who humble themselves will be exalted"
- Matthew 23:12.

To get ahead, leaders often have to promote themselves. Once they get started, leaders can begin to believe they deserve the honor and perks that come with being a leader. When the honor doesn't come, leaders can seek it and resent those who don't give it. To stay grounded, leaders must realize first and foremost that promotion comes from God. Then they must realize that they are successful because they are part of a team. They are unquestionably important team members, but nonetheless not indispensible or worthy of all the credit they may receive when things go as planned.

LEADERSHIP STEP: *Your Step today is to consider whether you are self-promoting or well grounded in a team mentality. Think of one thing you can do to honor and thank those who are on your team. It may be a handwritten note, a verbal thank you, or some token of your appreciation. These acts will serve to do what Jesus said in today's verse - they will keep you humble and prevent you both from promoting your own role in your team or expecting your team to honor you.*

Decision Making   April 16

"Because Joseph her husband was faithful to the law, and yet did not want to expose her to public disgrace, he had in mind to divorce her quietly" - Matthew 1:19.

As far as Joseph knew, Mary had violated their engagement covenant and violated their values as Jews. Joseph had to make a decision, but he was mindful of Mary, her family and their feelings when he did. With all that to consider, he decided to divorce her with as little fanfare as possible. When leaders make decisions that involve people, they don't have to humiliate others to prove the leader is correct. This also pertains to interpersonal dealings that don't need to involve sarcasm, verbal harassment, public ridicule or correction. Leaders' decisions affect many people and they need to keep that in mind as they make them.

LEADERSHIP STEP: *How well are you considering people as you make your decisions, especially about personnel? Your Step today is to reevaluate your termination policy to make sure it is as sensitive as possible to that traumatic experience for those being let go. Are you generous with your severance? Do you help those being released to find other work? Remember, you reap what you sow, so be merciful and God will be merciful to you if you are ever in that position.*

Communication   April 17

"After this letter has been read to you, see that it is also read in the church of the Laodiceans and that you in turn read the letter from Laodicea" - Colossians 4:16.

Paul used the technology of his day - letters and the Roman system of roads and ships - to communicate with his followers and inform them of his latest plans and insights. When he sent this particular letter to Colossae, he made sure they would circulate it among the other local churches. The point is that leaders use whatever means possible to spread their 'word' to those who need to hear or can benefit from it. If Paul were alive today, he would probably use all the social media channels to disseminate his message. Modern leaders should do the same.

LEADERSHIP STEP: *Are you up to speed on the media available to you to communicate with those who need or want to hear from you? Your Step today is to stop talking about learning the technology and do it. Get with someone or take the time to learn about and register for Twitter, online conference calling or any other media that you could benefit from using. If you have an account for those social media, then spend your time today planning how you will use them more effectively.*

Spiritual Growth   April 18

"These commandments that I give you today are to be on your hearts" - Deuteronomy 6:6.

Leaders should fill their hearts with good things because leadership is not only a head but also a heart matter. The Lord expects leaders to store His requirements for righteous leadership in their hearts so they can readily find their way into daily decisions and work relationships.

The Leadership Walk

While the Bible does not give specific directions for how to build a business, it does give specific directions for ethics, business practices and fairness.

LEADERSHIP STEP: *Your Step is to do a quick search on the topic of leadership in the book of Proverbs. Go to any online Bible and do a search for the words* **king** *and* **prince** *in Proverbs. Then substitute the word* **leader** *wherever you find king or prince, and see what Proverbs has to say to the one in charge or who is overseeing other people. What can you learn from those verses to apply to your leadership work? Print and carry that list with you for the rest of the week.*

Personal Development April 19

"The king assigned them a daily amount of food and wine from the king's table. They were to be trained for three years, and after that they were to enter the king's service" - Daniel 1:5.

Daniel was taken from the security and comfort of his Judean homeland and sent to Babylon University, where he was given a new name and had to learn a new culture, which included language, customs, currency, property rights and religious practices. This was his preparation to lead in Babylon and God chose his course of study. Leaders must give themselves to education and training, which is a lifelong experience and practice. Without this, there is no growth and consequently those leaders will not be able to lead and embrace fresh new initiatives.

LEADERSHIP STEP: *Your Step today is to think about your personal development plan to prepare for the future. Does that plan include more education? What is stopping you from pursuing that education? Pretend that you have all the money and time you need, and then decide where you would go to obtain this education and training. Once you decide* that, begin to research how that can happen. Don't assume it's impossible; work like it is possible and it will happen!

Team Building   April 20

*"Even so the body is not made up of
one part but of many" - 1 Corinthians 12:14.*

Leaders understand that they are only as good as the team that surrounds them. Paul's analogy of the church being like the human body can also be applied to any business or organization. There are many interrelated parts that must function well together; if one part of that organization is sick or malfunctioning, then the entire entity is rendered 'sick' or 'wounded.' Therefore effective leaders pay close attention to the health and dynamics not only of the team but also of the individual members.

LEADERSHIP STEP: *It is common to have an annual physical checkup when your body is evaluated and problems addressed. Your Step today is to schedule your annual department or organizational checkup. This will take place at an offsite, away from the normal office or plant routine. It would also be helpful to enlist the services of a consultant to come in and help run the offsite to give leadership another set of eyes and ears to assess your team's health.*

Rest Stop 16   April 21

"'If you keep your feet from breaking the Sabbath and from doing as you please on my holy day, if you call the Sabbath a delight and the Lord's holy day honorable, and if you honor it by not going your own way and not doing as you please or speaking idle words, then you will find your joy in the Lord, and I will cause you to ride in triumph on the heights of the land and to feast on the inheritance of your

father Jacob.' For the mouth of the Lord has spoken"
- Isaiah 58:13-14.

There is a need for leaders to regularly step away from the pressures of their work to address other needs they have in their lives. This day of rest is not to be a time of dread when they have to step away from work, but a time of delight when they choose to give some thought to the Lord and to the needs of other people. When they do this, they will find their joy not just in their work but also in the Lord who assigned them their purposeful work. And what leader doesn't need this, for work can often be frustrating and a source of disappointing effort that does not yield its intended results?

LEADERSHIP STEP: *On your next rest day, your Step is to focus on "not doing as you please" or "speaking idle words." You will use that day to visit someone close to you - family member, friend, associate or whoever the Lord lays on your heart. Bless them by hosting them at a meal or over coffee. Your objective is simple: refresh that person with encouraging words and actions so that your needs are not your main focus when you take a day to step away from the pressures of labor.*

Strategy   April 22

*"Plans are established by seeking advice;
so if you wage war, obtain guidance" - Proverbs 20:18.*

Armies don't just show up one day and decide to fight it out with an enemy. They determine what their objectives are and then develop a strategy to accomplish their objectives along with strategies for each battle they will wage. Usually there is a war council of top advisers who are experienced and who also command resources that will engage in the battle. The same is true for leadership in any organization, whether a family or company. The strategic plans, however, are determined by the objectives and must be clear for all is the strategy is to have any chance for success.

LEADERSHIP STEP: *In order to develop a clear strategy, you must have clear objectives. If it is to get out of personal debt, you must have a strategy for that objective. If it is to launch a new product line, then be clear on the product, when it will be launched and what the sales goals are. Identify one objective today for your enterprise, and then assemble some trusted advisers to evaluate or map out the strategic plans that will enable you to reach that objective by a certain time.*

Change   April 23

"Then a voice told him, 'Get up, Peter. Kill and eat.' 'Surely not, Lord!' Peter replied. 'I have never eaten anything impure or unclean'" - Acts 10:13-14.

Up to this point in time, Peter had maintained a kosher diet according to Old Testament Law. Then a voice from heaven told him to change his diet and he said, "No!" Even though it was a heavenly directive, he was being asked to change a lifelong pattern and it represented not an opportunity but a loss in his eyes. When leaders announce well-thought-out change initiatives, people can often respond in the same manner. The leaders can be offended or perceive the followers as rebellious or uncooperative.

LEADERSHIP STEP: *If you are leading change, you must provide support services for those most directly affected, whether it's a move for your family or a new product for your company. Your Step today is to sit down and listen to those being impacted by change and better understand what kind of support you can provide for them. Perhaps you need to change your attitude toward those resisting the change so you can find out and understand why they are doing so.*

People Skills   April 24

" . . . and standing behind Him at His feet, weeping, she began to wet His feet with her tears, and kept wiping them with the hair of her head, and kissing His feet and anointing them with the perfume" - Luke 7:38.

The scenario of a woman wetting Jesus' feet with tears and drying them with her hair is apt to make most people uncomfortable. Yet what does this say about Jesus? It says that He was supremely accessible and approachable. The woman was not afraid of being embarrassed or rebuked. She could be herself around Him and be accepted. She could be honest and open with her feelings and not be concerned that He would react, take advantage of, or be dismissive of her emotional moment. Effective leaders create the same atmosphere for their followers that allows genuine honesty and transparency.

LEADERSHIP STEP: *Your Step today is to evaluate how accessible you are as a leader. First, look at your workspace. Is it fortified with closed doors and assistants stationed between the people and you, or is it open? Next, look at your calendar. How much time every week do you spend with others? Third, examine the content in meetings. Is time with followers spent talking about your agenda or what's on their minds and hearts? What did you learn from your answers?*

Purpose   April 25

"But the plans of the Lord stand firm forever, the purposes of his heart through all generations" - Psalm 33:11.

God doesn't just have a purpose for individuals or the Church, He has a purpose for every organization, including companies, government agencies, schools, and other enterprises. A leader's job is to clarify that organizational purpose and then help individuals express their purpose within the larger group purpose. Some call this vision, mission, calling or destiny, but when God's purpose aligns with group purpose and individual purpose is expressed, there is a flow of energy and alignment that stems from God's involvement, even if it's a bank or a garden club.

LEADERSHIP STEP: *Your Step today is to develop, reaffirm or clarify the purpose for each organization of which you are a leader, including your family. Does that entity have a purpose statement? If so, is it accurate? Is it operational? Do followers understand what it is? If your group does not have a statement, then you develop one. Gather people together and summarize why the organization (or family) exists in one short sentence that is accurate and life-giving.*

Goals — April 26

"Do not put your trust in princes, in human beings, who cannot save. When their spirit departs, they return to the ground; on that very day their plans come to nothing. Blessed are those whose help is the God of Jacob, whose hope is in the Lord their God" - Psalm 145:3-5.

Leaders are often charismatic people and their dynamic personality gets things done by sheer force of energy and vision. Yet all leaders have limitations and weaknesses, and their ultimate weakness is they are mortal. They get old and eventually pass from this life. While leaders and organizations need to set goals, they are working in a fallen world with people who have limitations, weaknesses and physical frailties. Therefore they must temper their aggressive goal setting and realize that their best-laid plans will oft go astray and lead to less than they had hoped.

LEADERSHIP STEP: *Are you grounded in your own mortality and limitations? Do you accept the limitations of* others? Your Step today is to begin to develop a succession plan for your position, realizing that you may move on to take a new one at some point, or move on to glory! Then examine where you put your faith. Is it in your abilities and experience, or in the God of your abilities and experience? Finally, evaluate how you react to other people's human weakness.

Organization April 27

"Brothers and sisters, choose seven men from among you who are known to be full of the Spirit and wisdom. We will turn this responsibility over to them and will give our attention to prayer and the ministry of the word"
- Acts 6:3-4.

As the early church grew, the apostles did not have an organizational problem as told in this passage; they had a people problem. They had too much work and not enough people. Rather than take on more work themselves, they opted to identify new workers. Leaders must face the challenge of how to organize their work not only when they start, but also as they and the organization grow. The answer is not always to do more or less, but to put the right people in the right places doing the things they do best.

LEADERSHIP STEP: *Today's Step is to conduct a staff assessment or an analysis of your own workload. Prepare to do a time inventory for your team (and yourself). Have them each do a time inventory log (a sample can be found in the Appendix) for the next week, keeping track in half hour groupings what they did every day for the week. Then have them total the amounts by category (phone, customers, reports, etc.) and have a meeting to discuss the workload and whether it's time to bring on more people.*

Rest Stop 17 April 28

"Blessed is the one who does this—the person who holds

it fast, who keeps the Sabbath without desecrating it, and keeps their hands from doing any evil" - Isaiah 56:2-3.

The Lord promises a blessing to anyone who keeps and refuses to desecrate the Sabbath. That does not mean rigidly doing nothing, otherwise pastors, church musicians, Sunday school teachers and anyone involved in church work are violating the Sabbath. And it is not a specific day, otherwise rescue responders, people in the military, doctors and nurses who work on Saturday or Sunday are 'doing evil.' Keeping the Sabbath is taking time to rest, worship, do good to the poor or breaking with normal workday routines to engage in activities that refresh and energize to then re-engage with normal work or family duties.

LEADERSHIP STEP: *Assuming you have a regular habit of worship, your Step today is to address your need for or lack of a hobby. Do you have one? What is it? If you don't have one, what's the reason? A hobby is something you do mostly because you enjoy it, even though it may cost you time and money to engage in it. Do you see that concept as frivolous or wasteful? If so, you may be violating a principle of the 'Sabbath,' which is to take time away from the routine and structure of work.*

Service   April 29

"Jesus knew that the Father had put all things under his power, and that he had come from God and was returning to God; so he got up from the meal, took off his outer clothing, and wrapped a towel around his waist"
- John 13:3-4.

Jesus knew who He was and that He had power and control over 'all things.' So what did He do as a result? He stripped down to His 'work clothes,' took a towel and washed the feet of His disciples. He used His power to serve the practical needs of others in this instance washing their dirty feet that had accumulated dust from walking life's messy roads. Leaders have power, but they are aware that the power can inflate their ego, so they look for opportunities to humble themselves, especially by serving others. And serving others is not being polite; it is doing for others what they cannot do or think to do for themselves.

LEADERSHIP STEP*: If you are not yet a leader, write out today some of the things you will do with your leadership authority and power when you receive them. If you are a leader, examine how effectively you serve others. List all the instances where you are using your power to serve other's needs. If your list is not adequate to suit you, then devote some creative time to think of practical things you can do to better serve others from your position of authority.*

Motivation   April 30

> *"Whatever you do, work at it with all your heart, as working for the Lord, not for human masters, since you know that you will receive an inheritance from the Lord as a reward. It is the Lord Christ you are serving"* - *Colossians 3:23-24.*

Motivation is an issue that leaders must face, addressing the needs of others as well as their own. Money, benefits, prestige, a nice office, reporting to an effective supervisor, loss of privileges, and demotion are all motivators, but they are called extrinsic, for they motivate from outside the worker or leader. Intrinsic motivators are much more effective and powerful, and stem from the reason for or satisfaction from the results of the work itself. In today's passage, the most lasting and effective means of motivation are to do the work for the Lord, because He is always watching and will ultimately reward with eternal benefits.

LEADERSHIP STEP: *Your best indicator of why you do what you do often shows when you are **not** rewarded for your labors as you deem appropriate. That disappointment can lead you to hold back your best efforts. Your Step today is to honestly reflect on why you do what you do. Is it for money, promotion, or attention? Do you have a vision that you are working for the Lord and not for your company or your board of directors? Do you need to adjust your attitude in this regard?*

Self-Awareness   May 1

> **"Whenever the spirit from God came on Saul, David would take up his lyre and play. Then relief would come to Saul; he would feel better, and the evil spirit would leave him"** - 1 Samuel 16:23.

Saul had an "evil spirit" that resulted in depression, anxiety and anger. This problem was a problem for everyone in the royal court, yet no one would dare confront or deal with this issue, including Saul himself. Instead, everyone tried to 'medicate' and placate him with music played by David. Saul became the focus and center of attention instead of God or the needs of the people. When leaders control their situation through moods or preoccupation with their own personal problems, an organizational dysfunction takes root that only grows bigger and stronger unless dealt with honestly and directly by the management team or the board of directors.

LEADERSHIP STEP: *As a leader, do people know which one of you will show up every day? Are you consistent with your moods and feelings, or do you have people walking on eggshells around you? Your Step today is to identify a counselor, whether you think you need one or not, and to schedule time to talk about any personal or personality challenges that may be impacting those with whom you* work. Then you should plan on meeting with that person at least once every quarter.

Knowledge   May 2

> "... then you will understand the fear of the Lord and find the knowledge of God" - Proverbs 2:5.

The verses preceding this one speak about the price leaders must pay to get the knowledge they need to do their job of leading. The price includes seeking, asking, digging and searching. In other words, knowledge cannot be a passive pursuit. Effective leaders must not only seek practical knowledge but also apply the same kind of commitment and diligence to obtain knowledge of God's will and ways. What's more, with the ever-changing nature of society and the organizations therein, leaders must always be seeking new knowledge and skill to remain relevant.

LEADERSHIP STEP: *It is said that leaders are readers, and reading is one way to obtain the knowledge that you need and seek for your leadership role. What are you reading? Do you have a reading plan for areas you need to explore or learn? You don't have to read to read, for you can listen and fulfill your reading requirement as well. Audio books or educational DVDs are also beneficial and allow you to make use of commute or down time to add to your body of knowledge.*

Influence   May 3

> "All the believers were one in heart and mind. No one claimed that any of their possessions was their own, but they shared everything they had" - Acts 4:32.

This verse shows the unity of purpose that was operating in the early church. That kind of unity could not be obtained by coercion or manipulation. It was present because of Jesus' influence that was established through His teaching and life example. When the people saw this and the apostles taught this, there was unity through influence. Leaders know and want this kind of unity in their organization; they often don't know how to get it or want it more quickly than influence can produce. In either scenario, they abandon their role to influence followers and begin to demand compliance.

LEADERSHIP STEP: *Let's examine your role as influencer in your organization or family. One way you can influence is through training and teaching. How much time do you spend instructing your followers in what's most important to you and your organization, and then equipping them to do what you are teaching? Your Step today is to map out a plan today that will provide you opportunities to teach and influence in your staff meetings, off sites and other corporate gatherings.*

Power   May 4

"Woe to the land whose king was a servant and whose princes feast in the morning" - Ecclesiastes 10:6.

Today's verse indicates that there are two categories of leaders who abuse power when they finally obtain it. One group are the former 'servants' - those who were abused by power and, now that they have it, are going to abuse it the way they had experienced it. The second group is made up of 'princes' - those who have always had power by virtue of the fact that they are royalty and were never followers. The princes use their power to feed themselves and their ego and not to serve the needs of others. Both groups are guilty of abusing power by not using it for the purpose it was given, and that is to lead effectively, not to use it to serve personal needs.

LEADERSHIP STEP: *The best time to determine how you*

will use leadership power is before you have it. If you already have it, you must learn to shift the benefit of your power to others and to the future good of the organization. Your Step today is to revisit an exercise from January 22 and develop your leadership philosophy that describes how you will use your leadership power. Once you have written it out, obtain some help from others in deciding how you will apply it on a daily basis.

Rest Stop 18 — May 5

"Remember that you were slaves in Egypt and that the Lord your God brought you out of there with a mighty hand and an outstretched arm. Therefore the Lord your God has commanded you to observe the Sabbath day" - Deuteronomy 5:15.

The Israelites were once slaves in Egypt, victims of a Pharaoh who subjected them to harsh labor under oppressive conditions. Then Moses came back to Egypt and ordered Pharaoh to set God's people free. After a bitter struggle, Pharaoh complied and the people made the journey to the Promised Land flowing with milk and honey. They were to commemorate their freedom every Sabbath day by remembering where they had come from and where they presently were.

LEADERSHIP STEP: *No matter how intense your work pressure to produce, God has set you free to labor for and with Him in your current position. Your Step today is to take some time to reflect on God's role in your current work and thank Him for His help and provision. You can honor Him by stepping away from your normal duties and trusting Him to take care of things in your absence, while you reflect and journal your thoughts on the way He has led you throughout your career path.*

Wisdom — May 6

> *"So I said, 'Wisdom is better than strength.' But the poor man's wisdom is despised, and his words are no longer heeded"* - Ecclesiastes 9:16.

Wisdom is a form of strength and competitive advantage, and that makes it a form of strength in itself. Leaders are expected to have wisdom and know how to apply it in their work or social settings. Yet if a wise person is 'poor' - has no position or authority - then his or her wisdom has no platform from which to operate and affect other people or their life situations. Therefore to be a good steward of wisdom, a leader must actively seek opportunities for that wisdom to be showcased and become an important corporate strength. That means a leader must not shy away from leadership!

LEADERSHIP STEP: As a wise leader, you must create platforms for your wisdom to make a difference. Your Step today is to be creative and think of ways for your wisdom to be released. One way is training. The other way is to speak up more often in meetings. The third is to write or broadcast. Think of some other ways with which you are comfortable speaking wisdom and then overcome any false sense of humility to speak up, for it will certainly help and bless many.

Persuasion — May 7

> *"The hearts of the wise make their mouths prudent, and their lips promote instruction"* - Proverbs 16:23.

Persuasion is a key component of servant leadership, for coercion and manipulation to force compliance are not acceptable to those who have the best interests of others at heart. This simply means that leaders must work to discover ways to paint pictures of new realities that allow people to see and accept them on their own terms. Jesus was clear that the source for gracious, persuasive words was the heart and not the brain, for He said that the mouth speaks out of the abundance or lack in the heart. Leaders must therefore work on their heart to increase their ability to influence others.

LEADERSHIP STEP: *If you are saying one thing and doing another, people see the inconsistency and it affects your ability as a leader to persuade them to change their own behavior. Therefore your Step today is to examine if you are modeling the behavior or practice you are attempting to persuade others to adopt. For example, are you tardy but urging others not to be? Spend some time in honest self-reflection and correct areas that detract from your credibility.*

Values   May 8

"Kings detest wrongdoing, for a throne is established through righteousness" - Proverbs 16:12.

Kings were the leaders in the Old Testament, so principles that applied to them can easily apply to modern leaders in any sphere or life. In this verse, the wisdom writer indicated that a leader's foundation was righteous deeds and active opposition to wrongdoing. Above all, a king was to stand for justice and leaders must do the same today. That means justice in human relations, in customer service, in employee affairs, in organizational commitments and in financial affairs. Absence of justice in any one of those areas can 'undo' leaders, no matter how much good they have done in the other areas.

LEADERSHIP STEP: *Your Step today is to do a justice audit of your family or workplace. Take a look at the justice level in each one of the areas mentioned above: human relations, customer service, employee affairs, organizational* *commitments and financial affairs. Give some thought to each area and then assign a score of 1 (poor) or 5 (excellent) in each area. Get three other people to do the same, then get together and compare your scores. What do they tell you?*

Ethics — May 9

"Love and faithfulness keep a king safe; through love his throne is made secure" - Proverbs 20:28.

When leaders act or make decisions, they would do well to be guarded and guided by the values of love and faithfulness. Those two principles would be a strong foundation for any ethical leadership philosophy. This verse also seems to imply that the leaders who give love get love in return, and that helps make their leadership tenure meaningful and longer-lasting. It may be strange to think of love in an organizational context, but God's ways are effective, not just in church but also in other life situations.

LEADERSHIP STEP: *Your Step today is to set aside 45 minutes to consider how love can play a more important role in your leadership decisions and behavior. Go to 1 Corinthians 13, the well-known chapter on love, read it and then re-read it. Look at the various components of love as Paul described them, and evaluate your leadership style in light of those components. Why doesn't love play a more important role in your work life? What changes do you need to make based on 1 Corinthians 13?*

Collaboration — May 10

"They tie up heavy, cumbersome loads and put them on other people's shoulders, but they themselves are not willing to lift a finger to move them" - Matthew 23:4.

Jesus condemned leaders of Israel who made heavy and

hard work for others, while not doing anything to help them. It is similar to Pharaoh when he ordered the people to make bricks, but also to gather their own straw to make them. When leaders act like this, they are reminding people who is in charge and that they have the right to order work while being exempt from that same work. Effective leaders see co-workers more as partners and not as someone to do the work they demand. These leaders also lighten the burden of their team members by eliminating needless rules and obstacles to creativity and productivity.

LEADERSHIP STEP: *Do you make your team's work easier or more difficult? Your Step today is to answer that question by circulating a memo to your team asking one question: if the organization could eliminate one thing - rule, procedure, meeting, role, behavior, or policy - to enhance your work effectiveness or happiness, what would it be? If you want honest answers, have people answer anonymously if they so choose. Be open to the fact that you are an obstacle!*

Relationships   May 11

"The righteous care for the needs of their animals, but the kindest acts of the wicked are cruel" - Proverbs 12:10.

The wisdom writer was describing farmers, who realize they must take good care of their work animals since they are the ones doing the work that feeds their families. If that was true of farmers and the relationships with their oxen and cattle, how much more should leaders take good care of those who make the leaders look good by doing good work? Yet some leaders feel it below them to give special treatment to those in their employ, feeling that somehow that makes them vulnerable or will cause the workers to take advantage of them and their kindness.

LEADERSHIP STEP: *Do you know what each of your*

team members needs to feel like they have received 'special treatment?' For one, it may be time off; for another, special recognition; for another, a bonus. Your Step today is to take some time to find out what you can do to take care of the needs of each of your team members, remembering that each person is different and what motivates or blesses you may not be true for them. Once you discover what it is, find a way to do it for them regularly.

Rest Stop 19 — May 12

"There are six days when you may work, but the seventh day is a day of sabbath rest, a day of sacred assembly. You are not to do any work; wherever you live, it is a sabbath to the Lord" - Leviticus 23:3.

There are some who focus on the seventh day Sabbath rest, but they are not so focused on the six days of work that was to take place from sunrise to sunset. It seems in this context that the seventh day was a day of rest that was 'earned' or required by the rigors of the other six days.

What's more, that rest was not a day of doing nothing, but a day for focusing at least in part on the Lord. Leaders should understand their need for a break in their routine because of the demanding and full schedule they have the remainder of the week.

LEADERSHIP STEP: *Is your rest based on the need to get away from work because you hate it, or because you love your work and need the energy your rest day gives you so you can dive back in as soon as possible? Rather than focus on your rest as today's Step, focus on your work. Are you happy and fulfilled? Are you doing meaningful work that gives you life, or work that is taking more than it gives? If it's the latter, rest is a necessary escape and not a the respite God intended it to be.*

Emotional Intelligence   May 13

"And Jacob noticed that Laban's attitude toward him was not what it had been" - Genesis 31:2.

Jacob was paying attention and saw that his father-in-law's attitude had changed toward him and his work, so he began to prepare for his departure from the "family business." Jacob did not ignore the signs and hope things would change. He did not try to talk to Laban or work out a new deal. He simply saw that it was a new season in his life, and he acted accordingly. Leaders must read other people and determine what to do to maintain, adjust or end business relationships, regardless of the past success, family ties, or difficulty of the transition. Yet it all started with Jacob paying attention and seeing the emotional state of his business partner and boss.

LEADERSHIP STEP: *One of the best ways to 'read' people is to observe them in meetings and to listen to their responses. When you notice someone say "yes" to a question, but draw out the yes, saying it slowly with their voice pitch rising as they say it, they are really saying "yes, but." You need to follow that with a question to clarify. Your Step for this week is to stop doodling or working on your computer during meetings to watch the people and probe deeper to draw them out.*

Coaching   May 14

"Listen to advice and accept discipline, and at the end you will be counted among the wise" - Proverbs 19:20.

"No man is an island" is a secular proverb that is not spoken much any more, but it remains relevant. No leader is adequate to see or know all that there is to see and know. Yet with leadership comes the wisdom from the experience of decisions, some that worked and some that did not.

That wisdom needs to be shared in the organization, not just within departments, but also throughout the organization. Leadership should adopt a coaching program where everyone in the company has access to and can draw on the advice and counsel from wisdom sources.

LEADERSHIP STEP: If you want your organization to have wisdom, you have to learn how to share wisdom and have it accepted and acted upon by all. Your Step today is to acknowledge that part of your role as a leader is to coach others, both in and sometimes outside your organization. Once you accept that fact, you must then establish a coaching program to be adopted throughout your department or organization. This can be formal or informal, but should be accessible to all.

Attitude — May 15

"For the word of God is alive and active. Sharper than any double-edged sword, it penetrates even to dividing soul and spirit, joints and marrow; it judges the thoughts and attitudes of the heart" - Hebrews 4:12.

It is remarkable that a book written thousands of years ago is still powerful enough today to evaluate leaders' thoughts and attitudes. Of course, that is because the Author of that Book is still alive, standing behind the words written to direct, convict, inspire, confront, and encourage those who submit to that Book called the Bible. Leaders do well when they not only study economics, accounting, strategy and change tactics, but also have a regular reading and study program in God's word.

LEADERSHIP STEP: What is your relationship like with God's word at this point in your leadership life? Your Step today is to evaluate whether or not you are learning and growing in the knowledge of God's word. Then you must identify a reading program, study group, coursework or some other way to become more knowledgeable and intimate with the Bible. Your goal is not just to learn about it, but also to allow the Word to shape and guide your leadership decisions.

Productivity   May 16

"But the fruit of the Spirit is love, joy, peace, forbearance, kindness, goodness, faithfulness, gentleness and self-control. Against such things there is no law" - Galatians 5:22.

There is no asterisk after this verse explaining that leaders are exempt from producing, or allowing the Spirit to produce, the examples of character fruit mentioned in this verse. It does not say here, "Leaders are permitted to be impatient, angry, unkind, unpredictable and undisciplined because they have important work to do, and have to get it done by being tough." In other words, leaders are expected to allow God to work in their lives so they can discover ways to lead while being an example of God's man or woman in their role at work, in ministry or at home.

LEADERSHIP STEP: *As you have done with other Steps, today you will do a self-evaluation. Write each of the examples of fruit in this verse on a sheet in your journal, and then evaluate yourself in each by assigning a number from 1 (missing in action) to 5 (almost always present in my life) for work and home. If you have the courage, have someone else do it also and compare his or her results to yours. Then pray and allow the Spirit access to your heart to develop that area.*

Finances   May 17

"But woe to you who are rich, for you have already received your comfort" - Luke 6:24.

When companies and organizations are successful, there is usually a monetary return and reward for that success. Effective leaders don't allow money to cover up the problems in their organizations, and those same leaders should also help their organizations be sensitive to the needs that exist in their communities and even among the families of their employees. They can then help direct organizational finances toward helping those in need, which may be in the form of cash or employees volunteering in the community among the poor. This will help keep greed and a money-only focus from infecting the organization.

LEADERSHIP STEP: *What is your organization's position toward the poor and needy? If your focus is only on the needs in your immediate world, you will lose touch with how people are suffering all around you in the community and world. Your Step today is to examine two things: what your company (or family) does to help the poor and what do you do personally? Then help lead a company discussion around opportunities that can make a difference where profit is not the main consideration.*

Time Management   May 18

"Now that you know these things, you will be blessed if you do them" - John 13:17.

Jesus was clear that not doing what you know to do renders your knowledge worthless. It is action that counts most and not good intentions or talking about what needs to be done. Leaders understand this and have a bias for action whenever and wherever possible. This means they know how to manage and direct the most limited resource of all, and that is time - both for individuals and the teams of which they are a part. To do this, leaders must help the organization prioritize its time so that the leaders are putting first things first and avoiding the urgent in order to perform important things.

LEADERSHIP STEP: *Today's Step involves examining your team's time management practices, and first you will look at time wasters inherent in your organization. Are the offices or plant laid out in a way that saves time? Do policies and procedures facilitate decisions or cause them to be delayed? How is the computer system? Filing system? Then go to the tougher evaluation: are you pursuing the highest priorities for the organization that will render the greatest returns?*

Rest Stop 20 — May 19

"These are the Lord's appointed festivals, the sacred assemblies you are to proclaim at their appointed times" - Leviticus 23:4.

Israel not only had Sabbaths to observe, they also had many high holy days on which they had to assemble "before the Lord." Depending on where they lived, they had to travel short or long distances to Jerusalem to participate. The Lord did not apologize for requiring the people to spend some money and exert some effort to take a break from their workaday world to go spend time with Him through those annual traditions. Leaders must also find ways to incorporate regular refreshment trips to conferences, seminars, and educational experiences of both a spiritual and secular nature that help them gain perspective on their world back home.

LEADERSHIP STEP: *Is there some place, speaker or travel or conference experience that you have found to energize you in the work you do? Your Step today is to make plans to attend whatever that may be as soon as possible. If you* don't have that in your life, then your Step is to search and find something that can become a tradition in your annual calendar. It can be across town or across the country; your Step is to find a way to get there as often as possible.

Humility   May 20

"Humble yourselves, therefore, under God's mighty hand, that he may lift you up in due time" - 1 Peter 5:6.

Being a humble leader is always a notable thing because there can be so few in the marketplace. Leaders and emerging leaders can become competitive and aggressive, seeking more notoriety and power as they move up the organizational ladder. Today's verse urges everyone, even leaders, to put their promotions and honors in God's hands while they humble themselves. When they do, God will promote them according to His will and timetable and not theirs. This frees leaders to serve others and not use them as steppingstones for leadership careers.

LEADERSHIP STEP: *How do you feel when someone else with whom you work closely is promoted or honored? If you can rejoice with them and celebrate, you have truly put your own career in God's hands. If you are envious or depressed, you are not humbling yourself. The best way to avoid this is to initiate the process of recognizing others for their work and contributions. Your Step today is to find someone this week to honor for his or her work in a way that is meaningful for that person.*

Decision Making   May 21

"With this in mind, since I myself have carefully investigated everything from the beginning, I too decided to write an orderly account for you, most excellent Theophilus, so that you may know

the certainty of the things you have been taught"
- Luke 1:3-4.

These two verses give insight into how Luke decided to write his gospel. Obviously, the Holy Spirit inspired him, but notice how naturally Luke described the decision-making process. He was a scientist so Luke did what was natural: conducted research and decided to write an orderly account of Jesus' ministry. Theophilus had commissioned this work, and Luke set as his objective the confirmation of what Theophilus had been taught. All the while, God was directing Luke's path in a most natural way, using Luke's skill, past history, gifts and professional training to accomplish God's will as he wrote the inspired word of God. Leaders should expect God to use and move on them in a similar way – using their personality and interests to do His will.

LEADERSHIP STEP: *Are you facing a decision of any magnitude as a leader? Then follow the same process today that Luke did 2,000 years ago. Start out by understanding who you are and what you do best. Consider from where or whom the opportunity is originating. Do some research. Get clear about the objective you have in mind as you make the decision and then trust that the Lord has been guiding you through your thoughts and the circumstances at hand.*

Communication   May 22

"So it is with you. Unless you speak intelligible words with your tongue, how will anyone know what you are saying? You will just be speaking into the air" - 1 Corinthians 14:9.

It is important that leaders are clear in their communications with others, and that includes their followers, peers, customers, clients, suppliers and the public at large. This requires that not only the proper words be used, but also that the message leaders communicate is clear - and that they use the appropriate media to relay the message. What's more, leaders must have the credibility that comes with being a role model and having integrity for the message to be believed and received by others.

***LEADERSHIP STEP:** The only way you can know if you are communicating effectively is to seek feedback from your audience and listeners. One practice you can use is a five-minute wrap up at the end of every meeting when everyone gives you feedback on what the group had just decided and who is going to do what by when. Another method is to ask people after a speech or memo to tell you what you just said and its potential impact on their work or lives.*

Spiritual Growth   May 23

"When Jonah's warning reached the king of Nineveh, he rose from his throne, took off his royal robes, covered himself with sackcloth and sat down in the dust" - Jonah 3:6.

The king of Nineveh was not part of the Jewish community but a worshiper of idols. Yet when the warning came from Jonah, he humbled himself, fasted and prayed, and ordered his subjects to do the same. Leaders cannot ignore their own spiritual side, or look past the spiritual life of those who follow. Leaders should consider the ethical implications of what they do and the decisions they make, and realize that they will answer to the Lord not only for what they do in their personal lives, but also what they do in their business lives. In other words, leaders need to keep in mind that God is watching them - all the time.

***LEADERSHIP STEP:** Are you paying attention to your spiritual side as you express your business side? Do you give* *people leeway to do the same? Today's Step is to find one thing you can do to raise the spiritual awareness of your team or company. That may be a seminar on values, a book on ethics, or a speaker for a staff meeting who will talk about creativity and the spiritual aspect of people that are just as important as business knowledge and strategy.*

Personal Development   May 24

"Moses was educated in all the wisdom of the Egyptians and was powerful in speech and action" - Acts 7:22.

Moses' foundation for leadership was his education; later on in life, God worked on his character. Yet without doubt he went to the finest schools and had the best teachers in preparation for what his foster mother assumed was a bright future in Egypt. Leaders cannot ignore their need for training and education, for leadership requires specific knowledge of the sphere in which they lead as well as a self-awareness that enables leaders to know their strengths and in what scenario they function best.

LEADERSHIP STEP: *Your Step today is to search for available education anyplace in the world or online, without judging whether you can afford the time or money. Just do the research. Perhaps a summer program or an intensive seminar would be possible? You need to make a significant educational investment in yourself, which will pay dividends to your leadership effectiveness for years to come. The time is now.*

Team Building   May 25

Keep on loving one another as brothers and sisters" - Hebrews 13:1.

There is no way to build effective teams without involving some measure of love and compassion. Today's verse indicates that there is a challenge to this, for the closer and longer team members work with one another, the more wrinkles and flaws they will see in one another. That will require that they have some bond beyond the mission of the organization that will keep them together and the grease that lubricates the machinery of teamwork is in part made up of love.

LEADERSHIP STEP: *How is the love quotient on your work team? Do people care for one another beyond the work of the group? Perhaps it is time to plan an offsite meeting, which can take place for part or all of a day, or for more than one day. During this offsite, plan fun things with your team like a movie, a play, shopping, team-building exercises or simply spending time talking about things other than work. Your goal is to build memories together as people, not workers.*

Rest Stop 21   May 26

"So, because Jesus was doing these things on the Sabbath, the Jewish leaders began to persecute him" - **John 5:16.**

Jesus did good deeds on the Sabbath day and the Jews persecuted Him. They preferred He did nothing rather than bring healing and help to people. Leaders are busy people and need their rest, but they also need to use their down time doing good deeds for the poor and needy for which they do not get paid. This enables leaders to use their holiday and Sabbath times to reconnect with their own humanity and to realize how blessed they are. By doing this, they put their leadership problems and positions of authority in proper perspective so they don't get overly impressed with who they are!

LEADERSHIP STEP: *What are you doing that can be called good deeds for which you do not get recognition or reward? Your Step today is to assess your work among the poor - no,* giving money does not count - and consider how you can be more personally involved with relieving the suffering and meeting the needs of the oppressed, just like Jesus did. This may involve a short-term missions trip, volunteering at a food bank, hospital or home for the elderly.

Strategy   May 27

"At Iconium Paul and Barnabas went as usual into the Jewish synagogue. There they spoke so effectively that a great number of Jews and Greeks believed" - Acts 14:1.

Paul had a strategy for his ministry work, which was to go to the major population areas of the Roman Empire. When he got there, he went to the synagogue first, where of course he found Jews, but also found devout Gentiles who believed in one God, but who would not abide by the rules of a kosher diet. When the Jews became abusive, Paul withdrew with his converts to a place where he could teach and nurture the new church that had been established. All this represented a clear strategy, and history would deem this strategy a success. Leaders must also help develop a similar strategy that will enable the organization to meet its objectives and be profitable.

LEADERSHIP STEP: *As you lead, how clear is your strategy for your business? Is that strategy clear to your team? Is it working or does it need to be tweaked or abandoned? Your Step today is to take a long look at your overall organizational strategy or the specific strategies for departments, products or services. If you have the wrong strategy, don't defend it because it's yours. Instead, abandon it in favor of one that has a better chance for success.*

Change   May 28

"So when Peter went up to Jerusalem, the circumcised

believers criticized him and said, 'You went into the house of uncircumcised men and ate with them'" - Acts 11:2-3

Peter was the leader of the apostles and had been directed by the Lord to go to visit a Gentile in Caeserea. When Peter returned home, he was met by a contingent of Jewish believers who were upset with him that he had spent so much time with a Gentile, which was against Jewish custom. Peter was leading the church into change and not everyone was happy about it. Leaders must often do what Peter did and they often get the same response Peter got - resistance, criticism, and second-guessing. Yet if progress is to be made, leaders must master the elements of organizational change.

LEADERSHIP STEP: *Is there a change (minor or major) in your organization that you want or need to institute? Your Step today is to formulate a plan for seeing that change through from start to finish. Pay particular attention to how you will communicate that change, for as you can see from today's passage, Peter had to spend a lot of face time with people explaining his rationale and motives for doing what he did. You will probably have to do the same.*

People Skills   May 29

"He grew up before him like a tender shoot, and like a root out of dry ground. He had no beauty or majesty to attract us to him, nothing in his appearance that we should desire him" - Isaiah 53:2.

This verse was a prophetic description of Jesus, who was not charismatic in the sense of being handsome, a dynamic speaker or a flashy dresser. Someone who would have been looking for those traits in His leadership would have misread Him and His capabilities altogether. Leaders learn how to read and assess people not by their outward appearances but by their capabilities and the size of their hearts. What's more, leaders should seek to develop their inner person and not pay so much attention to the trappings of power that speak to authority but may not deliver on what they appear to be.

LEADERSHIP STEP: *Are you judging people by their outer appearances or your first impression of them? This may cause you to miss their gifts and true value to the organization. Your Step today is to set up time this week to meet with people in your organization to whom you are not naturally drawn so you can get to know them better. You may not like their outer style (or lack thereof), but you want to identify their worth as a person and worker with experience and gifts.*

Purpose   May 30

"The one who plants and the one who waters have one purpose, and they will each be rewarded according to their own labor. For we are co-workers in God's service; you are God's field, God's building" - 1 Corinthians 3:9.

Not only do members of a team have diverse gifts and strengths, they also represent a variety of life missions that distinguish them from one another. This life work should play out most significantly in their work or ministry roles, for that is where they spend most of their time every day. Yet most organizations look past the purpose of the individual to focus on the purpose of the organization. Effective leaders capitalize on the purpose of each team member to fit it into the overall purpose of the organization.

LEADERSHIP STEP: *Are you maximizing the benefits of individual purpose for your organization? Today's Step is to help people identify their purpose or mission so they can be more engaged and effective in their work. In your next few staff meetings ask these questions: What would you do* with your time if you had all the money to live on? What compliment have you heard all your life? What gives you greatest joy? Then see how the answers can help your business.

Goals — May 31

"I press on toward the goal to win the prize for which God has called me heavenward in Christ Jesus" - Philippians 3:14.

This verse indicates the anatomy of a goal: 1) it causes a group to "press on" while the inertia of tradition and fear is working to keep it in the same place; 2) there is prize, which means there are winners and losers; 3) it is a "calling," something special that only this organization can embrace and accomplish; and 4) is "heavenward," which means the group pursuing the goal is elevated in its self-esteem and efficacy. Leaders understand these components; that is why they help their followers establish, clarify, focus and achieve group goals.

LEADERSHIP STEP: *Your Step today is to work on your goals. You can start by writing out the current goals for your department, family, organization or company. Ask those involved with those entities to do the same thing and compare notes. If everyone has the same goals written down, you have clarity and focus. If not, it's a good time to get everyone on the same page by establishing clear and measurable goals so everyone is pulling in the same direction.*

Organization — June 1

"Then Pharaoh said to Joseph, 'Since God has made all this known to you, there is no one so discerning and wise as you. You shall be in charge of my palace, and all my people are to submit to your orders. Only with respect to the throne will I be greater than you'" - Genesis 41:39-40.

The Leadership Walk

Joseph's Pharaoh was the "good" Pharaoh in Scripture because he recognized talent, knew how to delegate responsibility and then got out of the way so his people could do their jobs. Today's verses describe how he set up clear duties along with a clear chain of command that took full advantage of Joseph's insight into the problem and the solution. What's more, Pharaoh wasn't threatened by Joseph's insight or wisdom, eliminating Joseph's need to be political or careful not to be too talented or too "in charge" around the throne. Leaders can learn many lessons from this good Pharaoh about organization, handling gifted staff, delegation and crisis management.

LEADERSHIP STEP: Today's Step involves taking a closer look at this good Pharaoh to see what else you can learn about how to lead, manage and organize. First, take some time to read the story of Joseph and Pharaoh in Genesis 41-50. Second, revisit the article in the Appendix that highlights aspects of Pharaoh's leadership style from the biblical narrative. Finally, identify some takeaways from the account and article to apply to your own leadership situation.

Rest Stop 22   June 2

"Therefore, since the promise of entering his rest still stands, let us be careful that none of you be found to have fallen short of it" - Hebrews 4:1.

The concept of rest in this verse does not seem to be a day or event, but a lifestyle. What's more, the rest doesn't appear to belong to the person resting but to the person giving that rest, who of course is Christ. The rest is a rest of faith, achieved when a believer ceases striving to make something happen but rather rejoices in what God causes to happen. That kind of rest leads to joy and the joy leads to strength, a supernatural strength that comes from God. While leaders are often looked upon to make things happen, in Christ they can take comfort and rest in the fact that God has their back in their struggles to lead.

LEADERSHIP STEP: *Your Step today is to take a break from the pressures of leadership and life. You will not only make a decision to put things in God's hands, but you will actually physically get away from the stress. Go somewhere you enjoy or love and don't check your email, don't accept phone calls and don't allow yourself to think about what happened last week or what needs to happen next week. Put it in God's hands and walk away in body and mind.*

Service   June 3

> "... **Instead, the greatest among you should be like the youngest, and the one who rules like the one who serves. For who is greater, the one who is at the table or the one who serves? Is it not the one who is at the table? But I am among you as one who serves**" - Luke 22:36-27.

Jesus' last words to His disciples before His crucifixion contained lessons about leadership and its connection to service. Jesus confronted their thinking that service is below leadership and that the two were mutually exclusive. Jesus saw service as the antidote to leadership abuse and power. What's more, He indicated His "greatness" did not emanate from position or power, but from His mission, which was one of service. Leaders must define their attitude toward service and, if they are to be great like Jesus indicated, position themselves to serve others as the youngest in a family could be the servant of all his or her elders.

LEADERSHIP STEP: *One way to serve others is to take an interest in their future and use your position, power and experience to help them see it come to pass. This requires you being a good listener and taking time to hear the dreams and* aspirations of those closest to you. Today's Step is to schedule time with one or two of your closest followers to talk about them and how you can help them get where they believe God wants them to be professionally.

Motivation   June 4

"Woe to you experts in the law, because you have taken away the key to knowledge. You yourselves have not entered, and you have hindered those who were entering" - Luke 11:52.

In today's verse, Jesus rebuked the leaders because they were being harsh on themselves and then on the people, actually demotivating followers from pursuing the highest good. Leaders must pay attention to motivation in their workplace (or family). Followers and team members are motivated by a variety of things and leaders should provide an atmosphere where motivations can flourish so people can do their best work. Leaders can watch what followers do and listen to what followers say to find what motivates them and work to remove obstacles to those motivations.

LEADERSHIP STEP: *Are you demotivating your workers or peers? Your Step today is to find out. Distribute an anonymous survey for people to return to you, asking them what they need from you to do their best work. Ask them to freely describe anything in your company - policies, relationships, budgets, communications, recognition practices - that demotivates. When they do, don't tell them they should not feel that way; simply remove those de-motivators!*

Self-Awareness   June 5

"In the month of Nisan in the twentieth year of King Artaxerxes, when wine was brought for him, I took the wine and gave it to the king. I had not been sad in his

presence before, so the king asked me, 'Why does your face look so sad when you are not ill? This can be nothing but sadness of heart'" - Nehemiah 2:1-2.

These verses are a good example of self-awareness - on the part of the king. The king noticed something was wrong with his trusted servant and did not hesitate to ask what the problem was. First of all, it was impressive the king noticed, with all the trappings of royalty surrounding him. Second, it was significant he cared enough to ask what the problem was. Finally, anyone who did what the king did was probably aware of his own emotional state and that enabled him to be in touch with that of others - to empathize and identify with those who are depressed and hurting. The king attention to Nehemiah's funk set off historical events that touched many lives and helped restore Jerusalem.

LEADERSHIP STEP: *The king in today's story knew his "employee" so when Nehemiah did not look happy, the king noticed and spoke up. Is there anyone on your team, staff or family that does not look like their usual self? Your Step today is to gather courage, ask to see them and spend some time talking about how they are doing and what is going on. Then, if it is in your power, do something to help alleviate their sadness, even if it costs you or the company something.*

Knowledge   June 6

"My people are destroyed from lack of knowledge. 'Because you have rejected knowledge, I also reject you as my priests; because you have ignored the law of your God, I also will ignore your children'" - Hosea 4:6.

Leaders must be carriers and distributors of all kinds of knowledge. They must have general knowledge about the economy and business in general. They should be growing in the knowledge of their own business, their people and their own organization. And perhaps most importantly, leaders should have knowledge of themselves and their people - what motivates and demotivates, personalities and how they mesh (or clash) and strengths and weaknesses. In order for this growth to occur, leaders must be constant learners and students, drawing on their past but never relying solely on it for their leadership decisions.

LEADERSHIP STEP: *Your Step today is to assess your knowledge level and growth in the areas mentioned above. Give yourself a 1 (poor) to a 5 (excellent) in these five areas: general knowledge (science, history and the like); business knowledge (finance, marketing, fundraising); knowledge in your particular field; self-knowledge; and knowledge of your followers (their strengths, weaknesses, etc.). In what areas do you need improvement and how will you do so?*

Wisdom   June 7

"See, I have chosen Bezalel son of Uri, the son of Hur, of the tribe of Judah, and I have filled him with the Spirit of God, with wisdom, with understanding, with knowledge and with all kinds of skills—" - Exodus 31:2-3.

God filled Bezalel with skill and wisdom, then He chose him to work on the tabernacle. Leaders need to follow the same pattern. First, they need to recognize the gifts and talents of those around them. Leaders need to be acquainted with where and when their followers can be counted on to perform best and even lead. Second, leaders need to identify those who are not only gifted but who also have wisdom, which is knowledge practically applied. Finally, leaders need to promote people who can perform and flow well in a team setting under the leader's guidance.

LEADERSHIP STEP: *You know what it feels like to be promoted. Today's Step is to promote others. Are there those* who have performed well on your team and who also have wisdom to get along with others? Then recognize their skill and wisdom by promoting them, even creating new positions and titles to acknowledge both their skill and wisdom. If you don't promote those whom God has specially gifted to perform great work, you will lose them and their talent.

Influence — June 8

"As Jesus went on from there, he saw a man named Matthew sitting at the tax collector's booth. 'Follow me,' he told him, and Matthew got up and followed him" - Matthew 9:9.

Jesus was a leader who influenced other people. He did not manipulate or control others, and did not use His leadership power to force others to do His will or else there would be serious consequences. He persuaded, even commanded, but the people He impacted were always free to do as they chose, and some followed while others walked away. Leaders today would do well to study His example and use their power more as a spice and not as a club, flavoring their relationships but not allowing it to dominate them.

LEADERSHIP STEP: *You may be wielding power more often than you realize and people are following not because they want to, but because they are afraid of the consequences not to do so. Your Step today is to identify some roles where you can work on your ability to influence others. You can do that through writing (people can choose to read or not), volunteering with some civic group (youth would be perfect), or teaching something where you do not grade the students.*

Rest Stop 23 — June 9

"And to whom did God swear that they would never enter his rest if not to those who disobeyed?" - Hebrews 3:18.

In his discussion of rest and the Sabbath, the writer of Hebrews focused on the benefits of being in Christ for Jewish believers who were actually considering going back to Judaism without Christ. In this particular verse, the writer indicated that rest was something God granted or not, depending on whether the "rester" was obedient to God. The point is that for the author, rest was not a physical but rather a spiritual condition. Leaders who work hard but are disobedient to the Lord can take time off but not find rest, but those who work hard but are in Him can find rest even when they work!

LEADERSHIP STEP: *The key ingredient for true rest is obedience, which is doing God's will the way He wants it done. Your Rest Stop Step today is to evaluate your leadership role in light of God's word to see if you meet the requirements for God's rest. Are you leading God's way and following God's commands? Do you love your neighbor as yourself and are you treating your fellow workers fairly? Do you provide excellent customer service and tell the truth?*

Power   June 10

"He had been quarreling with the people of Tyre and Sidon; they now joined together and sought an audience with him. After securing the support of Blastus, a trusted personal servant of the king, they asked for peace, because they depended on the king's country for their food supply"
- Acts 12:20-21.

In this passage, Herod was feuding with a people from the region of Sidon and Tyre. The people sought an audience because Herod controlled their food supply and held the upper hand in negotiations. There is little doubt that the people would have paid Blastus a bribe to "secure his support," which indicates the royal corruption that impacted the lives of many and enriched a few. For Herod and Blastus, power was something to be used to control others while they benefitted personally from its application. Leaders who serve the people do not use their power to control others, but when they do, it creates all kinds of disorder, corruption and suffering.

LEADERSHIP STEP: *Because you have power, people may be telling you what they think you want to hear, which may not be the full truth. Your Step today is to set some meetings this week **away from the office** to talk to people who have the courage to tell you the truth about you or your organization. When they tell you, do not to take offense, but thank them for their candor and honesty. Repeat this exercise regularly so people are not intimidated by your power.*

## Persuasion					June 11

"Let your conversation be always full of grace, seasoned with salt, so that you may know how to answer everyone" - ***Colossians 4:6.***

Benjamin Franklin once said, "A man convinced against his will is of the same opinion still." The classic image of leaders has them barking out orders, reminding people who is in charge and what will happen if they do not comply with the leader's wishes and demands. Franklin's insight and today's verse seem to recommend a different approach. Leadership is all about influence and influence stems from persuasion - convincing followers of the rightness of a course or task as opposed to ordering compliance and obedience. Persuasion is achieved with the right words spoken in the right way by a credible source.

LEADERSHIP STEP: *How much do you rely on direct orders and commands to get your job done? Today' Step is to consider a better way. One way you can know if you are persuading is if you give followers a chance to ask you* questions - even difficult, challenging ones. You can make this practice a part of your regular staff meetings or have special one-on-one question-and-answer sessions. This means you will have to allow more time for these encounters.

Values   June 12

"When a king sits on his throne to judge, he winnows out all evil with his eyes" - Proverbs 20:8.

Leaders must pay attention to what is going on around them to ensure that the values they espouse are not just so many words on a company brochure, but are truly being lived out in the organization's daily activities. Tom Peters coined the phrase "management by wandering around," which indicated leaders should not isolate themselves in their office suite, but rather stay in touch with the company by going to where the action is and the work is done. By doing this, leaders can see the people and work for themselves and not rely only on reports from peers or subordinates.

LEADERSHIP STEP: *Are you a prisoner by choice in your own office, protected by a closed door and an administrative assistant who guards it? Today's Step is to have a coming out party. You will institute a regular regimen of going to where your people are for meetings or simply for impromptu visits and tours. By doing this, you can ensure that you evaluate the conditions, opportunities, problems, and people according to the company's values and objectives.*

Ethics   June 13

"By justice a king gives a country stability, but those who are greedy for bribes tear it down" - Proverbs 29:4.

Bribery is a way of doing business in many countries, but it is an endless pit of greed as people line up to get their share of loot for doing a job they are already paid to do. Leaders must set the moral and ethical tone and climate for an organization or country, because when leaders are corrupt, it has a trickle-down affect. When leaders pursue and enforce ethical leadership and practices in good times and in bad, they provide a stable, predictable environment where business and life has the chance to thrive.

LEADERSHIP STEP: *Are you setting the moral and ethical tone for your organization? Your Step today is to include a discussion of company ethics in your staff meetings on a monthly basis. At that time, you will look at things like pay levels for staff and leadership, truth in your publications, living up to your mission and values, staff diversity, community service, truthful staff evaluations, nepotism, and financial reports. Are you performing ethically in these areas?*

Collaboration   June 14

"Then Moses summoned Bezalel and Oholiab and every skilled person to whom the Lord had given ability and who was willing to come and do the work" - Exodus 36:2.

Moses had a significant project to work on - the tabernacle - and he built a team of creative people who had the skills to work on the task. Bezalel was the team leader and Oholiab was the assistant, while Moses was the CEO or director. The work was important and was completed according to the blueprints the Lord had given. Collaboration requires skill, leadership, and a level of cooperation among talented people who can produce exceptional results. Too often leaders rely solely on their leadership to produce remarkable results, but if leaders want world-class results, they must employ and build teams of people with world-class talent and gifts.

LEADERSHIP STEP: *Do you have the people with the*

right skills on your team, or are you trying to get exceptional results from people who don't have exceptional skills or who cannot work well with a team of equally or more talented people? Your Step today is to assess each team member you currently have on a scale of 1 (poor) to 5 (excellent) based on their attitude, skill level and willingness to learn. What are you prepared to do to improve the quality of your team?

Relationships — June 15

"That day Herod and Pilate became friends— before this they had been enemies" - Luke 23:12.

The nature of political relationships is that they come and go based on what the parties involved can do for one another. They use one another for personal and selfish ends to obtain desired results that will make the achiever look good. These are not the kind of relationships that godly leaders should pursue and nurture. The relationships that matter are those based on love and service. Leaders who pursue those are following in Jesus' footsteps, who avoided political entanglement with the Pharisees and Romans in order to serve the people and to seek and save the lost.

LEADERSHIP STEP: *Are you in business or ministry relationships because of what you can get or what you can give? Your Step today is to draw a circle and insert the names of people who are in your circle of influence, who are those you are to serve. Then map out a strategy for the next three months to enhance and deepen your work relationships with those people. That may include social events or regular meetings - anything that enhances your ability to serve them.*

Emotional Intelligence — June 16

"He [Jacob] said to them, 'I see that your father's attitude toward me is not what it was before, but the God

of my father has been with me'" - Genesis 31:5.

In this verse, Jacob talked to his wives and informed them of the shift he had noticed in his working relationship with his supervisor and father-in-law, Laban. Laban's attitude had changed and Jacob took this to mean that their work contract was coming to an end. Jacob declared his trust in the Lord in the midst of this work shift and then went on to make a transition that brought him back to the land of his fathers. Leaders must learn to read people and the signs that things change and not cling to what was, but respond to what is so they can help create what will be - all the while trusting the Lord for their decisions and future.

LEADERSHIP STEP: *Your Step today is to face the reality of what your gut or instinct is telling you about a relationship with one of your team, perhaps even your supervisor. If you sense tension or a change of attitude, then it's time to address it. If the change is permanent, then you as a leader must develop a new plan for the future (and perhaps your future). You must face the truth, however, that something has changed and determine to get to the bottom of it.*

Coaching   June 17

"And he has given both him and Oholiab son of Ahisamak, of the tribe of Dan, the ability to teach others. He has filled them with skill to do all kinds of work as engravers, designers, embroiderers in blue, purple and scarlet yarn and fine linen, and weavers—all of them skilled workers and designers" - Exodus 35:34-35.

The Lord gave two men in this passage ability to do two things: produce excellent works of art with their hands and teach others. They were not only to do the work, but were to find and prepare others to do creative work themselves. It is interesting that those coaching and teaching gifts were from God, so those two men had a responsibility to teach. Leaders have the same mantle, for it is not enough for them to lead. Leaders must also equip others to lead and prepare for the day when a successor takes over for them.

LEADERSHIP STEP: *Today's Step is to plan for the day when you will be replaced. This may not happen for quite some time, but that is not in your control, for it may happen sooner than you expected through promotion, resignation, an unforeseen setback or even death. Identify three or four people whom you can coach and into whom you can pour your experience and knowledge. Don't hold back out of fear or overconfidence in the future; prepare your successor(s).*

Attitude   June 18

"Therefore, since Christ suffered in his body, arm yourselves also with the same attitude, because whoever suffers in the body is done with sin" - 1 Peter 4:10.

Author Peter Drucker once wrote that leadership's effectiveness is often determined by their ability to endure pain and suffering and still lead. Leadership can indeed be a painful experience, for leaders must deal every day with the uncertainties of life and business, the fickleness of employees and customers, and the nature of leading that makes them targets for criticism, competition and people who chafe under anyone's authority. This is where Jesus can help leaders, for He certainly understands what it is like to suffer while not responding, and instead stay the course, which will end up producing exceptional leadership.

LEADERSHIP STEP: *How is your attitude toward suffering? Are you bearing up under the pain of leadership and still leading? Your Leadership Step today is to search your heart and see if any bitterness has crept in toward anyone who has betrayed or offended you in your work* (or family) and if that has caused you to retreat for self-protection. If they have, forgive them - perhaps even set up a meeting with them – ask God to forgive you and get back to being a forgiving leader.

Productivity   June 19

"Be diligent in these matters; give yourself wholly to them, so that everyone may see your progress. Watch your life and doctrine closely. Persevere in them, because if you do, you will save both yourself and your hearers" - 1 Timothy 4:15-16.

Leaders are role models. People tend to emulate them not only what they do but also what they are and are becoming. Thus leaders are the standard bearers for the organization and set the tone for ethics, attitude and productivity. In today's passage, Paul urged Timothy to make progress by giving himself wholly to the work at hand and to have a public posture so that everyone could see his progress. Leaders must model humility, but must do it in a public kind of way so followers can know what humility looks like in action and be able to watch leaders as they respond to the pressures and temptations of daily work.

LEADERSHIP STEP: *Your Step today is to open up your life for the benefit of others. While everything in you might want to hide your growth, productivity and decision-making process, you have a responsibility to work in a glass office so others can see into it. How can you do this? A few examples would be teaching at staff meetings, holding special teaching sessions via video or in person, writing a book, starting a blog or being more transparent with those you mentor.*

Finances   June 20

"No one can serve two masters. Either you will

> *hate the one and love the other, or you will be devoted to the one and despise the other. You cannot serve both God and money" - Luke 16:13.*

When leaders begin to serve money or money interests, their leadership is often compromised. Obviously every business must make a little more money than they spend or it is out of business, so there is nothing wrong with maximizing profits. When leaders try to maximize their own profits or when they maximize profits at the expense of quality or people, however, then decisions can be made that will serve money and forget or minimize God and integrity. Once that happens, it is difficult to dethrone money as the supreme ruler when personal or corporate decisions are made.

LEADERSHIP STEP: *There is only one antidote to greed and that is generosity at both the individual and corporate level. And this value must be developed and expressed* **before** *you deal with large sums of money. What can you do as your Step today to help your organization make a decision that is not in their best financial interests, but rather the interests of the poor or your community's welfare? Do you have a chance to do that in your personal finances? Don't delay; act now!*

Time Management   June 21

> *"When his father-in-law saw all that Moses was doing for the people, he said, 'What is this you are doing for the people? Why do you alone sit as judge, while all these people stand around you from morning till evening?" - Exodus 18:14.*

Moses was a busy man, but he did not have to be. He had no vision or concept of the importance of and strategy for involving others. In other words, he tried to do the work of 100 people rather than find 100 people to do the work.

It was not only hard on Moses, but also on the people who were affected by this bottleneck he had created. Leaders must not believe they are indispensible, - the only ones who can do certain things - or that their way of doing things is the only correct way. When they have any of those attitudes, they can act just like Moses and actually wear out their people who are waiting for the leader's decision so they can do their work!

LEADERSHIP STEP: *Your Step today is to start a time inventory, keeping track of how many hours you are working every week. Then do a careful assessment of the work you are doing, keeping only those things that are part of your job description or that only you can do better than anyone on your team. In other words, get as many things off your desk and mind as possible so you can focus on the important work you have to do - and that's leading!*

Rest Stop 25 — June 22

"Then, because so many people were coming and going that they did not even have a chance to eat, he said to them, 'Come with me by yourselves to a quiet place and get some rest'" - Mark 6:31.

Jesus kept a busy schedule, even on the Sabbath day when He usually appeared and often spoke and healed at Sabbath services. In this verse, Jesus and his team were so busy that they did not even have time to eat! Jesus' recommendation was that they get away to a quiet place and get some rest. In this instance, their rest was not in response to a specific day but to a especially busy period in their ministry life. This verse indicates that leaders must watch their followers to make sure they stay fresh and refreshed, that rest is earned based on the work they doing and that rest is taken to re-engage work with new energy and enthusiasm.

LEADERSHIP STEP: *Your Rest Stop today is to take a look at your people and determine if they are in need of rest. If so, schedule a day off for them where possible and maybe even the same day off for everyone involved! If you can't do a day off, what else can you do to make sure your people get away from the pressures of the busy schedules you all maintain? If your people are weary, however, but the schedule isn't that busy, perhaps they don't need rest but more meaningful work!*

Humility   June 23

> *"It is to be with him, and he is to read it all the days of his life so that he may learn to revere the Lord his God and follow carefully all the words of this law and these decrees and not consider himself better than his fellow Israelites and turn from the law to the right or to the left. Then he and his descendants will reign a long time over his kingdom in Israel"*
> *- Deuteronomy 17:19-20.*

These words of Moses were directed to the future kings of Israel, who were admonished to follow the words and laws of the Lord just all the other people. They were not to consider themselves better than their followers and thus exempt from morality and integrity just because they were leaders. A philosopher once said, "There is no worse heresy than that the office sanctifies the holder of it," which means that somehow the person with the title "leader" is somehow special or superior to others. Leaders must not see themselves in a class by themselves, because then they may act like it and the results are almost always negative.

LEADERSHIP STEP: *Do you have this attitude that as the leader you have special rights? The only special rights are those that help you do your job. If a corner office helps you do your job, then it is warranted. Otherwise it is a leadership perk. The same applies to a reserved parking space, special* *food or a private bathroom, just to name a few. Your Step today is to do a "perk" review and eliminate those that came from or lead to an elite leadership mentality.*

Decision Making   June 24

"After Paul had seen the vision, we got ready at once to leave for Macedonia, concluding that God had called us to preach the gospel to them" - Acts 16:10.

Paul was trying to make an important decision as to which direction his ministry should take. He had tried several options but felt God's resistance. Then one night he had a dream, which caused his team to make a decision to immediately depart for Macedonia. Leaders are expected to make decisions or at least facilitate team decisions. Paul understood that staying where he was (doing nothing) was a decision in itself, and it would cause him to lapse into ministry effectiveness. As risky as it was, he set off in a direction he had not anticipated and the result was that he took the gospel to the continent of Europe.

__LEADERSHIP STEP__: Are you or your team settling on the status quo because it is safer and less risky, especially if you have a team member who has stopped producing? You must see there is a cost to doing nothing - that making no decision is a decision! Your Step today is to identify about what or whom you are making a decision __not__ to decide, to determine what that is costing you in lost credibility with the rest of your team, why you are so hesitant, and then act quickly!

Communication   June 25

"Utterly amazed, they asked: 'Aren't all these who are speaking Galileans? Then how is it that each of us hears them in our native language?'" - Acts 2:8-9.

The Leadership Walk

In Genesis 11, God confused language and therefore people could no longer understand one another. In Acts 2, God reversed that and caused people to understand one another even though they were speaking different languages. The differences: God got involved and people were speaking about the things of God. Leaders must also help their people communicate and understand one another so everyone is on the same page. This can be a time-consuming, frustrating process, but well worth the effort. Those refusing to make the effort resort to orders, edicts and memos, relying on power to get their way as opposed to building a consensus or allowing people to struggle to obtain understanding and communication breakthroughs.

LEADERSHIP STEP: *How much do you involve yourself as a leader in the communication process in your organization? Do people have access to you for clarification and deeper discussions? Your Step today is to set a time this week for an informal gathering, but the agenda is not of your choosing. Anyone from your department or company can come and they set the agenda of what you will talk about. They can submit topics in advance or simply ask questions.*

Spiritual Growth   June 26

"Do not be deceived: God cannot be mocked. A man reaps what he sows" - **Galatians 6:7.**

No matter how anointed or effective leaders are, they are not exempt from the laws of nature or of God. For example, if a great leader steps off a cliff, he or she is subject to the law of gravity and will plummet to the ground below, no matter how loved or successful that leader is (or was). Leaders are also subject to the law of reaping and sowing. If they sow kind words, they will reap encouragement. If they sow into others, they will reap followers. If they sow into the community, they will reap friends. If they sow negativity, they will reap suspicion and distrust. Leaders cannot ignore or circumvent the law of reaping and sowing without serious repercussions to their leadership harvest.

LEADERSHIP STEP: *Where in your leadership or your organization are you not reaping what you would hope to reap? Then perhaps you must examine if you are reaping what you have sown. Today's Step is to examine your sowing habits where others are concerned. Look at the time, effort and money you are investing into others to see if they are sufficient to reap exceptional followers. If not, what more can you do to ensure that you will have an abundant crop of exceptional teammates.*

Personal Development June 27

> *"When Moses was forty years old, he decided to visit his own people, the Israelites. He saw one of them being mistreated by an Egyptian, so he went to his defense and avenged him by killing the Egyptian. Moses thought that his own people would realize that God was using him to rescue them, but they did not. The next day Moses came upon two Israelites who were fighting. He tried to reconcile them by saying, 'Men, you are brothers; why do you want to hurt each other?'" - Acts 7:23-26.*

Moses knew he was the rescuer of Israel. In Moses' younger days, however, he was full of himself and his own ways. Just in these few verses, we see that Moses decided, *went, avenged, killed, thought, came upon, tried to reconcile,* and *spoke.* Moses was trying to save the world, or at least the Israelites, in his own power. When he killed the Egyptian, perhaps he thought, "One down, three million to go!" God had to take Moses on the backside of the desert for 40 years to deliver Moses from himself. When God was finished, Moses did not even want to return to Egypt let alone lead. Leaders must be set free from themselves if they are going to do great things, and sometimes God must remove them from leadership in order for them to become great leaders.

LEADERSHIP STEP: *Are you removed from power or not at the leadership place you thought you would be at this point in your life? Your Step today is to map out a personal development plan or assess the one you currently have. That plan should include reading, education, new skills, understanding of power and authority, journaling, self-reflection, and Bible study. Evaluate yourself in each area (1 is poor, 5 is excellent) and set course to improve and develop.*

Team Building   June 28

"Moses my servant is dead. Now then, you and all these people, get ready to cross the Jordan River into the land I am about to give to them—to the Israelites" - Joshua 1:2.

The Lord addressed these words to Joshua who was poised to take over leadership of the Israelites after Moses' death. Notice that there was a clear succession plan in place so that there was no lack of leadership when Moses "retired." Then Joshua became the leader not for some of the people but for all of them, and they probably numbered in the millions. Therefore Joshua had to lead them into their vision or goal - The Promised Land - as one unit, which required clarity of purpose, good communication and delegation of duties and responsibilities.

LEADERSHIP STEP: *You will not have your current position forever, which begs the question: Are you training your successor for the job or role you currently hold? Your Step today is to give thought to who that person may be and set out a plan to transfer your knowledge, systems and expertise to them (there may be more than one) without holding back. Then for the sake of the team and organization, have everyone on your team do the same for their position.*

Rest Stop 26 — June 29

"But in the seventh year the land is to have a year of sabbath rest, a sabbath to the Lord. Do not sow your fields or prune your vineyards" - Leviticus 25:4.

Israel had to raise its own food and livestock, thus the Bible gave instructions about how to cooperate with God's laws of creation in order to be successful. One of the concepts was to give land rest, allowing it to lay fallow, once it had been farmed for seven years. This "Sabbath" rest was not legalistic, that somehow the land had to stay inactive for one year to please the Lord for some reason known only to God. The land had earned the rest after seven years of use, and the year off gave the land a chance to replenish what it had lost in producing food so that it could produce more. Leaders must keep in mind that they cannot keep themselves or their teams running at a frenetic pace - at some point, each component of the business needs to shut down and take some time off in order to function effectively.

LEADERSHIP STEP: *Your Step today is to assess how long you have been pushing hard at work to see if you have "earned" some additional time off. How many years have you been working with only minimal breaks and vacation? In academia, it is permissible to take a sabbatical every few years, and you need to consider doing the same. Be creative and find a way to take off a month, or two or six, and use that time to replenish what's been lost in your tendency to work long and hard.*

Strategy — June 30

"Later they sent some of the Pharisees and Herodians to Jesus to catch him in his words. They came to him and said, 'Teacher, we know that you are a man of

integrity. You aren't swayed by others, because you pay no attention to who they are; but you teach the way of God in accordance with the truth. Is it right to pay the imperial tax to Caesar or not?'" - Mark 12:13-14.

The leaders of Israel had a strategy to discredit Jesus by trapping Him in words that would inflame the Romans, causing them to arrest Jesus and rid the Pharisees of their nemesis. First, they flattered Him and then they publically posed a tough question. The strategy backfired, actually increasing Jesus' stature with the people when He gave His famous "Give to Caesar" response. This strategy failed because the leaders arrogantly thought they could outsmart Jesus, their competitor. Leaders must help come up with strategies that will enable their organizations achieve their change and business goals. These strategies should not be an attempt to outsmart competitors, but to achieve what is most important to the organization according to its values and business objectives.

LEADERSHIP STEP: *Is your business strategy to outthink others, thus beating them at their own game, or is it to provide the most beneficial goods and services and market them so people know they exist? Your Step today is to assess the complexity of your business strategy and look for ways to make it more simple and easy to understand. Eliminate any aspects of the strategy that are based on you winning and others losing, and focus on what your company does best.*

Change   July 1

"There is a time for everything, and a season for every activity under the heavens: a time to be born and a time to die, a time to plant and a time to uproot, a time to kill and a time to heal, a time to tear down and a time to build . . ."
- Ecclesiastes 3:1-3.

This well-known passage from Ecclesiastes reminds readers that life is full of activities and events that are diametrically opposed to one another. Being born and dying are at opposite ends of the life spectrum and involve a series of changes leading from one to the other. The transitions can be traumatic, however, and each change in these verses represents an end or a new beginning. Leaders must help followers deal with change and sometimes that change is terminal - the end of a product, service or staff position. When something ends, it doesn't indicate that someone made a mistake; it is simply part of the cycle of life and death, beginning and end.

LEADERSHIP STEP: If you are like most leaders, you love "life" but avoid "death" - you embrace the new but dread ending something that has been an important part of so many lives. You may even be avoiding the termination of someone on your team whom you love, but whose time to end his or her current position has come. Your Step today is to face the fact that there is a time for everything and to initiate that change with courage and resolve, even though you know it will cause pain.

People Skills   July 2

"Jesus knew that the Father had put all things under his power, and that he had come from God and was returning to God; so he got up from the meal, took off his outer clothing, and wrapped a towel around his waist. After that, he poured water into a basin and began to wash his disciples' feet, drying them with the towel that was wrapped around him" - John 13:3-5.

Jesus' relationship with His followers was not simply to teach them or to build a ministry network of workers. He was their boss or "Lord," friend and mentor. To break down any barriers between them, Jesus stripped Himself of any pretense (along with most of His clothing), took a bowl and towel and washed their feet. This practical act of service was to rinse away the dust that gathered from walking through life. No one in that group wanted to perform this act except Jesus, who was the leader. Leaders must work to build close relationships with their followers, and that means treating them like real people with real needs and not just workers to get the job accomplished.

LEADERSHIP STEP: *Your Step today is to check out the "feet" of those you are called to lead, work or live. When you see their feet, use your leadership power to wash and refresh them where they are with what they need. For one, maybe it's an extra day off. For another, it may be time off to do school work, or praise or recognition. For yet another, they would like to spend time with you, going to a conference or trade show, or help in finding a new and better job.*

Purpose   July 3

"About noon, King Agrippa, as I was on the road, I saw a light from heaven, brighter than the sun, blazing around me and my companions. We all fell to the ground, and I heard a voice saying to me in Aramaic, 'Saul, Saul, why do you persecute me? It is hard for you to kick against the goads'" - Acts 26:13-14.

In today's passage, the Apostle Paul was standing before the king and other Roman officials describing his encounter with the Lord on the Damascus Road. That encounter launched his ministry to the Gentiles, which was the foundation for his leadership in the early and modern church. Notice the clarity with which Paul spoke about something that had happened decades ago. A leader's leadership should emanate from his or her call or purpose, and that purpose should be easy for any leader to explain and for others to understand. Without purpose, leaders are simply "hired guns," doing a job for money and benefits, often without passion and creative energy.

LEADERSHIP STEP: *Do you know your purpose? Can you describe it in one simple sentence or brief explanation? Are you fulfilling your purpose in your current leadership role? Your Step today is to take the purpose assessment found at www.purposequest.com. The assessment is made up of 20 statements to which you will respond and receive back an evaluation of where you are in your quest for purpose. The follow up will have advice to help you be more purposeful.*

Goals   July 4

"David had said, 'Whoever leads the attack on the Jebusites will become commander-in-chief.' Joab son of Zeruiah went up first, and so he received the command" - 1 Chronicles 11:6.

David offered a reward to help him accomplish his goal of conquering Jerusalem. Joab's goal was to lead the army, so his personal goal fit perfectly into David's bigger goal. Leaders must be clear on what goals the group, department or company are pursuing. Then the rewards must reinforce those goals, and the rewards must help motivate people to action. All corporate goals should offer a reward that someone wants and not an ultimatum that they must achieve the goals "or else."

LEADERSHIP STEP: *Your Step today is to examine the rewards system you have in place. First, do those rewards communicate what is most important to you and the company? Second, do the rewards provide a clear and desired incentive to those involved? Third, are your goals clearly communicated to those working to achieve them? The easiest way to discover the answers is to ask those involved to evaluate your goals for clarity and your rewards for relevance.*

Organization   July 5

"We took such a violent battering from the storm that the next day they began to throw the cargo overboard" - Acts 27:18.

When Paul's ship was heading to Rome, it encountered a terrible storm for many days. It became so bad that the ship had to jettison its cargo to be more nimble and maneuverable in the storm. There is a leadership lesson in that story, for leaders and their organizations often become too "heavy" and weighed down with rules, procedures and middle managers. Then when a 'storm' hits - an economic downturn, unexpected setback, new competitors, or a career change - they find it hard to compete under the new conditions. This often requires a re-organization, restructuring or a downsizing to restore the flexibility needed to navigate through stormy waters.

LEADERSHIP STEP: *Are you too "heavy" for the stormy waters you and your company are in? Then it's time to jettison some cargo! Your Step today is to create a change team that will look to reorganize your company or your personal world. This should include all aspects of your business, including personnel that may need to be released, and nothing is off limits. Your goal is not organization for its own sake or to reduce costs, but to become more nimble and capable of embracing current turbulent realities.*

Rest Stop 27   July 6

"Consecrate the fiftieth year and proclaim liberty throughout the land to all its inhabitants. It shall be a jubilee for you; each of you is to return to your family property and to your own clan. The fiftieth year shall be a jubilee for you; do not sow and do not reap what grows of itself or harvest the untended vines" - Leviticus 25:10-11.

Every fifty years, Israel took a year off from cultivating any crops, letting the ground go fallow. More importantly, mortgaged property was returned to its original owner and slaves were freed. The basic message of this jubilee year was *freedom* - freedom *from* debt, freedom *from* work, freedom *from* enslavement, freedom *from* bondage, freedom *to* serve the Lord. During that year, God reminded the people that He was their Source and Provider and that their main duty was not to make a living, but to serve Him. Leaders must also step back and realize that the work is not about them, or success or productivity.

LEADERSHIP STEP: *Your Rest Stop today is to step away from work and ponder the fact that God is in control of your work situation and your life. Are you free in Christ from the pressures of life and work? Can you step away every now and then and get a fresh perspective on life and service? Are you addicted to work or can you withdraw for a while to see that your worth isn't dependent on what you do, but rather who you are? How can you celebrate a jubilee?*

Service   July 7

"The greatest among you will be your servant. For those who exalt themselves will be humbled, and those who humble themselves will be exalted" - Matthew 23:11-12.

Greatness is not only measured by what leaders do but also by what level of service they attain in what they do. Service is not being polite by holding doors open for people, although courtesy and manners are an important part of team building. Leadership service is using power to help others achieve their highest priorities and potential. In other words, leadership power exists to empower others, not to build a personality cult around the leader. When leaders serve and please God, He will exalt and honor them on His own and in His own timing, which may only be after they are gone from the scene.

LEADERSHIP STEP: *Your Step today is to assess, as you have done at other times since the beginning of the year, your impact as a servant on your team (or in your family). Give yourself a score of 1 (poor) to 5 (excellent) in the following areas: listening to others, knowing their goals and challenges, time for others, daily involvement in helping teammates and time spent teaching and training (giving away who you are and what you know). How can you improve?*

Motivation   July 8

"You have loved righteousness and hated wickedness; therefore God, your God, has set you above your companions by anointing you with the oil of joy"
- Hebrews 1:9.

This verse describes the key element of Jesus' leadership effectiveness and that element was joy. The writer of Hebrews later tells us the joy set before Him caused Jesus to do Jesus did what He did. He was not forced or compelled to do the Father's will, He willingly chose to do it because of His love for the Father. There are important leadership lessons here, for leaders must help create a culture where people can find and function in the role with duties that give them joy. If they cannot find something, then it is either created for them or they are assisted in finding it someplace else with grace and all the assistance they need.

LEADERSHIP STEP: *Is joy a competitive advantage in your organization? Your Step today is to examine how joyful people are around you. Spend some time with your key staff and ask them whether or not they are happy. Find out what aspects of their current job give them the kind of joy that releases creativity, energy and enthusiasm. Then strategize* how they can do those things more often. If they are not happy, then you will need to have a different conversation.

Self-Awareness   July 9

"Have pity on me, my friends, have pity, for the hand of God has struck me" - Job 19:21.

Job was in the midst of his trials and he turned to his friends for help. Their lack of compassion and harsh advice are legendary as an example of how *not* to comfort someone going through a tough time. They could not empathize with Job because they had not done the tough work of recognizing their own weakness and emotional neediness, so they could not possibly identify with someone else's pain and sorrow. Leaders can learn to empathize with others only when they are in touch with their own shortcomings and humanity, and can be gracious to others when they learn and recognize that God has been gracious to them as well.

LEADERSHIP STEP: *Your awareness of others begins with your own self-awareness. Your Step today is to recognize your own emotional condition. This may seem awkward, but keep a journal today chronicling your emotional state for the day. If you feel fear, write it down and explain why. If you are happy, record that too along with what made you happy. Do the same with anger, surprise, joy and all other emotions along with the details of why they emerged. If you need more than one day, take it.*

Knowledge   July 10

"If you follow my decrees and are careful to obey my commands, I will send you rain in its season, and the ground will yield its crops and the trees their fruit. Your threshing will continue until grape harvest and the

grape harvest will continue until planting, and you will eat all the food you want and live in safety in your land" - Leviticus 26:3-5.

God made these promises of abundant provision and successful business operations to all who know and obey His commands. It is good for leaders to remember that it is not their business smarts, their shrewdness or their negotiating skills that bring their enterprise success and prosperity. While all those things play a part, it is God's involvement, blessing and grace that ultimately make the difference, and He is to receive all the glory and praise. All leaders will be held accountable for whether or not they did business in accordance with God's word, so it behooves them to know the decrees and commands for which they are being held accountable.

LEADERSHIP STEP: *Do you know what the Bible says about your business and your behavior in and toward that business? If not, it's time to increase your knowledge and find out! A good place to start is the book Proverbs. Start today and read a chapter of Proverbs every day (there are 31). As you do, pay attention to all the business behaviors, practices and advice that are contained therein. Take notes in your journal as you learn what will release God's business blessings as you obey.*

Wisdom   July 11

"God gave Solomon wisdom and very great insight, and a breadth of understanding as measureless as the sand on the seashore. Solomon's wisdom was greater than the wisdom of all the people of the East, and greater than all the wisdom of Egypt" - 1 Kings 4:29-30.

While wisdom can come from experiences of both success and failure, it is also a divine gift. While there is a "wisdom of Egypt" that is relevant and pertinent, there is the wisdom of and from God that is superior to any other source. What's more, it is a gift that seems to vary in scope and topic from person to person, according to God's sovereign plan. Solomon's wisdom surpassed all his contemporaries and was "measureless." If leaders are going to lead well, then they need to find people who are sources of this divine wisdom - gifted people doing what they are gifted to do. It is not enough that those people have the knowledge or skill in their area of expertise, but also have wisdom of how to apply that knowledge to the organization itself.

LEADERSHIP STEP: *Your Step today is to evaluate your current team for their wisdom - ability to apply their knowledge in their current setting with the team you now have. Once you have critiqued them, establish a "wisdom team" and make them a member. You don't have to officially form or name that team; only you have to know it is a group of people who seem to have insight beyond their years or work area that can help your department or business prosper.*

Influence   July 12

"Whoever aspires to be an overseer desires a noble task. Now the overseer is to be above reproach, faithful to his wife, temperate, self-controlled, respectable, hospitable, able to teach, . . . " - 1 Timothy 3:1-2.

Leaders in the early church were to model the Christian behavior that made them leaders in the first place. In some sense, they were teaching through and by their lives so that followers could not only hear the truth being taught, but also see the truth being lived. Leaders cannot overestimate the importance of their posture as a role model, for followers will be quick to see when leaders talk the talk but don't walk the walk. When followers see that disconnect of action from words, they can become cynical and are encouraged themselves to behave in a careless and undisciplined manner, thus depriving the organization of their best work and creativity.

LEADERSHIP STEP: *Your Step today is to determine if you are walking your walk. Since you are the leader, it may be difficult to get accurate feedback since people fear possible retaliation. With that in mind, identify a 360-degree feedback tool (almost any HR department or online search can help you find one). Invest in having a 360 done and study the results to see how people view you and what areas you need to improve to influence others through your behaviors.*

Rest Stop 28 — July 13

"Consecrate the fiftieth year and proclaim liberty throughout the land to all its inhabitants. It shall be a jubilee for you; each of you is to return to your family property and to your own clan" - Leviticus 25:10.

If a Jew had mortgaged or abandoned his family's land inheritance, he was to return to that land debt free in the year of jubilee. This was to preserve the family's ability to have the economic means to raise crops for generations to come, even if at some point the family's land inheritance had been mismanaged. There is some aspect of the Sabbath that was to focus on the family, for leaders are no good to their family if they are never home. What's more, if leaders so exhaust their resources at work that they have nothing left for their families, it is almost the same as them not present even though they are there.

LEADERSHIP STEP: *Are you taking care of your "ground" so that it will last for generations? Today's Rest Stop is to consider your exercise habits. How is your weight? How are your eating habits? Do you exercise regularly? Once you look at those health habits, take some time today to map out some* *goals and a plan for how you can improve. What is your ideal weight? How can you obtain and keep it? To get things started, why don't you go for a walk right now?*

Power   July 14

"When Herod realized that he had been outwitted by the Magi, he was furious, and he gave orders to kill all the boys in Bethlehem and its vicinity who were two years old and under, in accordance with the time he had learned from the Magi" - Matthew 2:16.

The hallmark of authoritarian leaders is anger. They believe they own what they lead (sometimes they do) and they are infuriated when someone does something to their "baby." This anger can be expressed verbally or in actions that let everyone know who is in charge and the consequences for failure or disobedience. What's more, in this verse we see that Herod did not have a succession plan, except that his sons would take over, but only upon his death. In some ways, authoritarian leaders believe they will live a long time, if not forever.

LEADERSHIP STEP: *Today's Leadership Step is for you to reflect on the role that power plays in your leadership role. You can measure that by your anger level. How angry do you get when people do "dumb" things or when they disappoint or fall short of your expectations? How do you express that anger? Do you show it and you don't even know it? If your anger level is high, then ask God to show you the root source of your anger and determine to change your style.*

Persuasion   July 15

"We must pay the most careful attention, therefore, to what we have heard, so that we do not drift away" - Hebrews 2:1.

The Leadership Walk

Everyone has a tendency not to pay attention when their mind wanders or zones out. That is why leaders need to be mindful of their need to communicate often and well. It is not how well leaders speak or write that is most important, but how well followers and listeners understand and retain what leaders say. Leaders should accept responsibility for making sure good communication occurs. That means leaders must say important things more than once, using different media to say it, and must work to help listeners pay attention and retain.

LEADERSHIP STEP: *How are you most effective at holding people's attention? You cannot persuade them if they are not listening to or reading what you have to say. Your Step today is to establish feedback on all your communication that is accurate and meaningful. You can watch your numbers of readers if you write or blog, use surveys for feedback if you speak or teach, take questions whenever you communicate, or simply watch to see if people are doodling, sleeping or listening when you talk.*

Values   July 16

"Everything they do is done for people to see: They make their phylacteries wide and the tassels on their garments long" - Matthew 23:5.

The Pharisees performed their religious rituals with one thing in mind: be noticed by other people. Their desire was to draw attention to themselves so people would honor them as leaders and consider them spiritual men. Jesus commented that they did ***everything*** to attract the attention of others. Leaders cannot get away from their values; what they consider important is what they will do every time. Authoritarian leaders are doing things for one reason, no matter what they do: to establish that they are in charge and worthy of the position.

John W. Stanko

LEADERSHIP STEP: Why do you do what you do as a leader? Is it to draw attention to yourself? Your Step today is to reflect on your motivation for leadership. Are you offended when people don't treat you with the respect you think they should? Do you need the best office and parking space because you are the leader? Do you do the things you do to serve others or to promote yourself? It is important that you be honest with yourself concerning these answers.

Ethics   July 17

"Whoever can be trusted with very little can also be trusted with much, and whoever is dishonest with very little will also be dishonest with much. So if you have not been trustworthy in handling worldly wealth, who will trust you with true riches? And if you have not been trustworthy with someone else's property, who will give you property of your own?" - Luke 16:10-12.

Jesus did not preach a complicated gospel. It was and is easy to understand - impossible to do without God's help, but not hard to grasp. In these verses, Jesus laid out three principles that make for good ethics: 1) be faithful in the little things; 2) be trustworthy in money matters; and 3) handle the possessions of others with integrity. The last of the three includes just not physical property of others, but also their reputation, gifts, future, time and career. In other words, the proper handling of people is not just a matter of efficiency but rather it is an ethical matter, along with the proper handling of money.

LEADERSHIP STEP: Do you see proper management of people as not just a management/leadership matter, but also an ethical one? Your Step today is to meditate on that truth and assess your ethics where others are concerned. How many people are you mentoring? How many have you helped promote to other positions? Do you waste people's time by being chronically late? Do you use your power to empower others? Are you keeping someone in a position they are ill suited for to protect yourself? What can you do to improve?

Collaboration — July 18

"Jonathan said to his young armor-bearer, 'Come, let's go over to the outpost of those uncircumcised men. Perhaps the Lord will act in our behalf. Nothing can hinder the Lord from saving, whether by many or by few.' 'Do all that you have in mind,' his armor-bearer said. "Go ahead; I am with you heart and soul'" - 1 Samuel 14:6-7.

Jonathan proposed a bold plan to attack the Philistines (something his father Saul with the army refused to do) and his armor-bearer agreed wholeheartedly to accompany him. Jonathan provided the leadership and his armor-bearer the followership and together they were able to create such a stir that eventually the army of Israel moved out of fear and attacked as well. Here we see that: 1) leaders provide adventure and purpose; 2) leaders need at least one follower to be a leader; 3) the armor-bearer also became a leader of Israel through his courageous followership; 4) courageous leaders and followers operate in faith; and 5) courageous followers encourage leaders to act on their leadership vision.

LEADERSHIP STEP: *Are you creating enough exciting opportunities for people to express their followership? Today's Step is to identify your followers and their reasons for following. Are they willingly following your vision or are they motivated by fear? Do they have faith or are they living off your faith? Can you speak to them and they respond with their own courage and vision? One other thing to consider: have you been a poor follower in your current position so that you are reaping what you have sown?*

Relationships   July 19

"So Jonathan made a covenant with the house of David, saying, 'May the Lord call David's enemies to account'"
- 1 Samuel 20:16.

Jonathan and David had a close relationship through which they served and encouraged one another. Jonathan knew he was to be David's right-hand man in David's administration and David valued Jonathan's friendship above any other relationship. Unfortunately, Jonathan's premature death in battle prevented their friendship from maturing beyond what it was. Leaders must not fall into the flawed thinking that they do what they do in isolation. Rather, they should acknowledge their need for many others to help them do the work, and some to be close enough to serve as confidantes, comrades and friends.

LEADERSHIP STEP: *Your leadership is not threatened but rather enhanced by a core of close followers who are also friends. Your Step today is to sit down and make a list of your closest associates in any of the work you do, including family. Then take time to write a note or pay a personal visit to say, "Thank you," for their help and support. Then use this list to pray for those people regularly. If your list is short, then you have work to do to build your network of relationships.*

Rest Stop 29   July 20

"Nehemiah said, 'Go and enjoy choice food and sweet drinks, and send some to those who have nothing prepared. This day is holy to our Lord. Do not grieve, for the joy of the Lord is your strength'" - Nehemiah 8:10.

Nehemiah saw that the people were burdened with grief and despair, and he ordered them to party as a nation. The day was "holy," which simply meant God had set it apart for a special purpose (it was not a day to do nothing as some interpret a Sabbath to be; it was a day to cultivate and express joyful hearts). What's more, Nehemiah ordered them ***not*** to grieve but to do what they had to do to get in touch with and maintain their joy, which was the source of their strength. Leaders should work to maintain the joy in their own lives and then help others discover and nurture theirs, for joy is the secret energy source of all productive and healthy people.

LEADERSHIP STEP: *You can take time off from work, but if you don't have joy, you won't find the strength and rest you crave and need. Your Step today is to read my article Joy Inventory found in the Appendix and follow the process I describe for a week or even just a few days. Then look at your inventory list to see what it reveals to you. When was joy present in your heart? What were you doing? When did joy run away and hide? What does tell you about your work at this time?*

Emotional Intelligence — July 21

> *"Then Nathan asked Bathsheba, Solomon's mother, 'Have you not heard that Adonijah, the son of Haggith, has become king, and our lord David knows nothing about it?'"* - 1 Kings 1:11.

At that point in his career, King David was pretty much out of the day-to-day operations of the kingdom. His staff was preoccupied with meeting his personal needs and that left a vacuum at the top of the nation, which Adonijah tried to fill through a political coup. David almost died before he installed Solomon as the rightful king. The point is that David inflicted much anxiety and angst upon his people by refusing to deal with his age and who would take over the throne, insisting that death was to be the only cause of his retirement. Leaders must realize that the nation, organization or company does not exist only to serve their needs and provide their comfort, but should do the same for as many in the entity as possible.

LEADERSHIP STEP: *Are you training your successor? Your Step today is to recognize that you may be the source of pain and suffering in your organization through your refusal to delegate or plan for the future. Then you must develop a plan to identify your successor or at least to begin to train others in some of the functions you perform in your company. Just talking about your eventual departure will help people with that reality and give them less cause for concern.*

Coaching   July 22

> *"So the Lord said to Moses, 'Take Joshua son of Nun, a man in whom is the spirit of leadership, and lay your hand on him. Have him stand before Eleazar the priest and the entire assembly and commission him in their presence. Give him some of your authority so the whole Israelite community will obey him. He is to stand before Eleazar the priest, who will obtain decisions for him by inquiring of the Urim before the Lord. At his command he and the entire community of the Israelites will go out, and at his command they will come in'"*
> *- Numbers 27:18-21.*

Joshua had served Moses and been close to him as Moses led Israel out of Egypt and through the Wilderness. Now it was time for Moses to help Israel make the transition to Joshua's leadership after Moses had ruled for 40 years. First, notice Joshua had the spirit of leadership on him, so he was obviously God's choice to lead. Then Moses was to establish Joshua in front of the people so people could mentally and emotionally make the transition to a new leader. Finally, Joshua was to have access to the priest so he could make decisions with God's guidance and assistance. Leaders must pay attention to the issue of succession, making sure that their successor has everything he or she needs to do the job effectively and is known and accepted by the people.

LEADERSHIP STEP: *No matter what position you have in your organization, you must realize you will not have it forever. Some day you will have to turn it over to someone else - and you are not always aware of what day that will be! Your Step today is to make a decision to begin training one person (or a team) in what you do, or at least preparing a document outlining your job duties so that someone (or a team) can replace you when the time is right to do so.*

Attitude   July 23

"If I preach voluntarily, I have a reward; if not voluntarily, I am simply discharging the trust committed to me" - 1 Corinthians 9:17.

When you replace *preach* with *lead* in today's verse, it can provide a new perspective on leadership. The age-old question of whether leaders are born or made is changed to whether or not leaders are **called** to lead. When leaders lead, they are fulfilling a mandate or assignment from the Lord, regardless of whether they head a Fortune 500 company or their garden club. In the context of this verse, leadership is its own reward - the knowledge of being used by God for a unique role and purpose. If nothing else, leadership is fulfilling a trust or stewardship that God assigns the leader to fulfill and complete. Thus leaders do not lead for what they can get - although there are rewards - but for what God has called and singled them out to do.

LEADERSHIP STEP: *Are you leading voluntarily? Do you see your leadership role as a duty or a calling, or both? Today's Step is to examine your attitude toward your leadership, whether you are leading now or preparing to in* the future. Are you protecting yourself from hurt or criticism by laying low or are you actively engaging opportunities to lead? Do you see your service to others as service to God, regardless of how they receive or treat you when you lead?

Productivity   July 24

"Where there are no oxen, the manger is empty, but from the strength of an ox come abundant harvests" - Proverbs 14:4.

An ox is a big animal capable of working hard and moving heavy objects. While a valuable asset to have, the ox creates its own problems because it has to be fed and then creates a lot of manure. This verse is not about care for oxen, but rather teaches that leadership is sometimes a messy process. Leaders cannot always play it safe, keeping their world simple and their manger clean from all manure. At times, they must work with people and processes that, while complex or creating their own problems, bring tremendous opportunities for growth and innovation. Fear of risk or change can keep a company and its people stuck in a rut that can lead to serious problems down the road.

LEADERSHIP STEP: *How prone are you to play it safe? Do you realize that deciding to do nothing, thus keeping your manger clean, is actually a decision that has serious implications? Your Step today is to ponder whether or not your aversion to risk is costing your organization future opportunities and growth. You can do this by listening to others who are less fearful of risk and carefully considering what they say, not only focusing on what can go wrong, but also on what can go right.*

Finances   July 25

"For the love of money is a root of all kinds

> *of evil. Some people, eager for money, have wandered from the faith and pierced themselves with many griefs"* - 1 Timothy 6:10.

Money is not the problem in the life of a company or an individual. It is the *love* of money that causes all kinds of problems. Leaders must first be aware of this personal danger for, if they do their job well, they will probably be rewarded financially. If their organization is successful, then the company will also have abundant financial resources. The only antidote for the love of money is generosity and giving, so leaders must develop this trait in their own lives and then help their companies develop a corporate sense of community service and generosity. This isn't just good business, this is a moral necessity!

LEADERSHIP STEP: *Let's start today by examining your personal giving habits. Do you give your time, money, talent and expertise to other people and organizations? Do an audit of your organization's generosity, even if you are supported by the donations of others. Once you assess where you and your organization are, your Leadership Step today is to determine how you, your family or your company can be more generous in to escape the love-of-money's evil and dangerous hold.*

Time Management   July 26

> *"Then the king, with the queen sitting beside him, asked me, 'How long will your journey take, and when will you get back?' It pleased the king to sendme; so I set a time"* - Nehemiah 2:6.

Nehemiah set a time when he would be finished with the project of rebuilding the walls. He had never been to Jerusalem, did not really know much about building, and had no idea what he was going to find when he got there. How did he know how long it would take? He probably made his best guess, and it satisfied the royal couple. Leaders need to set time limits on what they set out to do, otherwise things may drag on and there is no urgency in the work being done either personally or corporately.

LEADERSHIP STEP: *You may be facing a similar situation, but are hesitant about making a commitment to a specific time. Today's Step is to look at your most important projects and make your best guess, get to work and trust the Lord! Where are you holding back because you cannot be as precise as you would like? Where would making your best guess as to the time it will take help you get started? Where can you have faith to get it done in even less time than you estimate?*

Rest Stop 30 — July 27

"Do not bring a load out of your houses or do any work on the Sabbath, but keep the Sabbath day holy, as I commanded your ancestors" - Jeremiah 17:22.

Every other nation at the time of Jeremiah worked to survive. Israel was never to be like those nations, but was rather to live for worship and God's service. That was represented by Israel taking a day off from work, a day that was to be devoted to family, rest, worship and the acknowledgment that the Lord was their God. The Sabbath was also a reminder to the Israelites that they were not to fit God into their work at their convenience but that He was Lord of their work. Leaders would do well to remember that there is more to their lives (or should be more) than simply work and production. They should also be mindful that they don't exist to work but the work exists to teach them about God and to fulfill His purpose and plan.

LEADERSHIP STEP: *Did you ever think that you don't exist to work but that the work exists to give something to you? Your Step today is to reflect on these questions: what has* your work given you (except money)? How has your work enriched your life and deepened your walk and relationship with the Lord? What has your work taught you about God and His purpose for you and the world? If you aren't happy with your answers, reevaluate what you do and why.

Humility   July 28

"If anyone thinks they are something when they are not, they deceive themselves" - Galatians 6:3.

Humility is not denying the truth of a person is, which is nothing more than false humility; it is that person having an accurate assessment of who he or she is and what he or she can do. Thus pride is the opposite of humility because it carries an inflated or exaggerated perspective and evaluation of one's importance or abilities. Leaders need an appropriate humility, which not only includes admitting who they are not, but also recognizing and confessing who they are and what gifts and strengths they can bring to a team. It never glorifies God for leaders to act or pretend like they are nothing when God has gifted and called them to be a person of significance and influence.

LEADERSHIP STEP: Your Step today is to determine if you suffer from false humility, which is denying who you are and what you do well to appear to be humble. What do you do when someone compliments you? Do you deny the truth of what they are saying, or do you simply say, "Thank you"? Can you admit you are good at some things without feeling guilty? Can you talk about your gifts without feeling self-conscious? If you answer yes, then you have healthy humility.

Decision Making   July 29

"He has performed mighty deeds with his arm; he has scattered those who are proud in their inmost thoughts.

He has brought down rulers from their thrones but has lifted up the humble" - Luke 1:51-52.

God brings down rulers who have proud thoughts, because that thinking leads to pro-ud decisions, which in turn manifest proud actions. If there is one thing to which God reacts strongly and quickly, it is pride. God expects all rulers or leaders - not just church leaders - to render just and righteous decisions. Therefore, leaders must take pains and steps to ensure that their decisions are not based on ego, self, insecurity or greed, but rather are rooted in humility - knowledge and admission that the leader has limitations and needs God's wisdom to succeed. Sometimes that wisdom will come through other people, which means that leaders must humble themselves and ask for help, thus causing them to follow rather than lead.

LEADERSHIP STEP: *Your Step today is to assemble your team one-by-one or together in the coming days (this can include your family). When you are with them, ask, "If you were me, what is the one thing you would change about this organization?" Also ask, "What do you think is the greatest opportunity for growth and development we have as an organization?" Then listen for common themes in what you hear and make humble decisions with input you obtain.*

Communication   July 30

"So Joshua ordered the officers of the people: 'Go through the camp and tell the people, 'Get your provisions ready. Three days from now you will cross the Jordan here to go in and take possession of the land the Lord your God is giving you for your own'" - Joshua 1:10-11.

Joshua had to communicate to millions of followers and did so by using others to communicate a clear and simple message: it's time to move on, so get ready. It would follow that these followers not only knew Joshua, but also the officers communicating the message to them. They therefore knew the message could be trusted and was important, so all were on the same page, so to speak. Everyone knew to get ready for change. Leaders need to develop this same kind of communication network, a clear and simple message and messages that hold and captivate people's attention.

LEADERSHIP STEP: Today's Step is to consider and evaluate your communication network. Are you paying attention to its upkeep? Are you credible, consistent, and clear in your communications? Does your leadership team spread the word with the efficiency and urgency you require? Are your meetings all they can be as a communication tool? Of course, if you don't have credibility as a leader, people won't pay attention no matter how regularly you talk.

Spiritual Growth — July 31

"Let us not become weary in doing good, for at the proper time we will reap a harvest if we do not give up"** - **Galatians 6:9.

Leaders must seize every opportunity to do good deeds, no matter what business they are in. This includes not only in their personal lives, but also business or community lives as well. What's more, Paul encouraged the readers to endure in doing those good deeds, for there is always a season when it seems like doing good deeds receives no notice or has no reward. It may seem like God doesn't notice, but He has a big book and a sharp pencil, so to speak, and never forgets or allows good deeds to go unrewarded.

LEADERSHIP STEP: Have you grown weary in doing good deeds? Does it seem like your deeds go unnoticed or unrequited? Your Step today is to encourage yourself and organization (or your family) in your benevolent strategies. First of all, make sure your strategy is clear. Then identify the causes to which you are committed to give time and resources. Finally, communicate your work not to trumpet your good deeds but to benefit your cause(s) even further.

Personal Development — August 1

"Be strong and courageous, because you will lead these people to inherit the land I swore to their ancestors to give them" - Joshua 1:6.

Since leaders are going to take people places they could not go without leadership, those leaders must prepare for the difficulties of the journey. One qualification or characteristic is strength, which includes mental, physical and emotional. The strength must be for a purpose, which of course is to reach a destination many thought impossible. Another is courage. Leaders cannot faint along the way, but must face the unknown and intimidation with resolve and wisdom, for sometimes those leaders need the courage to change course or admit mistakes.

LEADERSHIP STEP: *Your Step today is to consider strength and courage and how they factor into your leadership effectiveness. Start with strength. Do you have the strength to say "no," to be quiet and to persevere in the midst of difficulties? Then go on to courage. Can you reflect on personal examples of when you exhibited courage? Where might your courage be lacking now and what may it be costing your organization or your personal development?*

Rest Stop 31 — August 2

"Let us, therefore, make every effort to enter that rest, so that no one will perish by following their example of disobedience" - Hebrews 4:11.

This verse indicates it takes effort to enter the kind of rest God has in mind for His people. It also teaches that disobedience is a source of unrest, as was shown by the Israelites who had to wander the wilderness due to their unbelief. A poor spiritual condition is a source of hardship and labor no matter how much leaders rest their physical body. Things like worry, lack of personal discipline, anger and greed can take away a leader's strength and lead to fatigue, which if left unchanged, can cause health problems.

LEADERSHIP STEP: *Your Step today is to determine your state of rest beyond your need for a day or two off from work. Do you ever say that you need a vacation? Are you tired when you get up even after a good night's sleep? Do you rejoice when it's your day off and dread the day when you have to return to work? Do you overeat or have other physical symptoms caused by anxiety? If your answer to any is yes, you need to make an effort to get to the root cause of your fatigue.*

Strategy   August 3

"Where there is no vision, people cast off restraint; but blessed is the one who heeds wisdom's instruction"
- Proverbs 29:18.

This verse is regularly quoted to point out the importance of vision. Without vision, people tend to do whatever they think is best, without regard to how their actions fit into the overall picture. There is no vision because there is no clear, compelling picture being communicated by leadership. This verse goes on to explain that providing a vision is wisdom that will light the way forward. Leaders should always communicate a vision beyond what they know how to accomplish, for this "vision wisdom" will show up and provide the answers to the "how" questions that always result when vision is cast.

LEADERSHIP STEP: *We have discussed vision in previous entries, but let's pay another visit to this important concept. Your Step today is to take a look at the vision that is spelled out for your family, company or organization? Is it clear as to why you exist? What are you trying to accomplish? Someone once said that vision is where you are going and mission is how you will get there. Are both your vision and mission clear enough to guide the steps of those involved?*

Change   August 4

> *"But Joshua spared Rahab the prostitute, with her family and all who belonged to her, because she hid the men Joshua had sent as spies to Jericho—and she lives among the Israelites to this day"* - Joshua 6:25.

Rahab protected and saved the Israelite spies, and her reward was that her family's lives were spared. She had to undergo massive changes, however, for she had to transfer cultures from where she had been to live with Israel in order to survive. What helped Rahab deal with the change was that her life was in danger. Leaders must help followers understand the need for and price of change when the stakes aren't so high. While the need for change may not be as severe as it was for Rahab, adapting and accepting change is still an important part of survival at both an individual and corporate level.

LEADERSHIP STEP: *Your Step today is to focus on a change that you need to institute at the corporate or family level. First, be clear on what change you seek. Second, determine what it will look like when the change is implemented. Third, decide how you will communicate both the need for the change and how the change is progressing. Finally, how will you know if you were successful?*

People Skills   August 5

"Then people brought little children to Jesus for him to place his hands on them and pray for them. But the disciples rebuked them. Jesus said, 'Let the little children come to me, and do not hinder them, for the kingdom of heaven belongs to such as these'" - Matthew 19:13-14.

Jesus was always accessible and friendly (except to religious bigots). People felt comfortable enough bringing their children to Him for a blessing, knowing He would not shun or avoid them. Yet Jesus' administrative assistants and ushers tried to keep the people away, thinking they were acting in His best interests. Leaders are meant to be among the people and not over them. They must not allow themselves to become isolated from either the people they serve or their needs, and must make sure their assistants and procedures reflect values of openness and accessibility.

LEADERSHIP STEP: *Today's Step is to examine the image your followers and team are portraying to the public. Are they keeping people and information from you that you need to see and know? Are they friendly in their encounters with others? One way you can find out is to ask around and perhaps even distribute a survey to a broader cross section of staff or public to get a clear picture of how they see your administrative "world." Then take necessary corrective action.*

Purpose   August 6

"On the contrary, they recognized that I had been entrusted with the task of preaching the gospel to the uncircumcised, just as Peter had been to the circumcised" - Galatians 2:7.

Paul's purpose was clear to those with whom he shared it, which means it first had to be clear to Paul. And Peter's was so clear to him that he was able to share it with Paul.

Both men knew what they were created to do and therefore were able to clearly communicate it to others so they would know what to expect from those two leaders. This allowed both men to focus on their strengths and not interfere with each other's purpose. Leaders are people of purpose, not doing things just because they can do them, but because there are certain things they do that no one else can do - and that is and should be their main contribution to their team and organization.

LEADERSHIP STEP: *Your Step today is to hone your purpose statement to make sure it is clear to you, so you can make it clear to others. Start by taking the purpose assessment found at www.purposequest.com. Then follow through on the suggestions you will receive in a return email. You may also wish to do some additional study of Paul's purpose, and an article to help you do that is also found on my website. Don't stop seeking until your purpose is clear to you and others.*

Goals   August 7

"One who is slack in his work
is brother to one who destroys" - Proverbs 18:9.

If a person was to build something and someone else destroyed it, it would be seen as a criminal act. Yet if someone does not build something that was possible to build, no one would see that as criminal although the end result is the same. In both cases, the world is deprived of something that had the potential to help or bless many. The point is this: A leader's inability to be productive robs the world of what he or she has in them that is unique, giving them something in common with one who would destroy what another built according to today's verse. There is nothing better suited to help a leader be productive than the goal-setting process.

LEADERSHIP STEP: *It's time to get back on your goal-setting track. What is the world losing by your inactivity? Where are you excusing your slackness as "no big deal"? Where do you need a change of attitude to create more urgency and less slackness? Your Step today is to examine your usage and effectiveness of goals. Spend time and set two or three goals in a few areas - physical, personal, business or financial - or revisit and reset goals you have abandoned.*

Organization   August 8

"Now if it pleases the king, let a search be made in the royal archives of Babylon to see if King Cyrus did in fact issue a decree to rebuild this house of God in Jerusalem. Then let the king send us his decision in this matter"
- Ezra 5:17.

All royalty has to pay attention to the organization and efficiency of their kingdom. Today's verse indicates Babylon had accessible archives available for research. These archives had to have people overseeing them and a logical filing and storage method. Once the research was finished on the question at hand, the king had to communicate his decision about the way forward quickly and efficiently - again calling for organizational efficiency. Leaders must pay attention to matters of systems and structure so their organizations can have access to past decisions and communicate present ones to those who need to know.

LEADERSHIP STEP: *Your Step today is to tend to the organizational capabilities of your company (or family). Do you have archives of photos and important documents? Where are they stored and how public are they? Then look at the communication efficiency of your team or company. Are you structured and disciplined enough to get important messages to those who need to know? Make sure you are modeling the organizational skill you desire others to have.*

Rest Stop 32 — August 9

"For God does speak—now one way, now another—though no one perceives it. In a dream, in a vision of the night, when deep sleep falls on people as they slumber in their beds, he may speak in their ears and terrify them with warnings, to turn them from wrongdoing and keep them from pride, to preserve them from the pit, their lives from perishing by the sword" - Job 33:14-18.

It seems that while people sleep, God is at work to speak to them through dreams. It is interesting that sleep is not simply a down time by God's design. Rather it is a time when He can communicate with people when their conscious defenses are not active. The point is that rest and sleep are not a cessation of activity, but rather a change of pace God uses for His purposes. Leaders should use rest not just to disengage from activity, but also to allow God to speak to them in ways they cannot avoid. What's more, dreams often have important content for the recipient, so if God chooses to use rest to work in people's lives, those people should expect to hear God during their rest time.

LEADERSHIP STEP: *Your Leadership Step or Rest Stop is to use down time to hear from the Lord. Have you had any recurring dreams? Perhaps God is speaking to you about a theme and you would do well to seek Him for answers. Do you go to bed or into a season of rest thinking about a problem? Perhaps you should have faith that God will provide an answer when you sleep. Don't see rest as a cessation of work but a change of pace to a different kind of work.*

Service — August 10

"The one who guards a fig tree will eat its fruit, and whoever protects their master will be honored" - Proverbs 27:18.

The Leadership Walk

Leaders often have many people serving them both personally and professionally. These people serve with distinction and are an important part of both the leader's and organization's success. Today's verse indicates that they are worthy of honor. Leaders must remember that any success they enjoy is not due to their efforts exclusively but rather to the efforts of the team. Therefore, leaders should proactively and creatively honor those who serve them day-in, day-out with distinction and excellence.

LEADERSHIP STEP: *Your Step today is to examine who in your world serves you well and is deserving of some special blessing or recognition. Make a list of everyone whom you need to recognize for outstanding service. Then be creative and think of personal and special ways to bless and honor them. Perhaps a personal note from you, a special gift, a small (or large) ceremony, something nice for their families, a group outing or simply some extra time off would be in order.*

Motivation   August 11

"Then the Lord said to Aaron, 'You and your sons are not to drink wine or other fermented drink whenever you go into the tent of meeting, or you will die. This is a lasting ordinance for the generations to come, so that you can distinguish between the holy and the common, between the unclean and the clean'" - Leviticus 10:8.

The Lord forbade the priests, who were the leaders in Israel, to partake of any alcoholic beverages before they went to work in the tent of meeting. This was not because the Lord was against alcohol, but rather so their judgment would not be impaired when they were dealing with spiritual things.
In other words, they were to take their work seriously and be motivated by a desire to serve the Lord. Leaders must also be careful not to self-medicate themselves to get through the anxiety and pressures of work, which can take

the form of many addictive substances like food, medicine, alcohol and almost any other activity that will help them escape their work rather than engage it.

LEADERSHIP STEP: *Your Step today is to do an honest evaluation of your recent approach to work and your leadership role. If it is strictly for the money, then you may be a candidate for adopting lifestyles and habits that help you get through your workday because of boredom or anxiety. Are you exercising regularly? How is your weight? Are you engaging in any habit that helps you get through the day but prevents you from giving your best efforts at work?*

Self-Awareness   August 12

"Let us not become conceited, provoking and envying each other" - **Galatians 5:26.**

Leaders are often in front of others because they are charismatic, dynamic, intelligent, visionary and skilled. They also enjoy some measure of success due to their strong ego drive to get things done, achieve and excel. A problem doesn't arise when leaders use their ego to get the job done. The problem comes in when leaders become egotistical, when they insist on getting the credit for everything, when they begin to "believe their own press clippings" that they are as good as others say they are. When that happens, leaders resent or envy anyone else's success and demand that they be the center of attention in all things.

LEADERSHIP STEP: *Your transition from ego to egocentric can be subtle but painful for those around you and dangerous for you. Your Step today is to take measures to keep this from happening: 1) surround yourself with people who will tell you the truth you need and not want to hear; 2) celebrate the success of others; 3) mentor others so they can* *excel and thrive; 4) serve others' needs; and 5) divest yourself of all privileges you get simply because you are the leader.*

## Knowledge	August 13

"All Scripture is God-breathed and is useful for teaching, rebuking, correcting and training in righteousness, so that the servant of God may be thoroughly equipped for every good work" - 2 Timothy 3:15-16.

The Bible is not a book about leadership but it contains many principles, stories and commands that would make any leader more effective. The Bible, however, is not to be approached lightly or without some understanding of how to interpret and apply its directives. Leaders would do well to study the Bible, not only in personal devotions, but also in some form of deeper, directed study that would aid in their ability to comprehend and incorporate what they learn into their everyday leadership style and decisions. Perhaps the Bible is best applied, however, in character formation, for this book written thousands of years ago can still interpret the motives and intent of a leader's heart with amazing accuracy.

LEADERSHIP STEP: *Your Step today is to recommit to a lifelong study of God's word, both from a devotional and academic perspective. First, make sure you choose a good translation and assign it as your study Bible. Second, read through the Bible in one year. Third, look for classes in your church or online that will enhance your understanding of Bible history, language, types of literature therein and authors. Finally, apply what you learn to your work.*

## Wisdom	August 14

"God gave Solomon wisdom and very great insight, and a breadth of understanding as measureless as the sand

on the seashore. Solomon's wisdom was greater than the wisdom of all the people of the East, and greater than all the wisdom of Egypt" - 1 Kings 4:29-30.

Apparently there were people in the ancient world who made their living from and built a reputation on a special ability to obtain and dispense wisdom. The best of them all was Solomon, who God gave a gift of wisdom and understanding. There was a day when the world came to the church and its leaders for wisdom, teaching and insight. There was a day when great explorers, inventors and innovators came from the church, spurred on in their work by their faith. No matter how naturally gifted or intelligent leaders are, the best leaders still access supernatural wisdom to help them do the work God assigned them to do.

LEADERSHIP STEP: *Your Step today is simple. Solomon got wisdom in response to his prayer for wisdom, which God was only too eager to answer. From this day forward, you will do the same thing: Ask for wisdom, according to James 1:6: "But when you ask, you must believe and not doubt." After you ask, you must actively listen and watch for God's responses, and quickly apply them to your situation. "Believe, ask, listen and watch, apply" is now to be your daily ritual.*

Influence   August 15

"Before the spies lay down for the night, she went up on the roof and said to them, 'I know that the Lord has given you this land and that a great fear of you has fallen on us, so that all who live in this country are melting in fear because of you'" - Joshua 2:8-9.

Rahab was the woman speaking in this verse and was hiding the men Joshua dispatched to spy out the land on her roof. This woman had remarkable insight into what God was doing, even though she was not yet part of God's people.

Notice she indicated the spies and Israel had obtained quite a reputation in her land, so much so that people were terrified of their presence. Notice also she had insight that God was going to give her homeland to the spies and their people. Leaders must pay close attention to the reputation they and their organizations have, for a good reputation is a powerful tool for public relations and goes far beyond the effects of any advertising or marketing campaign.

LEADERSHIP STEP: *Your Step today is to get in touch with what the community, your neighbors, competitors, customers, clients and general public knows and says about your organization or company. Perhaps you need to attach surveys to any contact you have with the public. Then someone should monitor your organization for online and media mentions. Being involved in community activities and service organizations is another way to build and monitor your image with the public.*

Rest Stop 33   August 16

"It is a day of sabbath rest for you, and you must deny yourselves. From the evening of the ninth day of the month until the following evening you are to observe your sabbath" - Leviticus 23:32.

This verse describes the Day of Atonement, when Israel was to have solemn assemblies and offer sacrifices for the forgiveness of their sins. They were forbidden to work on this day to symbolize the importance and priority of their spiritual condition over work and relationships, and go through rituals to obtain remission for sins for another year. Today there is atonement available through the sacrifice of Christ, and anyone can obtain forgiveness and cleansing. Leaders must take time to address their spiritual condition and determine if there is sin in their lives for which they need to ask God and others for forgiveness.

LEADERSHIP STEP: *Your Leadership Step or Rest Stop today is to examine your heart with the Holy Spirit's help to see if there is any sin issue that you need to confront. If there is, then you need to ask God's forgiveness and repent, which simply means to change your behavior from this point forward. Then you may need to go to others whom you have offended and ask forgiveness. If you cannot go to them, then call or write, but don't put it off; take care of it now.*

Power   August 17

> *"Hear this, you leaders of Jacob, you rulers of Israel, who despise justice and distort all that is right; who build Zion with bloodshed, and Jerusalem with wickedness. Her leaders judge for a bribe, her priests teach for a price, and her prophets tell fortunes for money. Yet they look for the Lord's support and say, 'Is not the Lord among us? No disaster will come upon us'" - Micah 3:9-11.*

In this passage, God alerted the leaders to the fact that He knew what they had been doing and He was not pleased. Notice that each one of the leadership positions was doing what they were doing for money, and they had all in affect become mercenaries - giving their services to the highest bidder. What's more, they did this and felt like God was not going to judge this perversion of power; in fact, they felt confident the Lord was on their side! Leaders must all deal with the "big three" of temptations - sex, money and power - and in this case, the leaders had failed miserably in two of the three. The lesson is that God is watching leaders and will hold them accountable for any abuse of power.

LEADERSHIP STEP: *Your Leadership Step today is to examine your relationship with money and power. Why are you doing what you do? Is it for the money? Are you using your position and authority to enrich yourself? This is not to say that you cannot be rewarded handsomely for your work* or gifts, but you cannot allow money to be your main motive. Of course, the major antidote for greed is generosity, so also look at your giving habits during today's reflection.

Persuasion   August 18

"I plead with you, brothers and sisters, become like me, for I became like you. You did me no wrong"- Galatians 4:12.

Paul had a special relationship with all the churches he founded and that gave him some measure of authority in their lives. Yet he was always careful not to overstep that authority, but rather spent a great deal of time and energy appealing, even pleading with them (but seldom ordering them) to adhere to the standard of behavior he expected from them as believers. Effective leaders do the same thing, for they know that if they order someone to do something, they may get compliance for a while, but the people ordered will revert to old behaviors eventually, and true change and transformation will not occur once the leader's authority is removed. That means leaders must communicate a vivid picture of the benefits or necessity of the issue for which they are advocates.

LEADERSHIP STEP: *If you are not going to resort to power to get people to do what's best, you must develop the skill of effective persuasion to get the job done. Your Step today is to examine the tools you use for persuasion - speech, writing, media, meetings - and the effectiveness of the relationships you have with your followers that enables you to produce the results and changes you need to make. When you persuade, your people and company are both better off in the long run.*

Values   August 19

"What is more, I consider everything a loss because of the surpassing worth of knowing Christ Jesus my Lord, for

whose sake I have lost all things. I consider them garbage, that I may gain Christ and be found in him, not having a righteousness of my own that comes from the law, but that which is through faith in Christ—the righteousness that comes from God on the basis of faith. I want to know Christ—yes, to know the power of his resurrection and participation in his sufferings, becoming like him in his death, and so, somehow, attaining to the resurrection from the dead" - Philippians 3:8-11.

There is no more brilliant writing in the New Testament than Paul's letter to his favorite church in Philippi. In it he repeatedly explains his concept of leadership and the values that go with it. In today's passage, Paul acknowledged he experienced some loss in return for gaining Christ, but expressed no regret. He renounced any attempts at or gains from self-righteousness and determined only benefits in Christ really mattered. He also confessed he lived in the power of the Resurrection as he suffered in this life and looked forward to the life to come in his resurrection from the dead. Every leader should have a life philosophy and blueprint for living just like Paul described in this passage.

LEADERSHIP STEP: *Your Step today is to examine your thinking about the themes raised in this passage, along with how they are playing out in your life. You should especially look at two of them, suffering and loss, because there are no guarantees that your leadership will be successful and without pain. Are you prepared to risk losing what you worked for as you pursue God's will? Are you willing to suffer for His sake as a leader? Are you carrying out your plans or His as you lead?*

Ethics   August 20

"Dishonest money dwindles away, but whoever gathers money little by little makes it grow" - Proverbs 13:11.

Most ethical failures in leadership and business involve money. Those guilty are usually looking for a shortcut to obtain riches, although some are only involved in petty theft and pilfering. Yet stealing small is stealing still, no matter the size of the take, and God is watching to take away what someone unethically obtains. Leaders must learn to be content with what they have and work faithfully to make it increase, both personally and for their organizations. The Bible is clear, however, that anyone who is unfaithful in little things (or a small amount of money) is just a few steps away from being unfaithful in more significant things (like a larger amount of money).

LEADERSHIP STEP: *Your Step today is to reassess your heart where money is concerned. How faithful are you in the little things like small amounts of money or things that don't cost very much? Do you use the company postage meter for personal mail? Use company office supplies like they were your own? And how about the bigger things? Are you looking for shortcuts to get your hands on a lot of money? What price are you paying for that pursuit of a big payday?*

Collaboration — August 21

"You have increased the number of your merchants till they are more numerous than the stars in the sky, but like locusts they strip the land and then fly away" - Nahum 3:16.

Companies and organizations form alliances with clients, suppliers, customers, employees, donors, volunteers, neighbors, local and national governments and labor unions. These partnerships can be predatory, greedily vying to destroy the environment, competitors, rivals and other organizations. These partnerships can also do tremendous good and produce positive results for society at large and the people and companies involved in those relationships.

Leaders create or perpetuate the culture and mindset of these partnerships, so it is up to that same leadership to set the tone for the type of partnerships and collaborative efforts of which their organizations will be a part.

LEADERSHIP STEP: *Your Leadership Step today is to consider all the partnerships of which you are a part. Are you happy with the results they are producing? Do you like the spirit in which they function? What role can you play in helping to shape, mold and change these collaborations into forces for positive change and societal contributions? It all stems from the business philosophy with which you function and, as a leader, you get to mold that business mindset daily.*

Relationships · August 22

"You have increased the number of your merchants till they are more numerous than the stars in the sky, but like locusts they strip the land and then fly away" - Nahum 3:16.

In Nahum 3, the prophet spoke out against Nineveh because of a variety of sins. In this particular verse, he confronted their bad business practice of partnerships that were designed to take and not give. These partnerships were predatory and had only one objective in mind: maximize their profits and then move on to new fields that they could strip bare once again. This offended the Lord, so much so that the prophet, God's mouthpiece, spoke out against the practice to condemn it. Leaders must determine the nature of and reason for their partnerships in business, but these partnerships (including those with employees) should benefit many and not just the self-centered interests of the company and stockholders.

LEADERSHIP STEP: *Your Step today is to do a partnership assessment with your staff, suppliers, customers and other publics. Is the nature of these partnerships to take and serve* *self-interests, or do they exist to benefit the environment, the community, and the long-term interests of employees and their families? Is everyone better off due to these relationships, or do you need to adjust the purpose of some to reflect an attitude of servant leadership?*

Rest Stop 34   August 23

> **"For six days, work is to be done, but the seventh day shall be your holy day, a day of sabbath rest to the Lord. Whoever does any work on it is to be put to death. Do not light a fire in any of your dwellings on the Sabbath day" - Exodus 35:2-3.**

If the Sabbath is to be taken literally, then people cannot turn on a light in their homes, drive a car, ride an elevator or cook a meal on the Sabbath. All that may seem spiritual, but can simply represent a carnal desire to follow rules to make one feel spiritual. The true sense of a Sabbath is to take time to reflect on one's spiritual condition. In today's passage, the Sabbath was a time to live in the light that only God can provide. That light is to expose sin, give guidance, provide wisdom and give insight into God's word. Leaders must examine their business and leadership practices in the light of God's word and adjust anything that is contrary to or raises itself up against the knowledge or will of God.

LEADERSHIP STEP: *Your Rest Stop today is to not light a fire in your home. No, that doesn't mean you cannot turn on the heat or stove. Instead, spend some prolonged time in God's light, which is His word. Your assignment is to pick a book or epistle and read it today and every day this week. With your journal open, ask God both to evaluate your leadership performance in light of this reading and to give you new insight that will make you a more effective and godly leader or follower.*

Emotional Intelligence — August 24

"If we claim to be without sin, we deceive ourselves and the truth is not in us. If we confess our sins, he is faithful and just and will forgive us our sins and purify us from all unrighteousness. If we claim we have not sinned, we make him out to be a liar and his word is not in us" - 1 John 1:8-10.

Emotional intelligence is defined as functioning in self-awareness, knowing what one is sensing and feeling so that person can understand how their emotions are impacting their actions. Leaders of all kinds must function in that awareness, for they have the power to make decisions that can cause great good or pain. When leaders deny the reality of their emotions, they often operate in what is called their "shadow" and followers never know if they are relating to the real person or a hologram that appears real but is actually wearing a mask or functioning from motives that even the leader may not understand.

LEADERSHIP STEP: *Your Step today is to spend time probing your inner perhaps hidden being. You will do this by asking questions and making requests of the Lord you may not often make. Pray this prayer found in Psalm 139:23-24: "Search me, God, and know my heart; test me and know my anxious thoughts. See if there is any offensive way in me, and lead me in the way everlasting." Don't deny or excuse what you hear, but record it in your journal; then repent and determine to seek help.*

Coaching — August 25

"Then I will give you shepherds after my own heart, who will lead you with knowledge and understanding" - Jeremiah 3:15.

This verse points out several interesting things about leadership. First, God works through leaders. When the shepherds of Israel failed, God did not do away with leadership - He replaced the bad leaders with good ones. Second, good leaders are a gift from God for he *gave* shepherds to Israel. Third, there are leaders who have God's heart when they lead and others who don't. Fourth, God expects leaders to lead and not simply maintain or manage. And finally, leadership's most important tools are knowledge and understanding - of the people and organization they lead, its mission, the skill of leadership and of the work the organization was established to do.

LEADERSHIP STEP: *Today's Step is to meditate on the five points from this verse as they pertain to your relationships with those in your organization. It is assumed that a coach is going to help the organization win and the people reach their full potential. Do you have the knowledge and understanding you need to coach the people and the organization forward? Are you truly leading, or are you playing it safe by maintaining things as they are and have been?*

Attitude   August 26

"He is the one we proclaim, admonishing and teaching everyone with all wisdom, so that we may present everyone fully mature in Christ. To this end I strenuously contend with all the energy Christ so powerfully works in me" - Colossians 1:28-29.

Paul knew his purpose and mission in life, which was to establish the church of Christ among the Gentiles. He had a clear vision of what he was trying to produce in those Gentile believers and he knew his strategy for how to achieve his objective. The key for today is verse 29, in which Paul indicated his attitude toward his work: he did it with great energy and effort, not waiting for it to happen but pressing forward to help make it happen. Leaders would do well to emulate Paul's focus, purpose and attitude of actively and *strenuously* working for the cause that God had assigned him.

LEADERSHIP STEP: *Your job is not simply to maintain but to lead with purpose. If your attitude is holding you back, it's time to adjust your attitude - or your work. What is your attitude toward the work you are doing? Your Step today is to ponder that question. Do you have a positive attitude toward it? Are you actively engaged or is fear holding you back? Do you love your work or is your attitude and energy level telling you it's time to look for another opportunity?*

Productivity   August 27

*"All hard work brings a profit,
but mere talk leads only to poverty" - Proverbs 14:23.*

While it is important that leaders help set the vision for an organization and then communicate that vision far and wide, the leaders must do more than talk. They must help direct the organization and its people to activities that will most probably produce the vision they have designed. Leaders in particular must determine what they can do that few others (if any) can do to help bring about the desired results for which the organization exists. Then leaders help rally followers to a better future by continuing to keep the vision fresh and vibrant, all the while working and contributing, being careful not to become idle because others are doing much of the work.

LEADERSHIP STEP: *Today's Step is to evaluate your own productivity as a leader or follower. First, do some work to define your gifts and strengths - what it is that you bring to the team that others cannot. Second, reflect on how you can express those strengths more often. Third, think about how* you can keep the vision uppermost in your mind and the minds of your colleagues. Finally, determine how you will measure your productivity for the sake of accountability.

Finances   August 28

"You may say to yourself, 'My power and the strength of my hands have produced this wealth for me.' But remember the Lord your God, for it is he who gives you the ability to produce wealth, and so confirms his covenant, which he swore to your ancestors, as it is today" - Deuteronomy 8:17-18.

Leaders are often around a lot of money and have potential to earn a lot of money. It is easy for those leaders to assume their intelligence, leadership prowess, job skills and the like are the source of that wealth. That prideful thinking then leads to an attitude of ownership, which means they have to fight to protect what is rightfully theirs and to gain more. Today's verses remind leaders and all people to remember the Lord who is the source of all good things, including wealth. That wealth is not a sign of man's faithfulness but rather God's faithfulness. God bestows the ability to earn wealth on those He sovereignly chooses. That should lead to an attitude of stewardship and not ownership.

LEADERSHIP STEP: *Your Step today is to examine your attitude toward finances and wealth. It is important you be clear that God is the source of any wealth you may have earned. Has pride or a sense of entitlement set in that has caused you to be arrogant or to put your trust in your money or your ability to earn it? Do you thank God for your financial resources? Are you careful to give back to God by being generous to your church and the poor?*

Time Management   August 29

"You yourselves know that these hands of mine have

supplied my own needs and the needs of my companions" - Acts 20:34.

Paul had a governing value not to be a financial burden on his converts so that the gospel would not be criticized or associated with traveling teachers common in his day. He did not just talk or think about that value. That value impacted his calendar and determined how he was going to spend the hours in his day. Therefore Paul did not work first and foremost to make money; he worked to express his values and to support and further his apostolic mission.

Leaders are values-driven just like Paul was, and their values show up in their calendar and their checkbook. They know that their values must be translated into action or they are just useless words.

LEADERSHIP STEP: *Your Step today is to review the values you have written out from previous Steps to see if you are following through on your priorities in life. How are you spending your time? Is your time management values-driven, or do you sell yourself to the loudest, most urgent bidder? Why do you work and do what you do? Is it simply to make money? If so, money is your highest value! Is that how you want it to be known? What changes do you need to make?*

Rest Stop 35 — August 30

"It is a day of sabbath rest, and you must deny yourselves; it is a lasting ordinance" - Leviticus 16:31.

The phrase *deny yourself* was used by a now-famous carpenter-turned teacher many centuries after Moses wrote these words in Leviticus: "Whoever wants to be my disciple must deny themselves and take up their cross and follow me" (Mark 16:24). This act of self-denial was not to be a ritual perfoemd one day every week but was to become a lifestyle that distinguished Jesus' followers from everyone else on earth. Leaders are no exception to this edict, and must refuse their instinct toward self-indulgence by denying self. This denial takes the form of serving others, refusing to use power for personal gain, and refraining from revenge, gossip and theft.

LEADERSHIP STEP: *Your Rest Stop today is to meditate on your current level of self-denial in your walk with Jesus. What evidence can you provide that you are truly denying your tendencies toward selfishness and self-service? Do you refuse opportunities to talk about yourself or draw attention to your accomplishments, and accept working with others with whom you would naturally prefer **not** to work? Where may you be resisting the cross that Jesus is asking you to carry?*

Humility   August 31

"No one from the east or the west or from the desert can exalt themselves. It is God who judges: He brings one down, he exalts another" - Psalm 75:6-7.

Today's passage states that it is God who is the source of all promotion and demotion. There is nothing wrong with planning a career, but it can become a problem when ego, conceit or ambition take over and make it a ruthless or unrelenting pursuit of the next promotion, better office or bigger payday. Of course promotion is generally into leadership positions, and when leadership is sought simply as the next step on the career ladder, the pursuit often lacks a godly focus and understanding and involves pride. Leaders and aspiring leaders would do well to humble themselves by preparing to become leaders but trusting the process and the timetable to the ultimate Career Coach - the Lord Himself.

LEADERSHIP STEP: *Your Step today is to examine your motives for wanting to be a leader. Is it for money, prestige,* or power, or is it born from a desire to serve and make an impact through influence and empowering others? Perhaps the best test is your reaction to times you are overlooked for a promotion or when you are actually demoted. Did you feel hurt and slighted, or did you thank God, trusting in His perspective and will for your life and career?

Decision Making September 1

"They looked for a way to arrest him, but they were afraid of the crowd because the people held that he was a prophet" - Matthew 21:46.

The "they" in this verse was the leadership in Israel and the "him" of course was Jesus. The leaders wanted to do away with Jesus, for they were convinced He was a heretic and an enemy of God. There are two things that stand out here. First, *they* could not really lead because *they* were afraid of the people. If *they* truly believed this about Jesus, *they* should have done something about it. Leaders cannot make good decisions, however, when *they* are afraid of the people *they* are assigned to lead! What's more, the people or followers had more wisdom and insight than the leaders (they recognized Jesus for who He truly was), which leads to the second point: Just because leaders have the title doesn't mean they know everything and are necessarily smarter or superior to those who follow.

LEADERSHIP STEP: *Your Step today is to reflect on things that may be affecting your ability to make decisions. Of what or whom are you afraid? Failure? Losing your job or position? Other people? Today may be the day to be set free by facing your fears and making a decision you have delayed. Then ask if you have cut yourself off from the help, wisdom and insight your followers can provide because of an attitude that you are smarter than they are, simply because you are the leader.*

Communication — September 2

"The Lord called to Moses and spoke to him from the tent of meeting. He said, 'Speak to the Israelites and say to them: 'When anyone among you brings an offering to the Lord, bring as your offering an animal from either the herd or the flock'" - Leviticus 1:1-2.

As Israel's leader, Moses received special insight of how Israel was to worship. This insight was not just for him, but was to be communicated to all the Israelites. Several factors were involved in this communication. First, Israel had to know and trust Moses. Second, Moses had to be clear in his communication. Third, the message had to be communicated to millions of followers, so there had to be reliable lines of communication. Finally, Moses both spoke and wrote the communication, and repeated what he taught in one huge review found later in the book of Deuteronomy. Each of Moses' steps is just as relevant and important for modern leaders if they wish to communicate with their followers, regardless of the business they are in.

LEADERSHIP STEP: *Your Step today is to evaluate the communication practices of your leadership style. Do you have the credibility and recognition Moses had that will enhance your messages? Are you clear when you communicate? Do you have lines of communication in your organization through which messages flow quickly to those who need them? Finally, do you say things more than once using multiple media to ensure your messages are understood?*

Spiritual Growth — September 3

You, Lord, took up my case; you redeemed my life. Lord, you have seen the wrong done to me. Uphold my cause! You have seen the depth of their vengeance, all their plots against me" - Lamentations 3:58-60.

In this passage, the prophet Jeremiah was pleading his case to the Lord because of how his contemporaries had treated him. He was leading Judah as their prophet, but the people would not listen to him, even persecuting him for telling them the truth. It is only a matter of time before leaders encounter enemies, who for various reasons - jealousy, ambition, ignorance, greed, just to name a few - oppose, criticize, undermine, and even rebel against their leadership decisions or position. When this happens, godly leaders must learn to look to God for help and wisdom and not seek revenge, become bitter or carry a grudge.

LEADERSHIP STEP: *Today's Step is to prepare for the day when your enemies come after you, just like they did Jeremiah and Jesus. First, don't be surprised when it happens - it is part of man's fallen nature to rebel and be ambitious. Second, don't be naive, for it may be someone close to you. Third, be open that God may use your enemies to reposition you or teach you more about trusting Him. Finally, be prepared to use prayer as your primary means of defense.*

Personal Development September 4

"Dear friend, I pray that you may enjoy good health and that all may go well with you, even as your soul is getting along well" - 3 John 1:2.

The writer was not just concerned with the reader's spiritual well-being, but also the reader's physical health. Leaders often encounter stressful situations that require many hours of attention and work. It is easy to allow physical health to deteriorate under those conditions, but leaders need all the energy and stamina they can muster to produce and maintain excellence on the job. This includes exercise, having regular medical checkups, eating properly, getting enough rest, doing fun things, and maintaining healthy relationships. One more thing a leader must especially watch and maintain is an ideal weight for his or her age and body frame.

LEADERSHIP STEP: *Don't allow the pressures of and time invested in leadership to destroy your health. Your Step today is to assess your physical condition and health habits. Is your current weight what you desire or do you need to go on a diet and lose some pounds? Are you eating the right foods for you? What about your exercise program? Are you taking the time to stay in shape? Do you have a hobby that allows you to step away from work and do something you enjoy?*

Team Building September 5

"Dear friends, let us love one another, for love comes from God. Everyone who loves has been born of God and knows God" - 1 John 4:7.

Love is a popular topic for discussion these days in business circles. It is seen as a competitive advantage for teams who not only function well together but also have genuine affection for one another. This may be a revolutionary thought and concept for modern leaders, but it is not a new business idea, but rather an ancient God idea! The question of whether leaders are born or made is answered by today's verse, for it clearly states that anyone, including a leader, who loves is born of God. Therefore loving leaders are "born of God" and then made, for this kind of love is not a human but rather a divine characteristic that serves and gives just as God does.

LEADERSHIP STEP: *Your Step today is to ask yourself whether or not you have included love as one of your leadership values and characteristics. Do you agree that love has a role in your leadership? Does love mean simply doing nice things, or can tough love be part of the equation? What tangible evidence can you provide that shows love is a trait* that finds its way into your leadership style and decisions? What more can you do to manifest Christ's love as you lead?

Rest Stop 36 — September 6

"'You will drink from the brook, and I have directed the ravens to supply you with food there.' So he did what the Lord had told him. He went to the Kerith Ravine, east of the Jordan, and stayed there. The ravens brought him bread and meat in the morning and bread and meat in the evening, and he drank from the brook" - 1 Kings 17:4-6.

Many people believe they work to make money so they can eat, pay bills and support their families. Believers understand they work to carry out God's will and, when they do, it is God who provides for their needs and not their company, donor base or investments. God can use but does not need those entities to support His people. In today's passage, God directed nature to provide for Elijah His prophet, and birds brought him his food and a brook provided his water. Leaders who understand this principle can lead with courage and can rest when they must because God is their source instead of how hard or long they work.

LEADERSHIP STEP: *Your Rest Stop today is to consider the source of your provision. Is it the Lord or is the company for which you work? The answer to this question determines for whom you work. If it is the Lord, you can lead with courage, for the Lord has your back, so to speak, and can provide for you even if your enemies threaten to terminate you or your position. If it is your company, then you cannot enjoy any kind of rest, for you are driven to provide for yourself.*

Strategy — September 7

"Now the men had said to her, 'This oath you made us swear will not be binding on us unless, when we enter

the land, you have tied this scarlet cord in the window through which you let us down, and unless you have brought your father and mother, your brothers and all your family into your house If any of them go outside your house into the street, their blood will be on their own heads; we will not be responsible. As for those who are in the house with you, their blood will be on our head if a hand is laid on them."' - Joshua 2:17-19.

In this passage, the spies gave Rahab instructions about what she was to do when they returned to take the land so she and her family would be protected. As simple as those instructions were, they represented a clear strategy for the protection and survival of her family. Whatever goals or plans organizations have, leaders must help devise and communicate clear strategies that everyone understands, has bought into and has the capability of implementing. It all starts with a clear vision of the direction or end result that the strategy will hopefully accomplish.

LEADERSHIP STEP: *Your Step today is to take a look at the strategies you have for your personal and organizational goals. Are they clear and concise? If they are not clear to you, then they will not be clear to anyone else and the chances of achieving your goals are minimized. You may want to look at those strategies one-by-one, and tweak, adjust or abandon them depending on their usefulness. In any case, the old adage applies: "Change the strategy, keep the goal."*

Change   September 8

"Then the king ordered Ashpenaz, chief of his court fficials, to bring into the king's service some of the Israelites from the royal family and the nobility—young men without any physical defect, handsome, showing aptitude for every kind of learning, well informed, quick to understand, and qualified to serve in the king's palace.

He was to teach them the language and literature of the Babylonians. The king assigned them a daily amount of food and wine from the king's table. They were to be trained for three years, and after that they were to enter the king's service" - Daniel 1:3-5.

In today's passage, we read how Daniel and his friends were transported from their homeland of Judah and brought to Babylon. Because they had much potential, they were chosen to be leaders and enrolled in a three-year development program. They had to learn a new language, new culture, and a new way of living with new "foreign" names. After that, they were to enter a management-training program that involved direct service to the king, the same king who had ransacked their homeland and killed family and friends. Leaders not only have to lead and manage change, they must deal with and embrace change in their own personal and leadership lives.

LEADERSHIP STEP: *Today's Leadership Step is to read Daniel 1 with your journal close by. As you read, ask the Lord to show you the depth and pain of the transition Daniel endured. What price did Daniel pay for leadership? What other changes in addition to the ones mentioned above do you think he encountered? What was Daniel's main concern when he began his training? Describe his attitude. What do you see that can help you with your own approach to change?*

People Skills September 9

"Like a roaring lion or a charging bear is a wicked ruler over a helpless people" - Proverbs 28:15.

There are two similes used in today's verse to describe a terrible leader. Anyone who encounters either animal in their described posture would experience a rush of fear. That is exactly what "wicked" leaders use to lead and control their followers. Fear naturally exists between leaders and followers, and poor leaders exploit that to control and manipulate. When people live or function in fear, they cannot produce their best work, express their creativity or take calculated risks. Those wicked leaders have no idea what they lose when they create an atmosphere of fear. Some simply don't care, for it's usually all about them and what they want, and not about the people who follow.

LEADERSHIP STEP: *Remember when you were a child and told that the principal wanted to see you? Were you happy? Did you think, "Good, I have wanted to talk to her about some changes around here"? No, you were probably terrified! That is the fear that naturally exists between leader and follower. What Steps can you take to lessen that fear in your relationships? Hold some offsite social meetings? Have an open-door policy? Do some team-building exercises?*

Purpose — September 10

"Before I formed you in the womb I knew you, before you were born I set you apart; I appointed you as a prophet to the nations" - Jeremiah 1:5.

Jeremiah realized at the beginning of his career as a prophetic leader that it was his life's work. In other words, he was fulfilling his God-assigned purpose as he led. The Lord had known and appointed him to lead before he was even born. This changes the question of whether or not leaders are born or made to "Are leaders called?" In this case and many others in Scripture, it is clear that God called David, Joseph, Moses, Deborah, Esther and John the Baptist to lead. All leaders should have a sense that what they are doing is God's will for their lives and that God's purpose for leaders is not limited to church work, but covers every aspect of God's creation.

LEADERSHIP STEP: *Today's Step is to clarify your sense of purpose and calling in what you are doing now. If you are leading your garden club, a women's Bible study, a Boy Scout troop, or any aspect of your company, do you have a sense that God has called you to that position? And as you lead, are you fulfilling your purpose? If you can say "yes" to both questions, then you can truthfully say, "God called me to this!" If not, it's time to resign and refocus.*

Goals   September 11

"And David said, 'The Lord who delivered me from the paw of the lion and from the paw of the bear, He will deliver me from the hand of this Philistine.' And Saul said to David, 'Go, and may the Lord be with you'"
- 1 Samuel 17:37-38.

David knew how to draw on the power of past successes to propel him into new ones. He had faced other giants, so this slightly larger one would be another testimony when David brought him down. What's more, David had to go it alone, for Saul offered no support, advice or backup, except to try and have David fit into Saul's two-sizes-too-big armor. Yet David was not alone, for he knew God was with him from past experience and God was not about to fail him. This is what real leadership is all about: drawing on past experience to see what others can't and setting lofty goals that lift everyone's performance and possibilities.

LEADERSHIP STEP: *Your Step today is to see if you are leading by setting lofty goals or by playing it safe. One way to know is by examining the goals you have set for you and your organization. Do you have any past success stories? Do you know how to draw on your past successes to encourage you or your team to new ones today? If your goals lack the ability to stir the imagination and energy of others, spend time today crafting new ones, with or without your team.*

Organization   September 12

"(Hiram's ships brought gold from Ophir; and from there they brought great cargoes of almugwood and precious stones. The king used the almugwood to make supports for the temple of the Lord and for the royal palace, and to make harps and lyres for the musicians. So much almugwood has never been imported or seen since that day)" - 1 Kings 10:11-12.

Solomon's kingdom had to learn how to handle growth and expansion, which meant he and his advisers had to address how they were going to organize their work, inventory, logistics and supplies. Because it is more work and requires new knowledge and skills, some companies and leaders choose **not** to grow, considering it more trouble than it's worth. Yet there is nothing wrong with - and it may even be God's will - increase as seen in today's passage, so there must be an organizational strategy or philosophy that enables people to handle more. That means that it is not wrong, and may actually be God's will, to want "more."

LEADERSHIP STEP: *Your Step today is to examine your attitude toward increase. Your fear of handling more may be a roadblock to your company's expansion and your own growth as a leader. Thus, you may oppose new product lines, methods, acquisitions and services because you are not prepared to go through the changes required to organize a larger sphere of influence. Are you biased against more or bigger? If so, why is that? What can you do to change?*

Rest Stop 37   September 13

"For this is what the Lord, the God of Israel, says: 'The jar of flour will not be used up and the jug of oil will not run dry until the day the Lord sends rain on the land'" - 1 Kings 17:14.

The prophet Elijah met a widow and told her if she made him a meal in the midst of her need, God would provide for her and she would not lack for the duration of a famine. Of course, the woman obeyed Elijah and God was true to His promise. Most people drive themselves to work and not take a Sabbath or break often quoting 1 Thessalonians 3:10: "The one who is unwilling to work shall not eat." Paul was referring to freeloaders who refused to work and lived off others. The keys to rest, wealth and work are the same as they were for that widow: being generous, seeing God as the source of all provision and obeying His leading.

LEADERSHIP STEP: *Your Step today is to evaluate how well you are using the three keys mentioned above. Are you generous with your money? When you are, you testify to your faith that God is your source and will replace and even multiply what you gave. Can you take a break from your work and not worry about money? That shows if you can obey without questioning God's ability. And finally, do you see God as your provider or your company or abilities?*

Service — September 14

"Whenever the spirit from God came on Saul, David would take up his lyre and play. Then relief would come to Saul; he would feel better, and the evil spirit would leave him" - **1 Samuel 16:23.**

David was obviously a skilled musician and his talents did not go unnoticed by the royal court. He was recruited to play for the king, but these were no ordinary concerts. David had to play for a mentally disturbed king who had severe issues with depression and anger. Somehow David's playing soothed the king's foul moods as they sound temporary relief through music, instead of dealing with the real problem. The point here is that David was called to serve in an awkward and delicate situation, and his talents were put to use in a way that he probably never imagined. Leaders often have to devote their talents to difficult situations that do not always serve their career interests but contribute to some public good that helps other people.

LEADERSHIP STEP: *Your Step today is to examine your motives for service and excellence. Are you pursuing those two values for your own benefit or for the benefit of other people? Are you avoiding tough assignments to protect yourself and your career path? Do you feel bitter that you have somehow been used to make a bad situation better? Have you made your talents and gifts completely available to the Lord for Him to utilize wherever and whenever He chooses?*

Motivation   September 15

"Blow the trumpet in Zion; sound the alarm on my holy hill. Let all who live in the land tremble, for the day of the Lord is coming. It is close at hand—a day of darkness and gloom, a day of clouds and blackness. Like dawn spreading across the mountains a large and mighty army comes, such as never was in ancient times nor ever will be in ages to come" - Joel 2:1-2.

The prophet Joel was alerting Judah to an impending disaster caused by their lax spiritual ways. He was urging the people to take steps and prepare for the coming onslaught of enemies. Effective leaders help their organizations see opportunities in the future and begin to prepare to take advantage of those opportunities today. Those same leaders also help their companies see threats to their operation, vision and goals, and take action to avoid those threats or to minimize their damage. This involves foresight - leaders must be able to read current reality and see into the future - and persuasion - being able to convince those who cannot see the danger that steps must be taken to prepare for anticipated problems and downturns.

LEADERSHIP STEP: *Your Step today is to bolster your organization against threats to its work and existence. Dwell on scenarios that can help your organization prepare for the worst. For example, have your team work on budgets that reflect a 20% or more revenue drop. Do succession planning in the event of the loss of a key leader. Help your team consider other negative events and plan a response to them.*

Self-Awareness   September 16

"My ears had heard of you but now my eyes have seen you. Therefore I despise myself and repent in dust and ashes"
- Job 42:5-6.

Job summarized what he had been through and concluded that before losing everything he had only **heard** about God. After his loss, he had **seen** God and it gave him a better perspective of who Job truly was - insignificant in comparison. That is a lesson leaders impressed with who they are need to learn. Not only did Job see an awesome God and a relatively un-awesome Job, he was humble and admitted the error in his judgment and ways. Furthermore, he vowed to repent, which simply means he wanted to turn his thinking around and move in the opposite direction.

LEADERSHIP STEP: *Your Step today is to humble yourself before God to ensure that you, like Job, are not someone who has simply heard about God without an accurate vision of who God is. You can do this in several ways. Consider a time of fasting. Perhaps you can do some volunteer work that involves menial tasks. Maybe you need to seek reconciliation with someone from whom you are estranged, or ask forgiveness for a situation or relationship you botched.*

Knowledge   September 17

"When you come, bring the cloak that

The Leadership Walk

I left with Carpus at Troas, and my scrolls, especially the parchments" - 2 Timothy 4:13.

In the days of the Apostle Paul, there were few libraries and fewer books that could populate them, for writing materials and literacy were scarce. The Jews were all literate for one reason: so they could read and study God's word. Paul was a Pharisee, and that group devoted large chunks of their lives to reading and study. It is no wonder then that God chose Paul to be the lead apostle to the Gentiles, for Paul was not only learned but also kept on learning and growing. Leaders in any field should follow Paul's example and continue to grow and gather knowledge, both in their field of expertise and in the leadership skills they need to promote organizational and personal success.

LEADERSHIP STEP: *Your Step today is to map out a reading program for the rest of the year. Keep in mind that your reading can be "listening," for there are many great audio books on the market, and many ways to obtain or download those books. Once you choose your reading topics, you can identify the books of interest to you in that area. In order to read, you must make reading (or listening) a part of your daily routine, even if it is only for five minutes.*

Wisdom   September 18

"Who is wise? Let them realize these things. Who is discerning? Let them understand. The ways of the Lord are right; the righteous walk in them, but the rebellious stumble in them" - Hosea 14:9.

The prophet Hosea reiterated what other prophets and wisdom writers had written: true wisdom is to know and walk in the fear of the Lord and the ways of God. God's ways "work," for He is personally committed to be involved in any processes or relationships dedicated and committed to do His will. That does not mean the righteous (including leaders) won't be tested or even experience outcomes that in the short run do not work out for their personal gain or benefit. Yet wise leaders walk in God's will because it is the right thing to do and not because it always works out to their advantage.

LEADERSHIP STEP: Your Step today is to once again review and study wisdom where it is mostly found in the Bible and that is the book of Proverbs. Go to the BibleGateway site and enter a search for the words wise or wisdom and then scan the lists (there are many references). Choose three verses to reflect on today, and then choose three more every day this week. Jot down in your journal your insights into wisdom and how you can apply them to your current situation.

Influence   September 19

"This is what the Lord said to me: 'Make a yoke out of straps and crossbars and put it on your neck. Then send word to the kings of Edom, Moab, Ammon, Tyre and Sidon through the envoys who have come to Jerusalem to Zedekiah king of Judah'" - Jeremiah 27:2-3.

Jeremiah was a prophet in Judah but his purpose was to be a prophet to the nations (see Jeremiah 1:5). The challenge was that the nations did not recognize or worship Jehovah, Jeremiah's God. In today's passage, Jeremiah was sent to give a word to the envoys visiting Jerusalem to take back to their masters. In bringing the word, the Lord had Jeremiah wear around his neck a yoke worn by an ox in order to help get the message across to them. The best Jeremiah could hope to do was influence those envoys, for he had no authority over them or their masters. At times, that is all leaders can hope to do: influence others so they willingly choose to listen and follow God's leadership wisdom.

LEADERSHIP STEP: *Jeremiah became part of the message he brought to the envoys when he wore the yoke. You too must become part of your message, using whatever media possible and any illustrations necessary to influence others. Your Step today is to do an influence check. Are you using social media to communicate? Is your communication lively or dry? Do people pay attention when you speak or write? What can you do to improve?*

Rest Stop 38   September 20

"Truly my soul finds rest in God; my salvation comes from him" - Psalm 62:1.

This psalm of David begins with a declaration that salvation comes from the Lord. People who do not know or who have not experienced this salvation will be restless, for their soul will be searching for some way to earn this salvation rest that only God can give. This represents the true spiritual nature of a Sabbath rest, for it is a condition when people cease striving to gain what they cannot earn and accept God's grace of salvation with joy and gladness. Leaders who do not know this salvation try to earn their legacy through hard work, memorials, buildings named after themselves and nepotism - hoping that appointing their children as successors will help give meaning to meaningless lives without God as their focus and source.

LEADERSHIP STEP: *Your Step today is to ensure you have entered the true rest God had in mind for His people in Christ. Have you put your faith in Him for your salvation? Have you ceased from your efforts to gain that salvation through good deeds? Are your good deeds a **result** of your saving relationship with Christ or an attempt to **earn** benefits only faith can bring? Are you resting in God's love and forgiveness or are you futilely working to obtain them?*

Power   September 21

"When Herod realized that he had been outwitted by the Magi, he was furious, and he gave orders to kill all the boys in Bethlehem and its vicinity who were two years old and under, in accordance with the time he had learned from the Magi" - Matthew 2:16.

In today's verse, Herod was old, but nonetheless was not happy to hear that a king had been born in his kingdom, a king that Herod did not sanction or appoint. Therefore he set out to restore his will in his kingdom by ordering the execution of any male child in his region in order to wipe out any competition to the throne. Rome had appointed Herod and he had plans for his sons to succeed him, not this child about whom the Magi had told him. The hallmark of authoritarian leaders is anger. They believe they own what they lead (sometimes they do) and anyone who does anything to harm or damage what is theirs brings a volcano of emotion. That anger is how they control people and get them to do what angry leaders want.

LEADERSHIP STEP: *Your Step today is to examine the role that anger plays in your leadership style and role. Are you known for your outbursts of anger, disgust or sarcasm? How do you act when you become angry? Do you speak angry words or show your anger in some other way? Reflect on why you become so agitated when people don't do what you want or expect. Remember, God appointed you, and you don't own your position; you are simply a steward.*

Persuasion   September 22

"Get yourself ready! Stand up and say to them whatever I command you. Do not be terrified by them, or I will terrify you before them" - Jeremiah 1:17.

Jeremiah spoke as a prophet to Judah. He had no official

title, position or authority, except that he carried the word from God concerning what God's people should do at that point in history. Jeremiah had nothing but his credibility, the words he spoke and direction from God as he stood before the people, most of whom had little interest in what he was saying. Yet the Lord told him to stand there and speak without fear. Seldom are leaders without any leadership authority like Jeremiah, yet they are commissioned with the same task of standing in front of people and followers and using words to persuade them to take a particular course of action or adopt a certain attitude.

***LEADERSHIP STEP**: Leaders who use a command-and-rule style get results, but the results stop when their authority ends or the pressure is removed. Your Step today is to examine if you have influenced or controlled people as you lead. If you are afraid to stop controlling because people may not do what you desire, then you are using power to get your way. In that case, it's time to address your fear and adjust your style, using power to influence rather than rule.*

Values   September 23

> *"Son of man, prophesy against the shepherds of Israel; prophesy and say to them: 'This is what the Sovereign Lord says: Woe to you shepherds of Israel who only take care of yourselves! Should not shepherds take care of the flock?'"* - Ezekiel 34:2.

God was upset with the leaders in Israel because of their misguided values. Instead of taking care of their followers, the leaders were taking care of themselves and God was not pleased. God places leaders in the church and over other entities like business and government to care for people and meet their needs. When this doesn't happen, leaders use their power, which is given to empower others, to grab what is most important to them - money, position, or ego-inflating projects. One interesting point in today's verse is that God is watching leaders and holds them accountable for the attitudes and values they have - or don't have!

LEADERSHIP STEP: *Your Step today is to again revise or develop your leadership values, especially regarding how you relate to others. First, determine what kind of leader you will be, preferably before you start to lead anything. Then explain in two or three sentences how you will express those values as you lead. Then put those values in order of priority and attach a Bible passage that epitomizes that value. Finally, review those values regularly to hold yourself accountable.*

Ethics   September 24

"The Lord detests dishonest scales, but accurate weights find favor with him" - Proverbs 11:1.

In ancient times, items sold by weight, like flour, salt, or seed, were put on one side of a scale with a weight on the other side. Unethical vendors would tamper with the weights, making the buyer think they were purchasing a certain amount, but in actuality the weight was less than it appeared. Thus the buyer was paying for a pound but in actuality they were only receiving 14 ounces. Today's verse reports that God watches those false weights - business dealings that are fraudulent - and actually bestows favor on those who act with integrity. Leaders must be mindful of this fact and watch their business and leadership practices to ensure everything they do and produce is accurately portrayed, labeled and advertised.

LEADERSHIP STEP: *Your Step today is to assess the world you lead: 1) Are you faithful to your organization's mission or is it a nice slogan to which no one pays attention?; 2) Do you follow through on customer service and promises?; 3) Does your leadership team keep commitments to employees or* *volunteers and treat them with dignity?; 4) Are your services and products of high quality?; 5) Are there false weights in your own character or leadership style?*

Collaboration — September 25

> *"But Ruth replied, 'Don't urge me to leave you or to turn back from you. Where you go I will go, and where you stay I will stay. Your people will be my people and your God my God. Where you die I will die, and there I will be buried. May the Lord deal with me, be it ever so severely, if even death separates you and me'"* - Ruth 1:16-17.

The story of Ruth contains many lessons for the reader. Ruth stayed loyal to Naomi even though there was no apparent personal benefit to do so. Ruth left her homeland and went back to Israel with her mother-in-law and it was there the unexpected happened: Naomi helped Ruth identify and win a potential suitor. The widow Ruth was soon married and became the grandmother to King David and part of Jesus' family tree. Leaders should not always evaluate partnerships by their apparent benefits, but look to align with people who have similar values to theirs. Those partners can then bring new perspectives to situations that can produce unexpected and beneficial results.

LEADERSHIP STEP: *Your Step today is to examine your current business or ministry partnerships. Do you have enough partners to achieve your vision? Are you only collaborating with people who think or act like you do? Do these partners share your business values, or are they a mismatch? Have you evaluated your partnerships solely on what they can give you or have you considered those to whom you can contribute something to make them more effective and stronger?*

Relationships   September 26

"Then Moses brought Aaron and his sons forward and washed them with water" - Leviticus 8:6.

Moses was Israel's leader, but God directed him to install Aaron and his sons as priests over the worship practices of the community. Aaron's family business thus became ministry, and they served in that capacity for centuries while there is no report of what happened to Moses' sons. Leaders must keep in mind that the roles in their organization may go to family members, but only if those members have the experience, talents or interests that benefit the company. Otherwise, nepotism can weaken any organization when the leaders insist that their family receive preferential treatment in hiring. What's more, Moses remained over Aaron's family. When family is present, it's always a good idea to have an arbiter or a leader who can prevent and protect the family (and company) from interpersonal squabbles or preferential treatment.

LEADERSHIP STEP: *Your Step today is to assess the relationships in your organization and how they may be affecting results or morale. Are there family members serving in your company? Are they qualified? Do they have special privileges or are they treated as any other employee or volunteer? Do some need reassigned so other family members are not overseeing them, thus preventing favoritism? Are they promoted based on performance or last name?*

Rest Stop 39   September 27

"Whoever dwells in the shelter of the Most High will rest in the shadow of the Almighty" - Psalm 91:1.

If someone is in another person's shadow, it indicates that they are standing really close to that person. In today's verse, the person who dwells in God's shadow gets to enjoy the rest that comes from being close to God. How can one dwell in this house and rest in His shadow? This rest does not come from observing a day, but from practicing the disciplines God requires: **prayer, Bible reading, generosity toward the poor, hospitality toward the needy, and commitment to a local fellowship of believers.** No matter how powerful, busy, prosperous or famous they are, leaders are expected to do those things. When they do, they will enjoy rest because they live close to God - close enough to stand in His shadow.

LEADERSHIP STEP: *Your Step today is to determine if you are so busy that it is costing you the time you need to spend with God. If that's the case, then you are not resting properly and it has nothing to do with how much sleep you get. There are five disciplines mentioned in bold above. Grade yourself on a scale of 1 (poor) to 5 (excellent) in each area. Then look and see where you are not doing what it takes to say close to God. What is that low score or scores costing you?*

Emotional Intelligence September 28

"When I saw that they were not acting in line with the truth of the gospel, I said to Cephas in front of them all, 'You are a Jew, yet you live like a Gentile and not like a Jew. How is it, then, that you force Gentiles to follow Jewish customs?'" - Galatians 2:14.

Paul confronted Cephas [Peter] because he was living among Gentiles like a Gentile until other Jews arrived. Then Cephas withdrew from the Gentiles so as not to offend his Jewish friends, acting like there should be a separation between Jew and Gentile. Paul was angered by this hypocrisy and confronted Peter in front of others. There are two examples of emotional intelligence at work in this story. One is Peter, whose fear of criticism from the Jews caused him to act in a way inconsistent with the mission to the Gentile world. The other was Paul, who directed his anger at the situation into a positive confrontation that would hopefully turn Peter from his hypocrisy and warn others against the error of Peter's ways.

LEADERSHIP STEP: *Your Step today is to emulate the way Paul handled Peter's misstep. Here's how: 1) determine if there is anyone's behavior that is inconsistent with the values and mission of the organization you lead or serve; 2) recognize your own feelings toward their attitude or behavior; 3) speak up, either in a one-to-one session or team setting. Caution: you can only do the latter if the team leadership is secure enough to handle this type of confrontation.*

Coaching   September 29

"This is the dream that I, King Nebuchadnezzar, had. Now, Belteshazzar, tell me what it means, for none of the wise men in my kingdom can interpret it for me. But you can, because the spirit of the holy gods is in you" - Daniel 4:18.

In Daniel 2, the king trusted none of his advisers and demanded they tell him both his dream *and* the interpretation. In today's verse, the king trusted Daniel and told him the dream. Daniel had coached the king previously in what he needed to do and the king trusted Daniel with his inner secrets. In a sense, Daniel was coaching the king for he was giving advice and perspectives the king could consider when making life and kingdom decisions. Coaching leaders must first prove themselves trustworthy with secrets before they can establish themselves as coaches. Once they do that, followers or clients will trust them and open up more quickly and completely. Coaching leaders should expect this to happen, but must be capable of handling those secrets with skill and wisdom.

LEADERSHIP STEP: *Your Step today is to assess your effectiveness as a coaching leader. First, name all those with whom you have a formal or informal coaching relationship. Second, identify the goals that you both have established in your relationship. Third, are you making progress toward those goals: Is your coaching client opening up more and responding? What can you do to enhance the trust between you and your client(s)? How can you grow as a coach?*

Attitude   September 30

"Have I not commanded you? Be strong and courageous. Do not be afraid; do not be discouraged, for the Lord your God will be with you wherever you go" - Joshua 1:9.

The Lord spoke to Joshua and warned and commanded him to be strong and courageous and ***not*** to be afraid. Of course that meant that Joshua was going to encounter many obstacles and enemies that would tempt him to lose strength and be fearful. The main reason God told Joshua not to fear is that God Himself was with Joshua wherever he went, and God plus one other person always constitutes a majority. When God tells someone not to fear, however, it is usually too late, and He is really telling them to move past their fears. All leaders must learn how to manage their fear and muster courage, which must function not in the absence of fear but in the midst and in spite of fear.

LEADERSHIP STEP: *Your Step today is to see where fear is overruling courageous faith in your life. Are you afraid to make a personnel change because it may get messy? Are you afraid to make a decision, so you settle for the status quo, which is really a decision not to decide? Do you live in fear of losing your job, so you to play it safe and remain indecisive? Do you fear criticism that is sure to come as you lead? Does it help to remember that God is with you wherever you go?*

Productivity   October 1

"I will look on you with favor and make you fruitful and increase your numbers, and I will keep my covenant with you" - Leviticus 26:9.

God is not intimidated by increase and His motto is *not* "small is better." In fact God expects His followers to take what they have and make it "more," whether it be a church, a business, an idea, a family, a righteous behavior or attitude, generosity, hospitality, an opportunity, good deeds or excellent service. This means that leaders must equip themselves to think bigger, to handle more, to organize better, to produce more, to reach more, to touch more, to envision more, to build more, to speak more, to think more, to talk more, to lead more, to write more, or to handle more in general. Leaders who work to shrink their world down to the size with which they are comfortable are not always doing what God wants but what they prefer and with what they are more comfortable.

LEADERSHIP STEP: *Your Step today is to examine your attitude toward increase and see if it allows you to make more happen, or if your attitude is one of fear that causes you to keep things manageable. If it is the latter, why are you afraid of more? Do you agree that God is desirous of more? What do you need to do to grow your ability to handle more? Your "more" theology must align itself with God's will, and His desire throughout the Bible seems to endorse "more."*

Finances   October 2

"If anyone has material possessions and sees a brother or sister in need but has no pity on them, how can the love of God be in that person?" - 1 John 3:17.

God blesses individuals and companies with resources but

he expects those blessings to be utilized in part to meet the needs of individuals and communities. It is up to leadership to foster empathy and generosity within the ranks of their families or organizations through community involvement, grants, focused giving and volunteer initiatives. Leadership must also help focus those efforts, building relationships within their communities so they can oversee the successful deployment of their generosity. Thus any benevolent or community development work must not only involve money but should also involve the investment of people's time and effort, including those of the leaders.

LEADERSHIP STEP: *Your Step today is to look at your organization's community involvement beyond just doing business. You should work to be a good neighbor by looking for and then investing in community needs. Ideally these efforts should be tied to the mission of your organization if possible, but your staff can also direct and connect your investments of time and money to the causes that are most important to them - and they will love you for it.*

Time Management   October 3

"But select capable men from all the people—men who fear God, trustworthy men who hate dishonest gain—and appoint them as officials over thousands, hundreds, fifties and tens. Have them serve as judges for the people at all times, but have them bring every difficult case to you; the simple cases they can decide themselves. That will make your load lighter, because they will share it with you"
- Exodus 18:21-22.

Moses' father-in-law gave him some good advice to stop trying to do all the work and to establish clear time priorities based on what it was that only he (Moses) could do, allowing others to do what they could do. In other words, Moses needed to delegate more of his responsibilities and let go of the day-to-day operations. Most leaders need to delegate more, but there are many reasons why they don't or can't. Some are afraid that the work won't be done as well as it is when they do it. Others are perfectionists. Still others don't have a vision to develop other people through the work delegated to them. And finally, some have a faulty view of leadership that requires them to have their hands in all aspects of the work instead of releasing it to other trusted associates.

LEADERSHIP STEP: *Your Step today is to determine how many hours you are working every week. Keep track of your work hours for the next two weeks, including commute time. Then keep a general log of how you spend that work time. After two weeks, look at the patterns of work and see where you are investing time in projects that you can and should delegate to others. That will enable you either to work less hours or devote that saved time to other projects.*

Rest Stop 40   October 4

*"Return to your rest, my soul,
for the Lord has been good to you"* **- Psalm 116:7.**

The psalmist made an interesting statement in this one verse. First, he wrote that his soul needed to "return" to its rest. That indicates that rest is the natural state for the soul. Second, the psalmist commanded his soul to rest. That means that rest is a decision, within the capability of each person to enter and enjoy. Third, the soul is the realm of the emotions, so the rest to which the psalmist was referring was not a vacation on the beach. Fourth, the psalmist reasoned with his soul, providing it with an important fact: God had been good to the psalmist. It helps to remember what God has done in the past so that any current turmoil or confusion can be put into proper perspective and rest may be maintained.

LEADERSHIP STEP: *Your Step today is to reflect on your state of unrest in light of today's verse. First, confess or admit if you have lost your rest. Second, reason with yourself and produce facts that help your soul be at rest. This will include going over all things God has done for you in the past. If He did those things for you in the past, He can do them again! Finally, don't act like you have no role to play in your rest. It is a decision no matter what you are going through.*

Humility   October 5

"'Surely the day is coming; it will burn like a furnace. All the arrogant and every evildoer will be stubble, and the day that is coming will set them on fire,' says the Lord Almighty. 'Not a root or a branch will be left to them. But for you who revere my name, the sun of righteousness will rise with healing in its rays. And you will go out and frolic like well-fed calves'" - Malachi 4:1-2.

It is possible either to live a life full of pride or to limit pride to certain areas, like finances, professional accomplishments, or relationships with others. No matter the frequency or application, today's verse states that there is a day of reckoning for every proud person. Yet there is a promise for the un-proud or humble person in the next verse, for those who revere God's name will go out and frolic like well-fed calves! Leaders must especially guard against pride, for they have access to money and power that can make them smug and confident in their own intellectual and leadership skills. When they transition to pride, God can and will become personally involved to humble and even humiliate them.

LEADERSHIP STEP: *Your Step today is to read Daniel 4 and see what happened when Nebuchadnezzar refused to humble himself and acknowledge God. Note that the king* had a dream about a tree and today's verse refers to roots and branches – God was literally fulfilling the promise He made in Malachi 4:1! After reading, ask God to show you any area of life where you are proud and quickly humble yourself, remembering God will do it for you if you refuse.

Decision Making   October 6

"Do not take advantage of each other, but fear your God. I am the Lord your God" - Leviticus 25:17.

The Bible is practical and down to earth. While it addresses ethical issues like lying, adultery, stealing and relationships, it also may surprise some that it gives direction on basic activities, like child raising, humane treatment of animals, and personal hygiene. Today's verse addresses decision making in the context of what was called the year of Jubilee. In that year, all debts were to be forgiven and no one was to take advantage of that year by not loaning money the year before or by putting off land deals until Jubilee was over. Leaders must be mindful of the spirit of this principle and not make decisions that take unfair advantage of weakened or helpless competitors, employees or suppliers, simply to gain a competitive edge for their organization.

LEADERSHIP STEP: *Your Step today is to assess the spirit and attitude with which you make decisions when negotiating with others. Do you or your leadership team look to win at all costs, taking no prisoners as you drive a tough bargain? Or do you look for Win-Win situations, where your company can win and the union, supplier, employees and partners can also come away feeling like they got a good deal? Do you see your negotiations as war or chance for a partnership?*

Communication   October 7

"The Lord said to Moses, 'Speak to the entire assembly

of Israel and say to them: 'Be holy because I, the Lord your God, am holy'" - Leviticus 19:1-2.

It may sound simplistic, but God is a great communicator and understands how to get His message across. In this verse, He began talking to Moses about what are known as the Ten Commandments. He directed Moses to speak to Israel, and told Moses to put the message in writing. Then Moses repeated those Commandments, both in speech and written form, so there would be no doubt in Israel what was expected of them and what was important to the Lord. Leaders must follow this example and be clear in their communication. They must be willing repeat their message in more than one medium until the meaning takes hold in the minds of the listeners in the way the leader intended.

__LEADERSHIP STEP:__ Your Step today is to examine your ability to communicate the vision or mission of your organization. How often do you talk about the vision or mission? Can people repeat back to you what the vision is? Do you review and repeat to followers what is most important to you and the organization? Do you say those things using more than one medium, like video, articles or staff meetings? How can you be sure that the people are getting the message?

Spiritual Growth   October 8

"And without faith it is impossible to please God, because anyone who comes to him must believe that he exists and that he rewards those who earnestly seek him'" - Hebrews 11:6.

If it is true that without faith it is **impossible** to please God, then it is also true that with faith it is **possible** to please Him. Faith is the currency with which transactions with God are made. Believers spend faith, receive the object of their faith and the Lord fills their pockets with more faith, thus creating a faith cycle and lifestyle of which God approves. While leaders are required to take a rational approach to life and business, they must also look for ways to express faith - faith that people can do the work, faith that risk and hard work will be rewarded, faith that people can change, faith that God is watching their efforts and will bless the work of their hands. Faith is not to be an event, but rather a lifestyle, even for leaders who are working in non-faith-based organizations.

LEADERSHIP STEP: *Your Step today is to examine the role of faith in your work and leadership style. On a scale of 1 (poor) to 5 (excellent), rate yourself in the following areas: 1) delegating work to other people; 2) stepping out of your comfort zone to learn new things; 3) taking calculated risks; 4) investing money in people and new ventures; 5) hiring new people or promoting others; 6) allowing people to make and learn from mistakes; and 7) a succession plan for your role.*

Personal Development   October 9

I praise you because I am fearfully and wonderfully made; your works are wonderful, I know that full well"
- Psalm 139:14.

This verse does not just pertain to one's physical being - anatomy, life systems, organs and skeleton. It describes personality, as well as intellectual and emotional makeup. Some people try to change how they look and act, convinced they have serious flaws in both. There may be, but they may also be exactly as God intended them to be. What God is mostly concerned with renewing or changing is one's thinking, which will transform areas that need changed while enhancing and maximizing characteristics that are an important part of each individual's God-designed personality and physical appearance.

The Leadership Walk

LEADERSHIP STEP: *Your Step today is to read Romans 12:1-2 and remind yourself that your main focus for leadership and personal development is your thinking. If you can change your thinking, you can change your behaviors in any area, and bring about personal transformation that will enhance your leadership effectiveness. Where is your thinking most deficient and holding you back? Where thinking about finances is concerned? Public speaking? Learning new skills?*

Team Building   October 10

"Why do you look at the speck of sawdust in your brother's eye and pay no attention to the plank in your own eye? How can you say to your brother, 'Let me take the speck out of your eye,' when all the time there is a plank in your own eye? You hypocrite, first take the plank out of your own eye, and then you will see clearly to remove the speck from your brother's eye" - Matthew 7:3-5.

These words of Jesus are among His earliest and most famous in Matthew's gospel. His advice here is sound for anyone in any kind of relationship with another - whether in family, church, or work teams. In order to help anyone grow, develop or confront their issues (specks), one must first confront his or her issues (planks). This is important for team building, for leaders must not assume the role of superiority and authority unless they are willing to confront the areas of development that are most pressing in their own lives. If leaders don't do that, their vision is blurred when it comes to identifying issues that give them the credibility to speak into the lives of others. What's more, Jesus calls people who don't see themselves accurately while trying to fix others hypocrites.

LEADERSHIP STEP: *Your Step today is to see if you are guilty of hypocrisy. When there is tension on your team, do you tend to blame others and not look at the role you may* be playing? How often do you say, "I was wrong, forgive me" instead of "I was wrong, but . . ." and then launch into excuses as to why you acted or spoke as you did? Is there any team dysfunction that you need to take responsibility for right now, asking team members to forgive and help you?

Rest Stop 41 — October 11

"All their days their work is grief and pain; even at night their minds do not rest. This too is meaningless"
- Ecclesiastes 2:23.

In this verse the wisdom writer described people who cannot stop working and cannot enjoy the work being done. Even when they stop working, their minds are back on the work, which is not a pleasant experience, but one filled with grief and pain. Worry, anxiety, regret and anger can consume leaders, turning their rest time into an opportunity to run mental marathons. Leaders are especially prone to this type of experience, for the duties and responsibilities of leading people and organizations can cause sleepless, restless nights. The writer of today's verse described this scenario as meaningless, futile and pointless.

LEADERSHIP STEP: *Do you stay up nights or wake up early due to worry or anxiety about work-related issues? Do you find it difficult to leave work mentally even when you are on a long weekend or holiday? Then incorporate the following as a daily or regular ritual: Read Psalm 127:2, which states that God gives to those He loves even in their sleep. Then when you go to bed, take a day off or a vacation, saying, "Lord, I put you in charge while I am gone. Watch over my work."*

Strategy — October 12

"Then on the seventh day they rose early at the dawning of

the day and marched around the city in the same manner seven times; only on that day they marched around the city seven times. At the seventh time, when the priests blew the trumpets, Joshua said to the people, 'Shout! For the Lord has given you the city'" - Joshua 6:15-16.

Joshua and his army marched around Jericho 13 times, once a day for six day and seven times on the seventh day. As bizarre as that sounds, it was a good strategy because it worked and not a life was lost in the process. For this to work, many things had to happen. Joshua had to "sell" it to the people. Then the people had to commit and stay together as a unit, not grumbling or second-guessing what was going on. Everyone had a role to play and Joshua needed everyone to be all in, for he needed all voices to generate enough decibels so the wall would collapse. Finally, Joshua and the people had to have faith that God would do His part once they had obediently done theirs. When all that occurred, the strategy was effective.

LEADERSHIP WALK: *Your Leadership Step today is to consider how well your strategies compare to the one Joshua deployed to take Jericho. Are you clear about what needs to happen? Have you clearly and simply communicated that to those involved? Is everyone speaking one thing with one voice or is there division on the team? Does everyone have faith in leadership and the strategy? If not, then what changes - to personnel or strategy - do you need to make?*

Change   October 13

"Then the peoples around them set out to discourage the people of Judah and make them afraid to go on building" - Ezra 4:4.

When the Jews started to rebuild and repopulate Jerusalem, there were people with vested interests who tried to hinder the process. That is usually how it goes when people and leaders try to plan and implement change. The tactics are almost always the same, for the opponents of change use forecasts of doom and failure to instill fear and to intimidate the change agents. When this occurs, leaders must continue to remind followers of the reasons for the change and how it fits into the overall vision and values of the organization. While opponents use fear, leaders must "preach" faith; when opponents use discouragement, leaders must find ways to encourage those doing the change work.

LEADERSHIP STEP: *Your Step today is to determine if fear or discouragement are plaguing change efforts in your organization. Since people cannot yet see the results of the change, you must paint a vivid picture of the new reality you are pursuing as a team. How, where and when can you do this? Perhaps it's time to revisit the reasons for the changes or to encourage one another by celebrating small victories or successes along the way.*

People Skills — October 14

"If you bite and devour each other, watch out or you will be destroyed by each other" - Galatians 5:15.

Paul warned his readers in this verse that once you start down a road of backbiting, gossip and sarcasm, it is difficult to contain. All those behaviors only lead to more and more of the same, which eventually tears down the people with whom you work, minister or live. Leaders must be especially careful not to set the tone and example for negative talk, abusive humor and sarcastic remarks, but must be honest when there is a problem, confrontational when there are harmful attitudes and behaviors, and encouraging all day, every day.

LEADERSHIP STEP: *Your Step today is to set the course for the conversations you are in today. Try this and see how people respond. When you sit down with another person on your team or in your family (it can also be a group), seize control of the conversation by saying something positive about your organization or the people who are in it. Watch and see how people follow your lead and build on what you said. The key is to be proactive and start positive gossip and rumors!*

Purpose   October 15

"Even so the body is not made up of one part but of many"
- 1 Corinthians 12:14.

An organization is not much different from the church or body of Christ, for both are made up of parts that serve different functions and together serve a larger purpose. In the church, people have spiritual gifts; in a company, each person has talents or strengths. In the church, there is a purpose to spread the good news and strengthen and train the members. In business, the purpose is whatever the chosen end result of the company happens to be. When people in the church or business know the purpose and what they are to contribute toward that end - assuming they are gifted or talented in that expected contribution - usually things run smoothly and there are anointed results in the church, and effective and efficient results in business.

LEADERSHIP STEP: *Your Step today is to assess how well your team members understand who they are and how what they are asked to do contributes to the overall purpose of the organization. Go around today (or hold a meeting) and ask people what the vision or mission of your organization is. If they don't know or aren't clear, then perhaps it's time to redefine the vision or find ways to take the current statement and communicate it more regularly and clearly.*

Goals   October 16

"Now the Israelites had been saying, 'Do you see how this man keeps coming out? He comes out to defy Israel. The king will give great wealth to the man who kills him. He will also give him his daughter in marriage and will exempt his family from taxes in Israel'" - 1 Samuel 17:25.

Goliath and his people had been harassing the people of God, so the king offered a handsome reward for anyone who would successfully conquer him. Even though the reward was lucrative, no one took the king up on his offer except David. David was tantalized by the reward but ultimately brought Goliath down because the giant had taunted God's name and people. The point is that the reward for achieving this corporate goal was not enough until the reward was coupled with a personal value system that stimulated David to action. Leaders often struggle to find the right incentive plan, which must communicate the company's priorities but must also resonate with the worker's personal needs and wants. Until that happens, incentive plans are often ineffective and meaningless.

LEADERSHIP STEP: *Your Step today is to examine how you are structuring your incentive plans for your team members. Are the incentives truly working or are do employees expect the reward regardless of performance? Do your incentives represent and support what is most important to achieve? Are your company's goals clear enough for people to understand how their activities fit into the overall goal plan? What adjustments do you need to make?*

Organization   October 17

"A large population is a king's glory, but without subjects a prince is ruined" - Proverbs 14:28.

God has put the drive for increase in all of creation. Every species looks to increase and that is true for humans. They want not just to reproduce but also to expand and grow their skills, enterprises, influence and love. While this growth can be directed toward selfish gains, that does not mean that all increase must be avoided or is misguided. The key is not to avoid "more" but to do it for the right reason and that reason is to glorify the God who put the desire for more in every person. Leaders must help direct the "more" efforts in their organizations, keeping the motives righteous while honoring this God-given motive for increase that is found in all the earth.

LEADERSHIP STEP: *Your Step today is to examine how your company, family or ministry thinks about **more**. Do you avoid **more** just because it upsets the status quo and puts too much pressure on you or your team? Do you want **more** for the wrong reasons - to become the biggest or the best in order to win the **more** competition? Are you fearful of **more**, thus spinning **small** or **less** as superior spiritually or ethically to **more**? Are you averse to **more** or **more** friendly?*

Rest Stop 42   October 18

"On my bed I remember you; I think of you through the watches of the night" - Psalm 63:6.

The idea of a Sabbath rest was not to go to the beach and do nothing. It was to turn attention to God during rest time and in return, the thoughts of God would bring refreshment and rest. The psalmist was not waiting for a specific day to think about God; he was thinking about God during his *daily* rest and not just his weekly rest. The psalmist was a great leader still honored in Israel, so it is important for modern leaders to follow his example and remember and reflect on what God has done, focusing on God Himself - His attributes, His goodness and His mercies.

LEADERSHIP STEP: *Your Rest Stop today is to consider what you think about during your rest times. Is your mind focused on work, the business of life or your relationship with the Lord? To help you focus on the Lord, consider these practices: learning meditation skills, a Bible study group that will help keep you in the Word, some cognitive learning skills that will help you control your self talk and thinking, or regular family devotions to keep everyone's mind in the Word.*

Service   October 19

> *"When he had finished washing their feet, he put on his clothes and returned to his place. 'Do you understand what I have done for you?' he asked them. 'You call me 'Teacher' and 'Lord,' and rightly so, for that is what I am. Now that I, your Lord and Teacher, have washed your feet, you also should wash one another's feet. I have set you an example that you should do as I have done for you'" - John 13:12-15.*

It was customary for a host to provide water to help traveling guests refresh and clean up from their dusty travels on foot. Yet no one wanted to assume the role as servant to the others at the Last Supper to provide this kind of demeaning service. Jesus recognized He had a "superior" position to His disciples as Teacher and Lord, yet He did not use His position for personal gain. Instead, he gave them an example of how leaders should empty themselves of any rank or leadership perks and serve those who follow them. Jesus instructed them to replicate what he had done to one another as a rule, not an occasional exercise.

LEADERSHIP STEP: *Your Step today is to assess how deeply a spirit of service has permeated your family or organization. Is there a spirit of cooperation between departments? How do you know there is (or is not)? Do the leaders have elite privileges like parking spaces and special meals, or is everyone* treated the same? Is your customer service exemplary, going beyond the normal to the spectacular? What can you do to improve your culture of service?

Motivation — October 20

"This is the city of revelry that lived in safety. She said to herself, 'I am the one! And there is none besides me.' What a ruin she has become, a lair for wild beasts! All who pass by her scoff and shake their fists" - Zephaniah 2:15.

The interesting thing about this verse is that the prophet was not talking about Judah or Israel, but rather about Assyria. The entire chapter is God's indictment against nations that were not serving Him and not part of the Jewish covenant community. Yet God was holding them all accountable for their irresponsibility, selfishness, pride and arrogance. The lesson should be clear for all leaders: God is watching what is done and He expects everyone to behave in a manner that is consistent with His ethical and moral code. When that doesn't happen, the good times eventually end and what was once so promising becomes a shell of its potential due to greed and self-centeredness.

LEADERSHIP STEP: Your Step today is to make sure the same things motivating Assyria above are not motivating you and your team. Bring in an outsider and ask them to sit, watch and listen to your operations for a week. Have them sit in on leadership and staff meetings, read your promotional materials and observe customer service. Then have them produce a report on what they saw. Don't ignore their report if they find pride or selfishness in your work.

Self-Awareness — October 21

"But Peter declared, 'Even if I have to die with you, I will never disown you.' And all the other disciples said the same" - Matthew 26:35.

Peter is often remembered as the disciple who proclaimed his loyalty, only to deny Jesus hours later. Yet this verse states *all* the disciples did the same thing. They assumed they were one place in terms of loyalty and commitment but were really in a very different place. Leaders must be aware they are as susceptible to failure - bad decisions, fear, fickleness, betrayal, lying, exaggeration, misinterpretation and faulty memory of the facts - as anyone else in their organization. An accurate assessment of their dark side gives leaders a chance to face and overcome it. Denial only challenges God to devise a scenario where reality will be revealed, just like it was for Peter and his friends.

LEADERSHIP STEP: *Your Step on your Leadership Walk today is to face the fact that you, like everyone else, have a dark side, but need help to identify and see it. Armed with this realization, you may want to find a leadership coach, someone who can listen to you, observe and evaluate your performance and give honest feedback. You want to focus on your dark side so it is not functioning while you deny it even exists, thus becoming a source of dysfunction in your world.*

Knowledge October 22

"Woe to you experts in the law, because you have taken away the key to knowledge. You yourselves have not entered, and you have hindered those who were entering" - Luke 11:52.

Jesus condemned the leaders of Israel because of their role in hindering people gaining knowledge of truth. Not only did they hinder others from knowing, they also refused to find the knowledge for themselves. This indicates leaders and followers should be on a learning journey together, forming what some writers have called a learning or teaching organization. Those organizations are always sharing information throughout every level, constantly studying what they have learned from past experiences to do a better and more effective job to accomplish their mission. In a learning organization, followers learn from leaders and leaders also learn from followers, since neither group has a lock on all the answers of how to do business.

LEADERSHIP STEP: Your Step today is to ensure you are part of a learning or teaching organization. First, make sure your staff meetings are times when everyone shares information and insight, not just the leaders. Second, do what you can to encourage everyone to get more training through outside workshops and seminars. Third, debrief business activities to identify the good and the not-so-good. Fourth, set aside in-house days for training and vision casting.

Wisdom   October 23

"So Pharaoh said to Joseph, 'I hereby put you in charge of the whole land of Egypt'" - Genesis 41:41.

There are two Pharaohs prominently featured in the Bible. One was the "bad" Pharaoh who oppressed Moses and his people. The other "good" Pharaoh was the one mentioned in today's verse, who recognized Joseph's plan to save Egypt as sound, and promoted Joseph to the number two position in all the land. Keep in mind that Pharaoh had just met Joseph when the latter came into Pharaoh's presence to interpret two dreams. This appointment required great courage and wisdom, for Pharaoh turned to a convicted felon who had distinguished himself in jail rather than any of the other Egyptian advisers. Leaders must use wisdom in hiring the right people and if they cannot recognize talent, they need to have someone among their advisers who can.

LEADERSHIP STEP: Your Step today is to examine your hiring track record to see if you have wisdom where recognizing talent is concerned. Have the last few people you hired become productive members of your team? Are you sure, or are you ignoring their dysfunction because you hired them? Are you hiring too quickly? Is there someone on your team more adept at recognizing talent? What is stopping you from relying on their insight instead of your own? Is it pride?

Influence — October 24

"We did this, not because we do not have the right to such help, but in order to offer ourselves as a model for you to imitate" - 2 Thessalonians 3:9.

Paul worked to pay the expenses for all his ministry team, even though he could have expected the places where he ministered to pick up the tab. He explained in this verse why he did that: so people would learn from his example that it is better to give than receive. While Paul was a prolific teacher and writer, he also taught through example, thus using every means available to influence and persuade others to follow his revelation of Christ and the Church. Leaders must be aware that people are watching them and that they have a wonderful opportunity to model whatever behaviors they desire others to adopt and follow. To not model what they are asking others to be and do is inviting others to dismiss those leaders as insincere and irrelevant.

LEADERSHIP STEP: *Your Step today is to take a look in the mirror and see what you look like, so to speak. Are you a walking billboard for the attitudes, behaviors and skills that you have determined are most important to you as a leader and to your organization? Do you take shortcuts because "I am the leader"? The best way to determine this is to conduct a 360-degree profile, for which you will need the services of an outsider who will drill down and see how others see you.*

Rest Stop 43 — October 25

"Do not be one who shakes hands in pledge or puts up

security for debts; if you lack the means to pay, your very bed will be snatched from under you" - Proverbs 22:26-27.

Today's passage refers to a practice called co-signing for someone else's debt. If the borrower can't pay, the creditors come after the co-signer to collect the loan. There is more than one way to cosign for someone else's commitments. That occurs when people want something for others more than others want it for themselves. When any kind of co-signing takes place, the co-signer can easily lose his or her rest worrying and fretting over the state of the other person's affairs. Leaders must be careful to set boundaries on their emotional involvement with family members and the people they mentor or lead, for their leadership energy can be sapped when they co-sign for irresponsible people.

LEADERSHIP STEP: *Your Step today is to examine whether or not you have co-signed for someone else's responsibilities. Are you covering for someone on your team or in your family who refuses to be responsible? Are you more anxious or concerned for their situation than they are? Are you being unfair to other team or family members as you compensate for the irresponsible one? What is this costing you in emotional and creative energy? Make today the day you stop!*

Power   October 26

"'The Lord bless him!' Naomi said to her daughter-in-law. 'He has not stopped showing his kindness to the living and the dead.' She added, 'That man is our close relative; he is one of our guardian-redeemers'" - Ruth 2:20.

The "him" here is Boaz who was kind to both the widowed Naomi and Ruth when they returned from Moab because there was food in Israel. Boaz had resources and power and used them not only for business but also to help others. Because of his kindness, Naomi blessed him and God heard her words and blessed Boaz with a good wife - and that wife was none other than Ruth! Of course, all leaders have power and if they use it to help and bless others, it will put a "blessing cycle" into motion: leaders do good deeds, people are helped, people will speak good things about them and their organization, God will hear and the Lord will bless the leaders so they can bless more people.

LEADERSHIP STEP: *Your Step today is to create the right conditions that will put the blessing cycle into motion. How can you use your power and resources to bless your employees and your community? This will require that you discover what either group truly needs and then make a concerted long-term effort to meet those needs. All the while, you must be doing it for the right reasons: to please the Lord as a good steward of personal and organizational resources.*

Persuasion   October 27

"You are no longer to supply the people with straw for making bricks; let them go and gather their own straw. But require them to make the same number of bricks as before; don't reduce the quota. They are lazy; that is why they are crying out, 'Let us go and sacrifice to our God.' Make the work harder for the people so that they keep working and pay no attention to lies" - Exodus 5:7-9.

The Pharaoh of Moses' era was the quintessential tyrant, whose tyrannical ways impacted and devastated his country to such an extent that it never recovered its greatness or stature. He epitomizes the command-and-control leadership style that characterized the industrial revolution and is still in vogue today. The *boss* sits at the top and judges the capabilities and motivation of the workers. When the 'boss' is not happy, then the *boss* cracks the whip to get more of what the *boss* wants. If the people suffer in the process, the *boss* is not in the mood to care and sees the workers as replaceable and expendable parts of production. Contrast the *boss* with the servant leader, who exercises listening, persuasion and service not only to get production but also to build up the people.

LEADERSHIP STEP: *Your Step today is to determine which leadership style you prefer and exercise: **boss** or servant. Do you use servant tactics when they work but revert to **boss** mode when your own back is against the wall? What style would your followers say that you employ? Do you read and study the servant leadership model, or any model for that matter, to develop your leadership skills? Do you use command-and-control or **boss** techniques when you lead?*

Values   October 28

"But Ruth replied, 'Don't urge me to leave you or to turn back from you. Where you go I will go, and where you stay I will stay. Your people will be my people and your God my God. Where you die I will die, and there I will be buried. May the Lord deal with me, be it ever so severely, if even death separates you and me'" - Ruth 1:16-17.

Naomi and Ruth were widows and Naomi was in a foreign land. Naomi decided to return home to Israel, and urged Ruth to stay behind so she could remarry. Ruth refused to stay behind, but decided to relocate to a new land with her mother-in-law. This was a values-based decision, for it did not seem to be in Ruth's best interests to go. Yet in Ruth's mind, it was because she loved Naomi and had decided to tie her future with Naomi's. Ruth did find a husband in her new land and that couple became the grandparents of King David. Leaders must also learn to identify their values and then make decisions consistent with their values and not just decisions that are expedient or self-serving.

LEADERSHIP STEP: *Throughout the year, you have been*

encouraged to identify, clarify and review your values to ensure that you are acting on them. Have you taken the time to spell them out? Have you then put them in some order of priority? This may seem like a cumbersome exercise because it is new to you. Your Step today is to read the article in the Appendix and follow the steps to write out your values. If you have done that, then help someone else clarify theirs.

Ethics   October 29

"If a ruler listens to lies, all his officials become wicked" - **Proverbs 29:12.**

Proverbs is a practical book that contains guidance on finances, child rearing, relationships and leadership. Today's verse is directed toward leaders and warns them they will reap what they sow in the area of ethics. If leaders forfeit integrity, before they know it they will be surrounded by unethical followers, all telling the leaders what they want to hear. If that is true, the opposite must also be true - integrity and ethics will attract other ethical followers and employees. Leaders must pay attention not only to their bottom line, but how that bottom line is being achieved and what affect it is having on employees, customers, society in general and the environment.

LEADERSHIP STEP: *Your Step today is to build an ethical leadership framework by reading through the book of Proverbs. As you read, substitute the word leader any time you see the word king, prince, ruler, or any other leadership role. As you restate those verses, study to see what those verses say to leaders about communication, business practices, decision-making, or other leadership activity. Once you have your list, study it and diligently apply what you learned.*

Collaboration   October 30

"When Naomi realized that Ruth was determined to go

> *with her, she stopped urging her. So the two women went on until they came to Bethlehem. When they arrived in Bethlehem, the whole town was stirred because of them, and the women exclaimed, 'Can this be Naomi?'"*
> *- Ruth 1:18-19.*

On one hand, Naomi was ready to separate herself from what family she had and move back home. On the other hand, Ruth did not want to stay there by herself so she decided to collaborate with her mother-in-law and make the transition to a new place, which turned into a place of blessing for both women. The lesson is that those two women stuck together and it made the journey more tolerable for both of them. When Ruth met her husband-to-be, it was Naomi who recognized what was happening and gave the advice that helped Ruth understand and respond to that encounter. Leaders must avoid going it alone, for they need the encouragement, admonishment, and wisdom from others who are more experienced and seasoned than they are.

LEADERSHIP STEP: *Your Leadership Step today is first to recognize your need to collaborate with other people in your leadership journey. These people must be committed to you and the organization's vision and be as open to your input as you are to theirs. Who do you have in your world now with whom you can collaborate? Ask God to help you see people with whom you are supposed to partner, and then work to build meaningful, productive relationships with them.*

Relationships   October 31

> *"And now, dear lady, I am not writing you a new command but one we have had from the beginning. I ask that we love one another." - 2 John 1:5.*

Love is seldom discussed in leadership and management

circles. Instead topics like efficiency, vision, effectiveness and other technical topics are taught, written about and discussed. Yet the Bible consistently teaches that love is God's priority where relationships are concerned. When love is present, people speak truth, serve others, make sacrifices, put other's interests ahead of their own, and perform loving acts for others as evidence of their love for God. Leaders are not exempt from God's love commands, even though at times they must make tough decisions and have difficult conversations with people who will accuse them of not acting in love.

LEADERSHIP STEP: *Your Step today is to score your love motivation as a leader. Give yourself a score of 1 (poor) to 5 (excellent) in the areas mentioned above: 1) speaking truth to others, especially hard truth; 2) serving others; 3) sacrificial investments of money, time and energy into other people; 4) putting the interests of others ahead of your own; and 5) performing loving acts beyond job descriptions and business interests. Are you satisfied with your scores?*

Rest Stop 44 — November 1

"What I feared has come upon me; what I dreaded has happened to me. I have no peace, no quietness; I have no rest, but only turmoil" - Job 3:25-26.

Job was a righteous man and a leader in his community, but he had one problem: he was a worrier. By his own admission, what he had thought about and feared came upon him when he lost everything that he held dear. His worry and consequent fulfillment of his worrisome fears robbed him of his peace, quietness and rest. Leaders make decisions that involve risk and impact many lives, so it is easy for them to worry about the outcomes of their decisions or all the unexpected events that may be the result of those decisions. If they are not careful, leaders can forfeit their rest times away from their work because of worry and anxiety over the present and the future.

LEADERSHIP STEP: *Your Step today is to read a poem written by Rudyard Kipling entitled **If**, which you will find in Appendix 8. After you read it, go back and study what it has to say about worry, loss, risk, success, failure, and all the other consequence of a leader's life. Take Kipling's advice to heart and see where worry is robbing you of joy at work and the mental freshness needed to do your job effectively. What changes do you need to make to get some rest from worry?*

Emotional Intelligence — November 2

"At once Jesus realized that power had gone out from him. He turned around in the crowd and asked, 'Who touched my clothes?' 'You see the people crowding against you,' his disciples answered, 'and yet you can ask, 'Who touched me?'" But Jesus kept looking around to see who had done it"
- Mark 5:30-32.

In this passage, the crowd pressed Jesus from every side while He was also pressed by His schedule to get where He was going. His disciples were acting as ushers, helping him get through the crowd and focusing on the next event. Suddenly someone with a need touched Jesus and He immediately knew it. He felt the woman's need and her faith touch triggered His awareness. The disciples were incredulous that He could be that busy and pressed and still know when one needy person touched Him - but He did! Leaders are busy people but should work to stay in tune with the needs and feelings of those who come into their world and do what they can to alleviate their pain and encourage their progress.

LEADERSHIP STEP: *Your Step today is to work on your empathy and sensitivity to other people and their needs while* *still leading your organization. If you are in a faith-based group, start every meeting with prayer for anyone's needs in the room. If not faith-based, begin one-on-one or group meetings by asking for personal updates. When someone expresses a need, do what you can to follow up and check on their progress if you are unable to give them immediate relief, help or sympathy.*

Coaching — November 3

"Why do you look at the speck of sawdust in your brother's eye and pay no attention to the plank in your own eye?" - Luke 6:41.

Today's verse indicates that people who advise others must first do some work in their own life and heart to be effective and accurate in their prescriptive counsel. It has been said that leaders cannot lead or mentor anyone to a place that they have not gone themselves. That means coaches and mentors must pay the price and experience firsthand the necessary steps for personal growth, change, and professional development. When they do that, it gives them the understanding of what they are asking their followers to do and why it is important that they do it. Without paying that price, leaders can lay heaven burdens on followers without realizing the impact they are having, thus lacking in the empathy needed for effective leadership.

LEADERSHIP STEP: *Your Step today is to determine what more you need to become an effective coach and mentor. There are many great books and programs on the market that can help you engage your own development as you attempt to lead others into theirs. Is it time to go back to school? Is it time to write your book or develop a seminar? Do you have a coach as you attempt to coach others? What more can you do to gain credibility and skill to mentor others?*

Attitude — November 4

"For the Israelites will live many days without king or prince, without sacrifice or sacred stones, without ephod or household gods" - Hosea 3:4.

This verse was a pronouncement of judgment by the prophet, declaring that Israel would function for many days without any leadership. God is a "leadership God" - He works through leadership, speaks to leadership, gives vision and dreams to leadership and judges leadership, holding them accountable for what they do, say, don't do and don't say. Leadership must have the attitude they are serving by God's choice and will be held accountable to represent God by doing His will and manifesting His preferred attitudes and behaviors. That prevents leaders from building their own kingdoms or having attitudes of arrogance and pride.

LEADERSHIP STEP: *Your Step today is to understand that you are leading by God's choice and you are God's gift to your organization or family in that capacity. That means that you must humble yourself and learn about leadership from God's perspective. Identify a leadership book today - not necessarily a Christian one - and commit to read it before year's end. Then find another one and keep on learning and growing to be the best leader God had in mind for you to be.*

Productivity — November 5

"If you follow my decrees and are careful to obey my commands, I will send you rain in its season, and the ground will yield its crops and the trees their fruit. Your threshing will continue until grape harvest and the grape harvest will continue until planting, and you will eat all the food you want and live in safety in your land"
- Leviticus 26:3-5.

In this passage, the Lord promised to take care of the things His people had no power to control - like weather, growing conditions, crop yield - if His people would take of the things that were in their control - obedience to His commands and decrees. This was commonly known as a covenant in Old Testament times in which both parties outlined mutual responsibilities with the benefits and punishments for keeping or breaking the covenant clearly defined. Leaders must humble themselves and realize that, while they work hard and usually have tremendous skills and expertise, they are still dependent on God's help in what they do, for there is much out of their control. Consequently, they should recognize their dependence and thank Him for their ability to lead and be productive.

LEADERSHIP STEP: *Your Step today is to examine your productivity to recognize God's role in your accomplishments. Can you see God's hand at work in your work? When you do, thank Him for His protection and empowerment. Also acknowledge that He had a hand in the things that you do well, for He equipped you with the gifts and skills to get the job done. If your productivity has slipped, however, is it due to faulty obedience to God's commands?*

Finances — November 6

"The Pharisees, who loved money, heard all this and were sneering at Jesus" - Luke 16:14.

The definition of sneering is "to smile or speak in a contemptuous or mocking manner." The Pharisees were not sneering because they disagreed with Jesus' theology, but because they loved money, and their love of money caused them to have contempt for God and His word! What's more, they were showing their disdain in all probability by smiling at Him. Leaders must guard against this love of money, for it will cause them to look past what is best for the organization, the followers or the customers and focus solely on the bottom line - or their own paycheck. And leaders must make sure their love of money doesn't cause them to laugh at, speak against or mock God and His directives for their business behavior and practices.

LEADERSHIP STEP: *Your Step today is to examine how much you love money. How generous are you or your organization? Do you invest time and money into your employees, community or customer care? How much and to what causes? Do you pay the utility company whatever it wants but scoff at a $50 bonus for those who serve you or the company? Does your love for money cause you to ignore biblical principles because they are bad for business?*

Time Management   November 7

"Moses' father-in-law replied, 'What you are doing is not good. You and these people who come to you will only wear yourselves out. The work is too heavy for you; you cannot handle it alone'" - Exodus 18:17-18.

Moses' father-in-law served as Moses' life coach and consultant when he came to pay a family visit. He observed Moses' work habits and workload, and informed Moses that he was a workaholic who was incapable or unwilling to delegate his responsibilities as they increased. The result was that Moses was tired and the people were tired too, having to wait for Moses to attend to their cases and then decide the outcome. Leaders need to realize they cannot do it all and often need input from others to help evaluate their work habits. With the help of others, they must delegate duties and increase the responsibilities of others

LEADERSHIP STEP: *Your Step today is to get some outside input into your work habits, especially if what you are doing is "not good" as Jethro described above. Are you exhausted? Is not delegating the possible cause? Is it time you change your*

work habits and philosophy, which would mean changing the way you use your time? Why don't you trust others to do the work? Are you ready to let go of how you have done your work up to this point in time and do it differently?

Rest Stop 45 — November 8

"Therefore my heart is glad and my tongue rejoices; my body also will rest secure, because you will not abandon me to the realm of the dead, nor will you let your faithful one see decay" - Psalm 16:9-10.

God is in control, but often people try to take over and do His job and He allows them to do so. Usually the results are less than optimal but that doesn't stop people from trying to control things that are beyond their control. Thus people fret, worry and get angry over things like traffic delays, the weather, world economic collapse, other people's attitudes and behavior, and equipment breakdowns - all things that are beyond anyone's control. When people try to control the uncontrollable, their work and worry takes a heavy toll on them physically and emotionally, and they are often tired, even when they are not working. Leaders would do well to work hard, but then put God in charge of their responsibilities when they step away from work, allowing themselves to focus on family, hobbies, church work or any other activity that gives them rest, relaxation and peace.

LEADERSHIP STEP: *Your Step today is to learn how to step away from work and enjoy your life outside of work. To help you do this, here a prayer you must pray whenever you leave work for the day, weekend or holiday: "Lord, I put You in charge of this place and my work while I am gone. And I will be truly gone - emotionally and physically. I trust You and ask that You do the things that I cannot do - change hearts, generate business and watch over all my interests. Amen."*

Humility — November 9

"For everything in the world—the lust of the flesh, the lust of the eyes, and the pride of life—comes not from the Father but from the world. The world and its desires pass away, but whoever does the will of God lives forever"
- 1 John 2:16-17.

It can be difficult to keep an eye on the eternal when the temporary is all around, pressing in and demanding attention and energy. Leaders can get caught up in the urgency of life and the exhilaration of power, for they are often important people in their world who have command over people and resources. They can get accustomed to their own importance, losing track of the transient nature of their power and very existence. For that not to happen, they need to humble themselves and keep focused on the fact that they will not lead and live forever, all the while storing up treasures in heaven by using their power and resources to do God's will, help people and perform meaningful work.

LEADERSHIP STEP: *Your Step today is to determine where your treasure is - in the here or the hereafter. Are you mindful that your days are numbered, both in your current position and in your days on earth? What are you doing to build a godly legacy that will outlive you and your memory? Are you caught up in the excitement of power or grounded in the humility of your limitations? Is your inspiration the boastful pride of this life or the lasting joy of eternal life?*

Decision Making — November 10

"By me kings reign and rulers issue decrees that are just"
- Proverbs 8:15.

Leaders should "reign" or lead using wisdom in all they

do, especially when they make decisions. The Lord expects leaders to dispense justice when they make those decisions. What is justice? It is the process that involves leaders taking the time to listen to the input and perspectives of as many sides of a debate as possible and then rendering a thoughtful and timely decision that benefits as many people as possible, without bias or prejudice toward the rich, powerful or famous. These decisions involve money, salaries, restitution, the investment and promotion of people, hiring, firing and the wise use of environmental resources. With so much at stake, leaders should seek the Lord for the insight they need to dispense justice every opportunity they have.

LEADERSHIP STEP: *Your Step today is to reflect on justice in both your organization and your leadership style. Do you listen to people with divergent views and opinions on matters at hand? Do you ask God for wisdom as you consider facts leading up to decisions? Do you explain why you decided the way you did and give people a chance to debrief and even appeal your decisions? What can you do to improve the decision-making practices in your organization?*

Communication — November 11

> *"I have much to write to you, but I do not want to use paper and ink. Instead, I hope to visit you and talk with you face to face, so that our joy may be complete"* - 2 John 1:12.

The apostles did not hesitate to use the technology of their day - the Roman road system, ink and scrolls, commercial ships - to communicate their teaching and pastoral advice to their flock all over the known world. Yet in today's verse, John preferred to communicate via a face-to-face encounter as opposed to the written word. Leaders must not only be committed to communicate, they must be willing to use and be proficient in modern technologies. Yet there is still great value in personal meetings, and leaders must not rely too much on technology that eliminates the personal touch. Face-to-face encounters enable leaders to read body language, tone of voice and other physical clues and cues from those with whom they are communicating.

LEADERSHIP STEP: *Your Step today is to evaluate your use of technology in your communication strategy. Are you confident in your proficiency or do you take pride in your refusal to use it? If you are proficient, are you over-using it to the extent that you neglect or avoid personal contact and face-to-face meetings? Do you have a communications strategy, knowing what you want to share with followers, along with how and when you will share it?*

Spiritual Growth   November 12

"Be strong and very courageous. Be careful to obey all the law my servant Moses gave you; do not turn from it to the right or to the left, that you may be successful wherever you go" - Joshua 1:7.

Joshua was about to lead the people into the Promised Land, completing a journey that Moses had begun but could not finish due to his temper when he misrepresented the Lord (see Numbers 20:9-13). God gave Joshua five directives as he prepared to lead the people in: 1) be strong; 2) have courage; 3) be careful; 4) be obedient; and 5) walk in all the Law's commandments. Those five warnings are relevant for all leaders to heed, for there are times when their spirituality must translate into practical action that calls for obedient courage. Courage is never the absence of fear, but rather learning to function and act in the midst of or in spite of fear, as Joshua was to discover time and time again as he crossed the Jordan to enter God's inheritance.

LEADERSHIP STEP: *Your Step today is to reflect on*

whether or not fear is hindering your walk with the Lord and your obedience to His commands as you lead. The challenge is that fear seldom identifies itself, but appears rational and reasonable. "We don't have the finances" can really mean "I am afraid we don't and will never have them" or "I don't have time" is "I'm afraid I don't have time to do that well." Where is fear holding you back on your journey into God's Promised Land for you?

Personal Development   November 13

"And the word of the Lord came again to Zechariah: 'This is what the Lord Almighty said: 'Administer true justice; show mercy and compassion to one another. Do not oppress the widow or the fatherless, the foreigner or the poor. Do not plot evil against each other'"
- Zechariah 7:8-10.

Personal development also involves spiritual growth and development. In the verses above, the Lord spoke to His people through the prophet and outlined His plan for their development. That plan included: 1) dispensing true justice; 2) showing mercy to others; 3) being moved by compassion; 4) helping the helpless; 5) empowering the powerless; and 6) avoiding plots and plans that do harm to others. Leaders should adopt this outline as a list of personal values they can pursue and express that will make their leadership more tender and sensitive to the needs of other people.

LEADERSHIP STEP: *Your Step today is to develop a plan that includes the points mentioned in today's verses for your leadership development. For today, focus on one of the six points in the commentary above and think of ways you can develop that particular area or practice. For example, if you choose point six, consider how painful it is to "hatch" plans that affect people's lives without their input - and determine ways to be more inclusive in your communication with others.*

Team Building   November 14

"Warn a divisive person once, and then warn them a second time. After that, have nothing to do with them" - Titus 3:10.

The Bible makes it clear God hates pride but He also seems to have a strong dislike for anyone who creates division in teams or organizations. In today's verse, Paul directed Titus to confront a divisive person once, then again and after that eliminate them from the group or team. This can be difficult to do, for they may be valued, talented and committed team members. Yet talent does not excuse anyone who ruins the unity and harmony of a group, and who refuses to stop. Leadership sometimes has to make the tough decision to confront a bad attitude and, if once doesn't work, to do it again and again. Finally, after warnings and discussions, the leader may have to show the divisive one to the door.

LEADERSHIP TEAM: *Your Step today is to admit if you have been looking the other way to avoid confronting someone on your team, board, or organization who is sowing discord. They may be popular or intimidating, but your job is to sit down today and share how their behavior is affecting others. In your first meeting, set a date for follow up sessions. Eventually, if there is no improvement, you may have to make the tough decision to let them go.*

Rest Stop 46   November 15

"I said, 'Oh, that I had the wings of a dove! I would fly away and be at rest'" - Psalm 55:6.

It sounds like the psalmist was saying, "I need a vacation or holiday!" While it is good to take weekly breaks, it is also important to take extended periods away from the pressures of work to replenish, refresh and recharge. It is not only the actual vacation that is energizing, but the planning process itself is also a fun-filled time when the planner visualizes the end result and enjoys the benefits of the time away even before he or she departs. Obviously leaders can be under extreme pressure, and planning time to "fly away and rest" is an important part of their rest strategy, even if that plan to "fly away" includes staying at home and finishing up some renovation or repair projects.

LEADERSHIP STEP: *Your Step today is to plan your next few vacations away from work. Make one a stay-at-home break. Plan what you will do around the house or with the family close to home. Be detailed and plan out every day, visualizing the projects completed and family time enjoyed. Then plan another one to a destination you have always wanted to visit. Where is that? Who will be with you? What will you do there? Notice how exciting it is just to plan them!*

Strategy — November 16

"They make many promises, take false oaths and make agreements; therefore lawsuits spring up like poisonous weeds in a plowed field" - Hosea 10:4.

This verse sounds like a testament to modern life rather than a pronouncement from an ancient prophet. It seems that the strategy Hosea was referring to was one that included making a lot of promises and breaking them, thus leading to court cases to try and sort out who was responsible to do what. Leaders must be careful not to rely on the legal system to conduct their business and not to succumb to or be intimidated by people who threaten legal action. The key is not to make any promises that cannot be kept and to conduct business in such a way that, when examined under the scrutiny or lawyers, juries and judges, those business practices will be upheld as legal and ethical.

LEADERSHIP STEP: *Your Step today is to examine the nature of your promises to your volunteers and workers. Is your strategy to be transparent and honest, or are you trying to outfox your people by being shrewd and coy? Do you play fast and loose with the truth, stretching it to suit your purposes or are you open even when it reveals information not beneficial to your position? Would everything you do and say hold up if scrutinized by a legal team heading to court?*

Change   November 17

"He who was seated on the throne said, 'I am making everything new!' Then he said, 'Write this down, for these words are trustworthy and true'" - Revelation 21:5.

If God is making everything new, that means He is in the change business, transforming all things from how they were to how they are going to be. Therefore change is not something that must be tolerated or engaged when there is a crisis, but rather change must be seen as a business and life strategy. Technology progresses, people come and go, one market opens up and another closes down, a calamity affects world markets, and princes and politicians assume power and are deposed. Wise and effective leaders understand that they always address the need for change and must help their organizations and the people in them to adjust to and prepare for the reality of change.

LEADERSHIP STEP: *Your Step today is to examine your attitude toward change to see if you consider it an inconvenience or a God-ordained way of life. Do you talk about the good old days or have you kept up with the latest trends in technology and social media? Do you decide regularly to preserve the status quo or lead change initiatives to improve and modernize your operations and business strategies? Are you resisting inevitable changes in any area?*

People Skills — November 18

"He restored the chief cupbearer to his position, so that he once again put the cup into Pharaoh's hand—but he impaled the chief baker, just as Joseph had said to them in his interpretation" - Genesis 40:21-22.

Joseph gets most of the attention in the Genesis story, but his "boss" Pharaoh also deserves some attention for his ability to promote the right people and recognize talent. In today's verse, Pharaoh restored his butler while "firing" the baker as Joseph had predicted (both had been on "probation" in prison for some time). The butler, though silent for two years, eventually introduced Pharaoh to Joseph, whom Pharaoh immediately promoted to be his second-in-command. What's more, Pharaoh delegated all responsibilities for famine management to Joseph, staying out of his way and giving him all he needed to do the job well. Leaders either must be skilled at hiring or having someone who is, for an organization can only be as effective and productive as its workforce.

LEADERSHIP STEP: *Your Step today is to evaluate how effective you are as a talent scout for your organization. How are your recent hires working out? Are they a good fit, or are you trying to make the hire look good? Is there anyone in your organization who is better at hiring than you are? Why aren't you relying on them more often? Once again I refer you to the article in the Appendix about Joseph and Pharaoh to glean more insight into the importance good hiring skills.*

Purpose — November 19

"So give your servant a discerning heart to govern your people and to distinguish between right and wrong. For who is able to govern this great people of yours?"
- 1 Kings 3:9.

When Solomon discovered his purpose to lead Israel, he was confronted with the scope of the job and his own inadequacy to fulfill it. What was his response? Did he go to school to get an MBA? Enlist a mentor? Appoint a more seasoned cabinet of advisors? There is nothing wrong with any of those practices for a leader, but Solomon chose none of them. Instead, he prayed and asked God to give him wisdom. It was this wisdom in response to his prayer that has been Solomon's best-known trait through the centuries, and it came as a result of prayer. Leaders must pay attention to all sorts of personal development strategies and practices, but there is none more important than prayer as they carry out their duties with full awareness of how much they need God's help.

LEADERSHIP STEP: *When you realize your purpose requires more than you have to give, it should lead you to prayer. Your Step today is to make prayer a higher priority in your daily regimen. When do you pray? How long? Do you have a prayer list? For what and whom are you praying? As you reflect on these questions, also give thought to how you can deepen your prayer life. How can you increase your time in prayer? Have you considered a prayer retreat?*

Goals   November 20

"It took Solomon thirteen years, however, to complete the construction of his palace" - **1 Kings 7:1.**

Solomon was a builder and spent 20 years constructing the Temple and his personal residence. What he wanted to build could not be finished quickly, so he had to learn how to plan and work for the long term. Leaders are under tremendous pressure sometimes to produce short-term results, causing them to avoid or lose sight of the long-term benefits they can bring to their organizations. Thus they should be asking where the company wants to be in five, ten, fifteen or even twenty years - and what needs to happen today to hasten and contribute to those long-term goals.

LEADERSHIP STEP: Your Step today is to give thought to the long-term goals you would like to be associated with and remembered for in your organization. You don't have to do this by yourself, but you can convene various groups to deliberate the long-term company (or family) vision. Then facilitate a process to identify the goals that will make the vision a reality. Be prepared to stay the course as short-term urgencies try to steal your momentum and zeal.

Organization   November 21

> *"When the queen of Sheba had seen all the wisdom of Solomon, the house that he had built, the food of his table, the sitting of his servants, the attendance of his officials, their clothing, his cup bearers, and his ascent by which he went up to Yahweh's house; there was no more spirit in her"* - 1 Kings 10:3-5.

Solomon presided over what could be called the glory days of Israel, when resources were plentiful and royal activity was at an all-time high. Solomon was teaching, building, lecturing and expanding the kingdom, and he entertained foreign dignitaries who came to hear his wisdom. The Queen of Sheba "saw" Solomon's wisdom in how he had organized his kingdom to handle all this activity, and she was duly impressed - and this was a woman who had a large kingdom and operation in her own right. Leaders must at some point pay attention to how they will organize everything they do to maximize its exposure, profits or impact. Disorganization will cost any organization something and leaders must address this eventually, no matter how visionary or entrepreneurial they may be.

LEADERSHIP STEP: Your Step today is to evaluate your

company's organizational prowess - or lack of it. Are you more visionary or administrative? If you are visionary, then who is your counterpart in your world? Who handles the details and pays attention to the policies, human resources, and all the other unexciting but necessary practices for successful business? Do you honor this person and their gift or do you see it and them as necessary pain to be tolerated?

Rest Stop 47   November 22

"In peace I will lie down and sleep, for you alone, Lord, make me dwell in safety" - Psalm 4:8

God is watching over things when people are asleep because as the psalmist explained "he who watches over Israel will neither slumber nor sleep" (Psalm 121:4). It is God who watches over finances, relationships, business deals, family members and savings and retirement accounts while their owners and overseers sleep. Therefore leaders can take a vacation and rest because of this truth, and put and leave God in charge for a day or longer as needed. He is the only one who can provide and guarantee true rest to people because He Himself has no such limitation. He is always on duty.

LEADERSHIP STEP: *Your Step today is to put God in charge of your responsibilities and to resign as overseer of your life. This means you will make a decision to stop being self-reliant and be more God-reliant. That means today you will take a break from emails, contact with business associates, and not allow yourself to dwell on your challenges or problems. That will enable God to give you some supernatural rest as you trust and rely on Him.*

Service   November 23

"The idols speak deceitfully, diviners see visions that lie;

they tell dreams that are false, they give comfort in vain. Therefore the people wander like sheep oppressed for lack of a shepherd" - Zechariah 10:2.

God often chooses to accomplish His will through leadership. He expects leadership to give the people direction and care, not to dominate them for personal gain or mislead them through useless leadership strategies. In today's verse, the Lord spoke through the prophet to reveal what happens when people have poor or no leaders: they fall prey to oppression from the loudest voice or the latest fad. The Lord further revealed that the oppression comes from their lack of direction, so they wander like sheep. Leaders must be mindful of their God-given role to care for His flock regardless of whether or not they serve as leaders in or outside the church. This role can be most ably fulfilled when leaders have the mindset of servants and not of lords or masters immune from God's direction or judgment.

LEADERSHIP STEP: *Your Step today is to continue to grow in your understanding and application of servant-leader principles. You can become familiar with the writings of Robert Greenleaf, the father of modern servant leadership studies at www.greenleaf.org. Or you can read the article in the Appendix from my book,* **So Many Leaders, So Little Leadership,** *where I discuss biblical servant leadership so you can continue to grow in your role as a servant.*

Motivation   November 24

"See, the enemy is puffed up; his desires are not upright— but the righteous person will live by his faithfulness— indeed, wine betrays him; he is arrogant and never at rest. Because he is as greedy as the grave and like death is never satisfied, he gathers to himself all the nations and takes captive all the peoples" - Habbakuk 2:4-5.

The Leadership Walk

It is interesting the concept of living by faith actually appears in the Old Testament and the person who does not walk in faith is negatively portrayed in today's verses. People of un-faith can have some or all of the mentioned traits: be puffed up or proud, driven by unrighteous desires, arrogant, restless, greedy, unsatisfied and insatiable, and aggressively trying to take control of everyone and everything around them. Unfaithful leaders can do grave damage to people and organizations when their drive to win and conquer is on the loose and they are not even aware of what or why they do it. Leaders must develop faith habits that enable them to trust others, their teams, the future, their decisions, and the Lord and the promises in His word.

LEADERSHIP STEP: *Where faith doesn't exist, fear does, and it can lead to the negative traits mentioned above. Your Step today is to assess your leadership motivations as honestly and courageously as possible. Go over that list again and ask the Lord to show you where those traits are operating in your leadership style. Don't assume you know what's in you and why; just do a self-examine (or with a counselor) to determine if un-faith is motivating you in any way.*

Self-Awareness   November 25

"While Pilate was sitting on the judge's seat, his wife sent him this message: 'Don't have anything to do with that innocent man, for I have suffered a great deal today in a dream because of him'" - **Matthew 27:19.**

Pilate was in a leadership position and was sitting in judgment of Jesus. While there, his wife sent him a message that he should have heeded. She knew Jesus was innocent and she also knew Pilate should have dismissed the case. God gave him one last warning, yet he could not pay attention because he was about to make a politically expedient decision to condemn Jesus in order to please the Jews and keep the *Pax Romana* - the peace of Rome. If leaders want to get the wisdom and insight they need for good decisions, they only need pay attention to their heart, or listen to the insight and integrity of others closest to them. When they ignore these warnings they often stray into the land of poor decision making.

LEADERSHIP STEP: *Your Step today is to spend 30 minutes of quiet time to listen to your heart. Go where there are no distractions, turn off your cell phone, don't take your computer and only take your journal and Bible. If you aren't "done" after 30 minutes, then linger a bit longer. If you can't get away, then get with one or two trusted colleagues or advisers and ask them to share their heart about the direction of your organization or decisions being considered.*

Knowledge   November 26

"You have searched me, Lord, and you know me. You know when I sit and when I rise; you perceive my thoughts from afar. You discern my going out and my lying down; you are familiar with all my ways. Before a word is on my tongue you, Lord, know it completely. You hem me in behind and before, and you lay your hand upon me. Such knowledge is too wonderful for me, too lofty for me to attain" - Psalm 139:1-6.

Some of the most useful knowledge leaders can possess is self-knowledge. The most reliable source of self-knowledge is God Himself, for He created all leaders and is intimately acquainted with all their ways. He is willing to share that knowledge with all leaders who seek Him so they can understand the truth behind their thoughts, actions, words, and motivations. Leaders would be well served if they regularly sought the Lord to obtain accurate knowledge about who they are, for they can be easily fooled into thinking they are one way when in reality are quite another.

The Leadership Walk

LEADERSHIP STEP: *Your Step today is to learn about yourself as you truly are, not as you wish you were. Go back and find any report you received from any personality assessment (if you have not done an assessment, seek out a counselor or HR professional to identify one). Take that report or feedback and read and pray over it for the next four days. Record in your journal thoughts and insights you receive about your strengths, weaknesses and possible motivators.*

Wisdom   November 27

"If any of you lacks wisdom, you should ask God, who gives generously to all without finding fault, and it will be given to you. But when you ask, you must believe and not doubt, because the one who doubts is like a wave of the sea, blown and tossed by the wind. That person should not expect to receive anything from the Lord" - James 1:5-7.

Wisdom has been defined many ways, including knowledge in action. It is taking existing information and applying it to unique situations in creative ways. Today's passage directs anyone who lacks wisdom to ask for it, but then not doubt after the petition is made. It is easy to doubt, however, because the wisdom sent is often counterintuitive, or the mind of the asker is often so conditioned that he or she cannot even receive the wisdom God sends. Leaders need wisdom but because of their experience, they often dismiss new ways of doing things with a curt, "that won't work." Once leaders pray and ask, they must be open to what comes to them as an answer to that prayer, and not dismiss it too quickly.

LEADERSHIP STEP: *Your Step today is to choose one leadership situation you are involved in that isn't going well. Spend 15 minutes praying about that scenario, asking God to give you wisdom. Then pay close attention to your thoughts, being careful not to dismiss them too quickly as bizarre or* *impossible. Also be alert today to listen and watch for things that come your way to see if any are answers to your prayer.*

Influence — November 28

"For you yourselves know how you ought to follow our example. We were not idle when we were with you" - 2 Thessalonians 3:7.

Leaders are almost always teaching as they help frame decisions, equip workers and communicate vision and values. While much of this teaching is done using words, some of it is done by the leaders setting an example and modeling the desired behaviors, work habits, and relationships they believe are necessary for successful and ethical practices. While people may not heed or pay attention to the positive role model leaders play, they almost always identify a negative role model, and that poor example usually undermines the credibility of the leader and works against the desired goals or vision the leader sets.

LEADERSHIP STEP: *Your Step today is to examine the role model you are providing for those who work closest to you. Are you consciously trying to model your leadership philosophy? Do you accept the fact that you are held to a higher standard that others in the organization? Do you also accept that you are a teacher, for good or not-so-good, and your words carry more power if you have credibility in the eyes of the listener? Where can you improve as a role model?*

Rest Stop 48 — November 29

"How long will you lie there, you sluggard? When will you get up from your sleep? A little sleep, a little slumber, a little folding of the hands to rest—and poverty will come on you like a thief and scarcity like an armed man" - *Proverbs 6:9-11.*

Rest is not a right, but rather a necessity that follows performing the work that God has assigned. Rest is meant to refocus one's attention on God and to recharge for the work ahead. In other words, rest is to have meaning and focus and is not simply to be a time to do nothing. There are some who believe that doing nothing is a religious requirement and others who believe it is a God-given right. It is neither, but rather a time to acknowledge God's prerogative to rule schedules and work patterns, for on more than one occasion Jesus declared Himself to be Lord of the Sabbath. Leaders should acknowledge that God has the right to determine when and how rest is to be taken and that includes the possibility that He requires some type of work and worship on days when leaders would just as soon do nothing.

LEADERSHIP STEP: *Your Step today is to make Jesus Lord of your rest, for He knows what is best for you and your health, creativity and energy. That means on your "Sabbath," He can direct you to "work" in your church, have you visit a home for the elderly or do family visits or other family-related activities. He can also direct you to invest your vacation time into missions or other activity that will energize and refresh you, even though it does not involve physical rest.*

Power — November 30

> ***"Look! It is Solomon's carriage, escorted by sixty warriors, the noblest of Israel, all of them wearing the sword, all experienced in battle, each with his sword at his side, prepared for the terrors of the night"* - Song of Solomon 3:7-8.**

Today's passage describes Solomon's entourage passing by the writer. King Solomon had 60 men in attendance, all armed in battle regalia and prepared for action. The writer was quite impressed with Solomon's royal swagger. The problem was that Solomon eventually used that power to enslave his people and use treasury funds for personal building projects. Eventually he believed he was above God's law, marrying many wives and learning to serve their gods. His show of power ultimately split the 12 tribes into two nations and ruined any chance for the continuation of the glory days of his father David. Leaders must be careful lest, when they surround themselves with pomp and trappings of power, they think they deserve all the ceremony and hoopla that accompanies their presence - and then use that power for personal gain.

LEADERSHIP STEP: *Your Step today is to inoculate yourself against power going to your head and giving you an inflated estimation of your importance. One thing you can do is to write your funeral eulogy, for you must be doing today what you want people to say about you when you're gone. This also reminds you that you are mortal and will pass from the scene eventually, motivating you to plan for your succession and keeping you accountable for how you use your power.*

Persuasion   December 1

"Lord, let your ear be attentive to the prayer of this your servant and to the prayer of your servants who delight in revering your name. Give your servant success today by granting him favor in the presence of this man"
- Nehemiah 1:11.

Nehemiah was a servant in the king's court facing the daunting task of persuading his master to release him for a season to go and rebuild Jerusalem. Nehemiah knew he had no "leverage" with the king, except for his excellent service record in the royal court. What did Nehemiah do? He prayed God would give him favor so he could be persuasive in the king's presence. Leaders would do well to pray the same prayer, otherwise they will command people to perform, and probably see the followers comply. Yet there is no buy-in or transformation of hearts and minds when people are forced to comply. When they choose to follow based on a persuasive presentation, however, the follower and leader both see more lasting and effective results.

LEADERSHIP STEP: *Your Step today is to pray like Nehemiah prayed. For what are you praying? You are asking for a persuasive tongue that can paint a vivid picture of why someone should respond to or comply with the direction you see. Part of that is establishing a credible reputation among those with whom you work, just like Nehemiah did. The other part is framing your argument in such a way that people can see it, ask questions and then willingly agree to follow.*

Values — December 2

"The merchant uses dishonest scales and loves to defraud. Ephraim boasts, 'I am very rich; I have become wealthy. With all my wealth they will not find in me any iniquity or sin'" - Hosea 12:7-8.

Today's passage contains a description of business people who have prospered because of fraudulent and dubious business practices. They boast about their unethical behavior, claiming that being good business people has brought them success. The interesting thing is that God was watching them and of course condemned their practices, proving that God is interested in values-based behavior in the business world. Leaders would do well to remember this so they can develop and be guided by honesty and integrity when they are dealing with employees, suppliers, customers and the public in general.

LEADERSHIP STEP: *Your Step today is to examine your business practices. Look for areas where your talk and your walk aren't quite in sync. Ask yourself these questions: Do* *you encourage discussion around decisions to get various perspectives on their ethical impact? Do you have a set of values and standards for customer service, pricing, environmental impact and product or service quality? How often and how effectively do you audit the application and consistency of those values?*

Ethics   December 3

"Woe to those who plan iniquity, to those who plot evil on their beds! At morning's light they carry it out because it is in their power to do it. They covet fields and seize them, and houses, and take them. They defraud people of their homes, they rob them of their inheritance" - Micah 2:1-2.

The prophet had one word of warning to those who use their leadership power to steal, defraud, and rob people of inheritances and who plan evil at night and carry it out at first chance. His one word of warning was (and is) "woe"! God is watching business and leadership practices of people the world over and shows great interest in their ethical practices. The lack of ethics clearly spelled out in God's word should be a major concern for all, for their woe may be that what they do in secret God chooses to reveal for the world to see. Leaders must take into account how their decisions and business practices affect the poor, widowed and marginalized in society and consider the fact that God is watching what they do.

LEADERSHIP STEP: *Your Step today is to read the entire book of Micah (seven chapters), specifically studying it to identify the ethics contained therein. Look for what the Lord has to say about leadership, idolatry, business practices, justice, bribery, care for the poor and wealth. See if you can identify any other categories and then work to construct a set of business and leadership ethical guidelines based on what you have read. How can you apply those ethics in your work?*

Collaboration — December 4

> *"'Watch me,' he told them. 'Follow my lead. When I get to the edge of the camp, do exactly as I do'"*
> *- Judges 7:17.*

Gideon was leading a few men against a much larger enemy contingent and he needed to coordinate and direct their efforts for success. He did not send them out to do what he was not willing to do, while he stayed safely away from the battle line. Instead he led the troops, giving them clear instructions along with a visual example to follow. He was a true leader and did not ask his followers to do anything he was not willing to do himself. Leaders must work to build effective teams, fostering a spirit of collaboration if they are to achieve the organization's most important goals. That will not be achieved only by giving commands. What's more, they must also lead these teams by example and not delegate responsibilities that only the leaders can achieve.

LEADERSHIP STEP: *Your Step today is to assess your ability to foster collaboration. Ask yourself: 1) Can I identify the most important values and behaviors needed for organizational success? 2) Am I modeling those values and behaviors for my followers? 3) Am I clearly communicating what I require from my followers? 4) Do I lead them by being among them, or am I aloof and reserved? 5) Do I have courage to lead them to the edge of risk?*

Relationships — December 5

> *"These people are grumblers and faultfinders; they follow their own evil desires; they boast about themselves and flatter others for their own advantage" - Jude 16.*

Flattery is the exercise of publicly talking about the

characteristics and accomplishments of others, whether true or exaggerated, in order to gain favor with or to make a favorable impression on the one being flattered. Usually the flatterer needs something the flattered has, so the process is based on manipulation and deceit. The difference between flattery and paying a compliment is that the latter is sincere and truthful, and has no ulterior motive. Leaders must be aware that some want to flatter them to tap into their power for personal gain; leaders must also be careful not to use flattery to get what they want. Sincerity and speaking truth are safeguards against the use of flattery to establish or maintain relationships.

LEADERSHIP STEP: Your Step today is to learn to recognize flattery in your life, whether you are using or receiving. The way to avoid using flattery is to make a conscious effort to encourage people privately for who they are and what they do or to make it a regular habit to do that for all the people on your team in your meetings. The way to avoid flattery being used on you is to thank people for their comments and then remind yourself that you are not as "good" as they are making you out to be!

Rest Stop 49 — December 6

"The fear of the Lord leads to life; then one rests content, untouched by trouble" - Proverbs 19:23.

The fear of the Lord causes the one who fears to avoid evil as defined by the commands in God's word. This avoidance of evil will bring peace of mind, which in turn will enhance a person's ability to rest physically and mentally. Leaders must define for themselves how this fear of the Lord will be expressed in their leadership role. Since they are in the business of promoting, developing, and directing people, this fear should include a component that spells out how those leaders will treat the people with whom they work.

When they violate their people philosophy, they should expect their conscience to bother them and to have their rest affected, for that is how God created them to function.

LEADERSHIP STEP: *Your Step today is to reflect on and spell out your standards and values where the people you work with are concerned. How will you treat them financially? How will you promote them and make room for their gifts? What will you do when they exhibit harmful attitudes and behaviors? This exercise will actually educate and activate your conscience, which will then be triggered negatively when you violate those standards and values.*

Emotional Intelligence — December 7

"In the month of Nisan in the twentieth year of King Artaxerxes, when wine was brought for him, I took the wine and gave it to the king. I had not been sad in his presence before, so the king asked me, 'Why does your face look so sad when you are not ill? This can be nothing but sadness of heart'" - Nehemiah 2:1-2.

Nehemiah was the king's personal servant and came into the king's presence burdened for Jerusalem and the condition of his people back home. The king could easily have dismissed Nehemiah's countenance or missed it altogether. Instead, the king not only noticed how sad Nehemiah was but also asked the reason. The most powerful man in the kingdom was watching his people, made the effort to "read" them and cared enough to inquire what was going on. This is a classic example of emotional intelligence, for the king was not just observant, but also empathetic enough to probe the matter to see if he could help. When Nehemiah shared his grief, the king help set a plan in motion to relieve Nehemiah and rebuild Jerusalem!

LEADERSHIP STEP: *Your Step today is to improve your*

ability to read the people around you, especially those with whom you work. Try to do less business via email or phone and have more face-to-face time so you can observe the people while you chat. Pay attention to body language - when they cross their arms, wiggle in their chairs, get a sad or excited look on their face - and then question what's going on to see how you can help them.

Coaching   December 8

> *"Now Boaz, with whose women you have worked, is a relative of ours. Tonight he will be winnowing barley on the threshing floor. Wash, put on perfume, and get dressed in your best clothes. Then go down to the threshing floor, but don't let him know you are there until he has finished eating and drinking" - Ruth 3:2-3.*

Naomi gave Ruth the advice in today's passage when Naomi saw that Boaz was interested in Ruth, her daughter-in-law, who was a widow. In a sense, Naomi was coaching Ruth in a life situation that Ruth had never seen or encountered before, and the results were spectacular. Boaz married Ruth and they became the grandparents to King David, so you might say that God was in that coaching opportunity. Leaders should use their wisdom, experience and power, not only to benefit the organizations for which they work, but also for the people in and outside the company whom God brings them to mentor, guide and develop. This may or may not be part of their formal job description, but is part of their heavenly one as they embrace the fact God has given them power to empower others.

LEADERSHIP STEP: *Your Step today is to make a list of those you believe God has directed you to coach and mentor, whether it is formally recognized and established or more informal. Then pray for those people every day this week, Keep your journal handy to jot down thoughts you have for* their development. Then set a time next month with each one to talk about their plans, challenges, and how you can best serve them next year.

Attitude   December 9

"Do not put your trust in princes, in human beings, who cannot save. When their spirit departs, they return to the ground; on that very day their plans come to nothing. Blessed are those whose help is the God of Jacob, whose hope is in the Lord their God" - Psalm 146:3-5.

No matter how great leaders are, they are limited by the nature of change and their own limitation and mortality. Business changes, new opportunities arise and that requires that leaders move on or surrender roles they have become accustomed to. Then there are times leaders fall ill, are injured and even encounter the ultimate transition when they pass into God's presence. Leaders should carry that attitude of urgency in finding and training their replacement in **everything** they do so both the work of their business or ministry can continue seamlessly. It also keeps them from developing an attitude that they **own** their position, thinking they will do it for a long time - when tomorrow may be their last day.

LEADERSHIP STEP: *Your Step today is to create a sense of urgency in finding and training replacements for who you are and what you do. If you got sick tomorrow (God forbid) and could not work for three months, what would happen in your organization? Who would and could step into your role? If there is no one, then your objective is to give this some thought and set in motion a contingency plan if you had to be gone for three months - or longer.*

Productivity   December 10

"Very truly I tell you, whoever believes in me will do the

works I have been doing, and they will do even greater things than these, because I am going to the Father" - John 14:12.

Leaders with faith have as much right to claim and pursue the promises of God as anyone else, regardless of what field of endeavor they work, for the "the earth is the Lord's, and everything in it" (Psalm 24:1). Therefore they should look not simply to maintain what they do, but expand, broadcast, publish, multiply, innovate, create or change it for God's purpose and glory as He reveals His plans to them. Today's verse promises that those who know the Lord, even those in business, education, industry, ministry or social work, will actually do greater things than Jesus did because it is God's will that they do so to validate and extend the message and impact of God's kingdom.

LEADERSHIP STEP: Your Step today is to reflect on the greater things that Jesus would want you to do in your current position and leadership role. Once you stop fighting or talking yourself out of those things, it will be time to face your fears and misgivings, and allow that truth to set you free to lead, grow and develop your department, team, company or ministry. Then set goals for next year and beyond to help lead your people to do greater things.

Finances   December 11

"Besides, in my devotion to the temple of my God I now give my personal treasures of gold and silver for the temple of my God, over and above everything I have provided for this holy temple" - 1 Chronicles 29:3.

David was a great leader, who is still honored as the national leader in Israel today, 3,000 years after his death! His leadership capabilities positioned him to garner great wealth, power and honor. David did not shun those benefits or avoid the fact God had assigned those things to him. He used it all to honor the Lord and do great good. Leaders must not pretend to be insignificant or shy away from opportunities to do good because others (or their own thinking) consider those attitudes to be more consistent with Christian or biblical behaviors. That means God may choose wealth for some, and then expect them to be generous and carry out his wishes with those resources.

LEADERSHIP STEP: *Your Step today is to examine just how surrendered to the Lord you are. You are probably content that God may want you to be a relative unknown in your walk. What if, however, God wants you to be a household name? What if He has assigned you fame or even some money? Are you willing to sacrifice your privacy and lifestyle to live a life that is more public and is shared with many others beyond your family? How will you react to that cross?*

Time Management — December 12

"Then Jesus entered a house, and again a crowd gathered, so that he and his disciples were not even able to eat"
- Mark 3:20.

When Jesus went public, He was a busy man. He traveled, taught, discipled and trained his team, answered questions, dealt with opponents and critics, and healed all who came with a need. There were times when He tried to get away from it all, only to have the crowds eagerly pursue Him, so much so that He had to stay up all night to fit in His prayer times. Jesus was operating with a sense of urgency for He knew that ultimately He had to return to the Father so the disciples could continue the work. The point is that leaders are usually busy people because no one can quite match their experience, talents and gifts. Therefore leaders must learn to manage time by setting deadlines, delegation, priorities, declining opportunities and accepting the fact that their time is often not their own.

LEADERSHIP STEP: *Your Step today is to see if you have accepted the lifestyle that often goes with leadership. Have you made peace with your time often **not** being your own, but is needed and spoken for by others? Do you handle your calendar to make sure high priority tasks are performed well? Do you resent or accept there are things only you can do and you must sacrifice freedom for the needs of others?*

Rest Stop 50 — December 13

"All their days their work is grief and pain; even at night their minds do not rest. This too is meaningless"
- Ecclesiastes 3:23.

The wisdom writer of Ecclesiastes was on a mission to figure out what was meaningful in life and did not find much. He focused on work and did not discover much hope there, concluding all work was mostly meaningless and futile. Furthermore, the writer observed it was meaningless to fret and fuss over work that was likewise meaningless, destined to change and passed on to successors (along with wealth) who may or may not treat it with respect. He did come to one consistent conclusion: it is a gift of God to enjoy work and that meant in part to step away from work's frustrations and enjoy rest and recreation.

LEADERSHIP STEP: *Your Step today is to reflect on your relationship with your work roles. Are you expecting too much from them? Do you spend a lot of time fretting over the outcomes, which in the grander scale of things will pass away without much notice? Do you enjoy the work, or do you have to achieve a certain level of recognition or accomplishment to find any joy or sense of purpose? Is your mind free from work's pull when you are away and resting?*

Humility — December 14

"They are a feared and dreaded people; they are a law to

themselves and promote their own honor"
- Habakkuk 1:7.

Jesus is the model for leadership and all other leaders are compared to Him and found lacking. In today's verse, the Lord Himself qualified the Babylonians as His instruments, even though they were feared and dreaded because they were a rebellious and proud people. The Lord would evaluate and judge them according to His own standards and they like all others were woefully inadequate as leaders. Just because the Lord chooses a leader does not mean He endorses their leadership decisions or philosophy. They will be judged by one standard of righteousness that is best explained, revealed and described in the person, actions and humble attitudes of Jesus the Messiah.

LEADERSHIP STEP: *Your Step today is to determine that Jesus is your role model for your leadership style. What were the characteristics of Jesus' leadership style from your point of view? Are those traits present in your own life and leadership? For additional help, read Philippians 2, which beautifully sets forth Jesus' humble leadership behaviors and attitudes. Then set some goals that will enable you to develop those same characteristics.*

Decision Making — December 15

"When the princes in Israel take the lead, when the people willingly offer themselves—praise the Lord!" - Judges 5:2.

Leadership is a joint effort that involves both leaders and followers. There is a sense in today's verse that, when both parties do what they need to do willingly and enthusiastically, it is almost a spiritual experience - the people "praise the Lord." What does it mean that leaders "take the lead"? It means that they act like leaders and make decisions that set the direction and tone for the followers. The leaders in Jesus' day refused to take the lead because they were afraid of the people, arresting Jesus at night so the people would not know what was going on. They made poor decisions that cost Israel and her people dearly. The people had inadequate leaders to follow and consequently the Romans destroyed Israel, the main cause being poor leadership.

LEADERSHIP STEP: *Your Step today is to scrutinize your attitude toward leadership. Are you eager to lead, not so you can dominate others, but rather to contribute what only you can offer? Are you fearful, thus restricting your decisions and input, or are you confident and straightforward in presenting your ideas and experience? Are you political - trying to shrewdly maneuver your alliances - or are you acting in the best interests of your company and those you lead?*

Communication — December 16

"In the first year of Cyrus king of Persia, in order to fulfill the word of the Lord spoken by Jeremiah, the Lord moved the heart of Cyrus king of Persia to make a proclamation throughout his realm and also to put it in writing: 'This is what Cyrus king of Persia says: "The Lord, the God of heaven, has given me all the kingdoms of the earth and he has appointed me to build a temple for him at Jerusalem in Judah"' - Ezra 1:1-3.

Cyrus was king of a sprawling kingdom when the Lord moved on his heart to rebuild the Temple site. The first thing Cyrus did was to communicate his plans throughout his kingdom. How did he do that? He first wrote his plans down and then used the social media and technology of his day to disseminate the information to as many people as possible. Leaders must be committed to broadcast their messages as widely as possible on a regular basis, which means they must be good writers who appreciate and utilize the communication media available to them. That also means that leaders must work to stay relevant not only in what they communicate but also in how they communicate it.

LEADERSHIP STEP: *Your Step today is to conduct a personal communications audit. How much time do you spend communicating what is most important to you, along with your current insights and ideas? How do you communicate? Do you use recent social media? Are you a good writer and speaker or are you working to improve? Do you allow personal bias to discredit modern technology and its use? Would people say you are an effective communicator?*

Spirituality   December 17

"Though the fig tree does not bud and there are no grapes on the vines, though the olive crop fails and the fields produce no food, though there are no sheep in the pen and no cattle in the stalls, yet I will rejoice in the Lord, I will be joyful in God my Savior" - Habakkuk 3:17-18.

Every business, church, family, and organization will go through hard times from time to time. Life happens and when it does, it often brings with it the unexpected downturn, setback, loss, or failure. The role of leadership in those times is not to allow the down time to define the future by keeping it in perspective, keeping hope alive and helping to address any proactive steps the entity can take to lessen or soften the hard time. In times of difficulty, leaders must be purveyors of hope, keeping the vision alive and reminding people of the good times past and the good times yet to come - and to keep their own eyes on the Lord who will sustain them.

LEADERSHIP STEP: *Your Step today is to examine your spiritual resolve when tough times come. Do you panic or do* you keep your hope and faith alive by reminding yourself that this is not permanent, that God is up to and after something? Do you keep an optimistic outlook when talking with others? Do you keep everyone involved informed of the current reality without hiding the facts? Do you pray more and with a listening ear? Do you seek the Lord for wisdom?

Personal Development — December 18

"Praise be to the Lord my Rock, who trains my hands for war, my fingers for battle" - Psalm 144:1.

David was a leader in Israel who began his career as a warrior, taking down Goliath. Then he led troops in battle, which led to his fame and King Saul's jealousy. After that he led a band of misfits as Saul pursued David to kill him. Then David became king of the tribe of Judah, and eventually all of Israel. David recognized it was God Himself who trained him as a warrior in preparation to be a king. That led David to praise the Lord his Rock. Leaders must develop themselves for whatever role God wants them to play, but must recognize God directs their development program. This realization should lead them to worship the Lord as the source of both their development and ability to lead.

LEADERSHIP STEP: *Today's Step is to define your area of expertise as a leader. For David, it was for war; what is it for you? Is it technical expertise? People skills? Finance? Cross-cultural work? Training? Communication? Once you identify those areas, pray and ask God for His help and grace. Also ask Him to show you what you can do and where you can go to become the best "you" that you can be. Don't leave your development to chance.*

Team Building — December 19

"Then Haggai, the Lord's messenger, gave this message of

The Leadership Walk

the Lord to the people: 'I am with you,' declares the Lord. So the Lord stirred up the spirit of Zerubbabel son of Shealtiel, governor of Judah, and the spirit of Joshua son of Jozadak, the high priest, and the spirit of the whole remnant of the people. They came and began to work on the house of the Lord Almighty, their God" - Haggai 1:13-15.

There is an unseen, spiritual dynamic to teamwork that is described in today's passage. First, the prophet Haggai gave the people a vision: to rebuild the Temple. He described in previous verses what the current situation was costing them in lost crops and poverty. Second, Haggai assured the people that they would succeed and that God was with them. Third, God did His part by stirring the hearts of the people, who volunteered freely to do the work. This included all the "department heads" and the people themselves. Leaders must learn to tap into the inner life of followers, who if properly motivated will come together and do greater things as a team than they could ever accomplish as individuals.

LEADERSHIP STEP: *Your Step today is to see if you are tapping into that unseen, spiritual aspect of your team's work. Have you provided a clear vision of the new reality for which you are all working? Have you secured the support of key influencers and supervisors? Have you prayed for unity, energy and vision so that all the team are moving in the same direction and working toward the same end? Are you providing encouragement as the team moves forward?*

Rest Stop 51   December 20

"I lie down and sleep; I wake again, because the Lord sustains me" - Psalm 3:5.

The context of this verse is that the Lord sustained King

David even when his enemies were threatening him on every side. Part of that care was David's ability to lie down and sleep even when danger threatened to rob him not only of his rest but also of life itself. Most leaders will not face that kind of pressure, so if David could find a way to trust in the midst of his hassles, then all leaders should find a way to rest as well. Yet the enemies most leaders face - job security, good decisions, a healthy economy, ongoing donor generosity, office politics, the fickleness of boards of directors and staff - are every bit as real as David's wartime enemies. Therefore, the decision to rest is just that - a decision, based on trust that the Lord is protecting and watching out for leadership's well being.

LEADERSHIP STEP: *Your Step today is to assess your worry level that may be costing you rest and sleep. Give yourself a 1 (never) to 5 (always) in response to these statements: 1) I have trouble sleeping; 2) I cannot stop thinking about situations at work even when I'm away; 3) I'm pessimistic; 4) I can't stop thinking about a mistake I recently made; and 5) I think about what can go wrong at work. If you scored from 18-25, then you may need help to find rest from worry.*

Strategy — December 21

"Now this is what the Lord Almighty says: 'Give careful thought to your ways. You have planted much, but harvested little. You eat, but never have enough. You drink, but never have your fill. You put on clothes, but are not warm. You earn wages, only to put them in a purse with holes in it'" - Haggai 1:5-6.

The prophet was giving the people the word from the Lord and the word summarized a failed and flawed life strategy - or their 'ways' as the Lord described them. They planted, ate, drank, dressed and earned wages, but all of it was never enough to fill or satisfy them. Leaders must not only direct the decision-making process, they must also help formulate a meaningful and successful strategy through which the decision may be safely and successfully implemented. In other words, leaders must be committed to "what' needs to be done, but be flexible and ready to abandon the 'how' the 'what' needs to be carried out and pulled off.

LEADERSHIP STEP: *Your Step today is to honestly and ruthlessly evaluate the strategy you are currently using to implement your company's vision and decisions (and for your own personal life as well). Is your strategy working as you intended? Do you need to face reality and shift how you are doing things without tampering with what you need to do? Are you ignoring parts of your strategy that may be working because you did not intend them to work as they are?*

People Skills — December 22

"Now the Ephraimites asked Gideon, 'Why have you treated us like this? Why didn't you call us when you went to fight Midian?' And they challenged him vigorously. But he answered them, 'What have I accomplished compared to you? Aren't the gleanings of Ephraim's grapes better than the full grape harvest of Abiezer? God gave Oreb and Zeeb, the Midianite leaders, into your hands. What was I able to do compared to you?' At this, their resentment against him subsided" - Judges 8:1-3.

In today's passage, one of the tribes left out of the attack on Midian "vigorously" challenged Gideon's decision to go to battle without them. In other words, they angrily got in Gideon's face. Yet Gideon did not take the attack personally and skillfully soothed their anger by complimenting them on a past victory while minimizing his achievements. Leaders can expect to be "vigorously" challenged from time to time and must learn how to do what Gideon did - defuse a potentially volatile confrontation. When confronted, leaders cannot become competitive and try to win the argument, but must rather do what is necessary to keep their team on task as they all pursue the vision of the organization through the human dynamics that almost always threaten to derail the journey.

LEADERSHIP STEP: *Your Step today is to learn to listen when confronted and not become defensive, to not react but rather respond. Watch is your body language. Don't cross your arms or legs, but remain open to the confronters. Don't raise your voice, but rather lower it from your usual level. Listen intently and ask questions to clarify. You may want to practice these steps in your mind so you will ready when the confronter comes.*

Motivation   December 23

"The day of the Lord is near for all nations. As you have done, it will be done to you; your deeds will return upon your own head" - Obadiah 1:15.

The principle of reaping and sowing is applicable to all walks of life for both individuals and organizations. You cannot escape this universal principle, just like a farmer cannot plant wheat and expect to harvest corn. If an organization sows deception, then it will reap deception from its suppliers, publics and employees. If an entity sows good customer service, then it will reap a harvest of good public relations and positive word-of-mouth marketing. Leaders must help their organizations understand that the motivation to do the right things is not just a matter of ethics, but it is also vital for business or ministry success. Leaders who are motivated to make money or achieve short-term success may cut corners or take shortcuts, but those paths always lead to a dead end.

The Leadership Walk

LEADERSHIP STEP: *Your Step today is to check your seed bag to see what you are sowing as a leader and as an organization. You may need to engage the services of a consultant or an objective person such as a new employee or people from your board of directors to do that. Let them examine and report honestly on what they find in every area of your business operation. Look to see where your business practices may be the source of poor business results.*

Power   December 24

"The Lord turned to him and said, 'Go in the strength you have and save Israel out of Midian's hand. Am I not sending you?'" - Judges 6:14.

Gideon lacked power, or so he thought, when the Lord commissioned him to go and defeat the Midianites. Yet he did indeed have power - the power of God's choice and presence as Gideon carried out the Lord's assignment. There is no question that any leadership position has a certain amount of positional power - what the boss says goes. And there is also expert power, where leaders have greater experience or expertise, thus giving them power to direct other people's actions and roles. The power mentioned in today's verse stems from the leaders call to do something related to his or her God-given purpose. The source of that power is not authority or expertise, but the leader's partnership with God.

LEADERSHIP STEP: *Your Step today is to meditate on the source of your leadership power. Do you sense a call from the Lord to do what you are doing, or is it more of a career choice? If it is the latter, perhaps it's time to look for something more tied to your purpose? If it is the former, are you maximizing the relationship and partnership with the Lord, focusing less on your abilities and "power" and more on His? Are you looking for reasons to lead or excuses not to?*

Ethics — December 25

"Judah's leaders are like those who move boundary stones. I will pour out my wrath on them like a flood of water"
- Hosea 5:10.

Boundary stones marked out property rights, and the leaders of Judah were moving those stones to deprive people of what was rightly theirs. The Lord was watching those practices and transactions and disapproved, threatening to pour out His wrath on those unethical thieves. Because leaders have power, they can amass privileges, special treatment and powerful allies who will enrich the leaders with benefits not available to others without power. When those privileges provide opportunities to take what belongs to others, the Lord gets involved to protect the rights of the poor and powerless. Simply put, leaders must be careful not to use their position for personal gain.

***LEADERSHIP STEP:** Your Step today is to focus on Jesus as your model for leadership. Then evaluate what you have and have received simply because you are the leader. Do you need a reserved parking space? What about office space and staff devoted to serving you? Do you use your service staff for personal work and errands? More importantly, are you encroaching on the rights of the powerless to enrich yourself? What would Jesus do in your leadership position?*

Coaching — December 26

"When they had brought these kings to Joshua, he summoned all the men of Israel and said to the army commanders who had come with him, 'Come here and put your feet on the necks of these kings.' So they came forward and placed their feet on their necks"
- Joshua 10:24.

Joshua had just led the army in a defeat of five armies and their kings after the sun miraculously stood still to aid his campaign against them. The five kings fled but Joshua and his men captured them. Then Joshua had the commanders who fought with him come forward and put their feet on the necks of the captured kings to give those commanders a taste of what real battle against real enemies was supposed to feel like and how it was supposed to end. Effective leaders are always coaching and teaching others to prepare them for "battle," whatever the battle in their business represents. That means those leaders give interesting work assignments and opportunities that will allow their subordinates to grow and blossom.

LEADERSHIP STEP: *Your Step today is to identify the key leaders who are to be part of your organization's leadership team. Identify the strengths of each one, and fashion an action plan for each that will allow him or her to grow and develop. That should include interesting work assignments that will both stimulate and challenge them to develop and grow. Your plan may include additional schooling, for which your company should help pay the cost.*

Rest Stop 52   December 27

"Then the king returned to his palace and spent the night without eating and without any entertainment being brought to him. And he could not sleep"
- Daniel 6:18.

The king had been duped into sentencing Daniel to spend a night in the lion's den. Consequently, the king could not sleep because of worry, knowing he had made a bad decision that risked the life of his loyal servant. When leaders don't do right, they lose their ability to rest, for then they must worry about the results of their poor or misguided decisions. Contrast this to what David said in

Psalm 3:3: "I lie down and sleep; I wake again, because the Lord sustains me." Rest isn't dependent upon going to a nice vacation spot or spending time with family or friends. True rest depends on integrity, honesty and righteousness. Without those characteristics, leaders may close their eyes and sleep but they will not be able to find true rest.

LEADERSHIP STEP: *Your Step today is to keep track of your thoughts when you are supposed to be at rest. What are you thinking about? Are you playing out scenarios in your mind of what may happen because of what you have done, said or decided? When you should rest, is the Lord sustaining you or do you need sleep help, such as pills or alcohol? Do you have troubling dreams that disturb your rest? Is God empowering your rest times?*

Ethics — December 28

"Do not use dishonest standards when measuring length, weight or quantity" – Leviticus 19:35.

In the first books of the Bible, God addressed the issue of business ethics. He instructed Israel's business people not to cheat and advertise something as one standard when it was really inferior or less than promised. Leaders must help the people in their organizations think through the ethical implications of their decisions, realizing that God is watching and listening to the deliberations. One author wrote about how ethics needs to include three concepts: love, justice and holiness, in equal portions. The problem is that people will have varying opinions as to how those three concepts are expressed, so leaders have their work cut out for them as they attempt to forge an ethical consensus.

LEADERSHIP STEP: *Your Step today is to do some research on the concepts of love, justice and holiness as they pertain to ethical decision making. Then lead a staff discussion about* those three concepts and how well you apply them in your business setting. If you are not in a faith-based setting, then you will need to find creative ways to introduce those concepts as not just being right, but being good business as well.

Emotional Intelligence — December 29

"Then David said to Nathan, 'I have sinned against the LORD.' Nathan replied, 'The LORD has taken away your sin. You are not going to die'" – 2 Samuel 12:13.

It can be difficult for leaders to admit when they are wrong. They may be afraid of legal action being taken against them. They may feel like their admission will lessen their stature or authority with followers. Leaders may also be too proud or conceited to admit an error, looking for others to blame for the gaffe. Finally, leaders may not see their mistake, either through pride or through their own cognitive limitations. There is only one way to prevent these confession blocks and that is for leaders to always be open to the possibility that they may be wrong. When they are least open to that option, then leaders and circumstances don't have to wrestle and pin leaders to the ground in order to obtain a confession of weakness.

LEADERSHIP STEP: Are you open to the fact that you may be wrong today, that perhaps you were wrong yesterday and will in all probability be wrong tomorrow? There is one way to find out. Your Step today is to reflect on a recent problem and at least be open to your role in it. If you see where you may have been wrong, then go to the person or the team and admit it! If your role was clear-cut, then you will want to apologize to those whom you offended or caused pain.

Change — December 30

"No one sews a patch of unshrunk cloth on an old garment.

Otherwise, the new piece will pull away from the old, making the tear worse. And no one pours new wine into old wineskins. Otherwise, the wine will burst the skins, and both the wine and the wineskins will be ruined. No, they pour new wine into new wineskins" - Mark 2:21-22.

There are times when change must take place in a business or organization and there is no way to take halfway measures. The product or service must be discontinued, the department or plant shut down, or the people let go. When leaders try to avoid the pain of change, they tend to make things worse by trying to please everyone or perpetuate an inefficient or outdated procedure or person. Leaders need to be brutally open and honest during those times of extreme change and give people every consideration as they face what for them may be a death-like experience as they are asked to end what they know and walk into what they do not know. At that point, leaders must show how much they care, even if the people are angry with them for the changes taking place.

LEADERSHIP STEP: Are you putting off a decision to change something because you know how painful and difficult it will be? Your Step today is to gather courage to start the change process. Stop thinking about compromise and think about complete and total overhaul. Then be open and honest with people and give them time to get used to the idea. Where possible, get them onboard to help guide the changes, but don't let the implications keep you from being a change agent.

Goals — December 31

"But by the grace of God I am what I am, and his grace to me was not without effect. No, I worked harder than all of them—yet not I, but the grace of God that was with me"
- 1 Corinthians 15:10.

The Leadership Walk

Leaders must often work long and hard, and that can take a toll on their creative energy and health. Yet in today's verse, we read that Paul learned the secret of hard work. He learned how to cooperate with God's grace so that it wasn't just him working, but God working in and through him. In other words, Paul partnered with God to get a lot done as he worked hard. Leaders can also learn to be God's co-worker in order to tap into this supernatural energy that produces a positive effect for their companies, families and countries. Yet even with God's grace, there is no substitute for hard work, which has been God's will for mankind since the Garden of Eden when He commanded them to be fruitful and fill the earth.

LEADERSHIP STEP: *As you close out this year, your Step today is to give some thought to the coming year. What goals do you want to set? Where were you pleased with your performance last year? Where did it fall short of expectations? What goals can you set for next year that will energize you and cause you to work hard? How can you involve God in your work process? Where is God already partnering with you in your work? Where is He absent?*

APPENDIX ONE
My Leadership Philosophy

I was born to lead, but I work hard to be the best leader that I can possibly be. I exercise a team approach to leadership that values the input and worth of every individual. As a leader, I share finances, success and credit with all those who contribute. I also serve others so that they can become all that God wants them to be, using any power I have to empower them. I do this without concern for my title, remuneration or recognition. I find ways to influence and persuade others without resorting to power tactics or manipulative techniques.

1. What concepts or principles do you see that are a part of my leadership philosophy?
2. Which of those concepts would you like to include in your own statement? Which ones are missing that need to be included in yours?
3. What value do you see a leadership philosophy has for you? For your followers?
4. To read more about developing your philosophy, go to my website at purposequest.com and under the heading "Leadership," find the article titled "Developing a Leadership Philosophy."

APPENDIX TWO

Your Governing Values

As I've studied successful leaders, I've seen that they have often developed an inner set of values, whether they are aware that they have or not. Each one has a set of guidelines that help them make decisions, small or great. Some have written down these values and carry them in a notebook or planner; others carry them on the "tablets of their heart." Most often these values were developed and defined from:

- Family examples, both positive and negative
- Mentoring relationships
- Religious teachings
- Life failures
- Suffering through tough times
- Watching other leaders whom they admired
- Watching other leaders whom they did *not* admire

For instance, some who were taken advantage of have vowed never to do the same, and others, out of the same situation, decided to take advantage of as many people as possible. Both have developed values that guide their decisions and develop their leadership style. Others have felt the pain of domineering leadership and decided to perpetuate that style; some hold the value not to rule with an iron fist, but rather with an open hand. Both have developed values. And without realizing it, you have developed some values, too.

Robert Greenleaf, in his book, *On Becoming a Servant Leader*, stated "This is the ultimate test: what values govern one's life – at the end of it?" He poses an interesting question, don't you think?

Are you developing a set of values that adjust over your lifetime as your leadership grows and matures? You shouldn't wait until you're a leader to try to define these values, for by then you may not see the importance of such a task ("I'm already a leader; why sweat the small stuff now when big decisions await?"). If you wait too long to reflect on your values, you may find that you've already given your energy to values that weren't worth the effort you gave them.

As most successful leaders, the Apostle Paul had a set of values that guided his ministry and ministry decisions:

1. Not taking financial support from the churches he was starting
2. Not working where someone had already labored to start a church
3. Always visiting the synagogue first when arriving in an area
4. Traveling in the company of a team
5. Not insisting on a Jewish lifestyle as he visited diverse cultures and people.

Paul's success wasn't a matter of chance. At least part of his success came from the fact that he had a set of values that served to guide his life and work decisions. He didn't impose these values on others, for they belonged to him, having been shaped by his own experience and understanding of what God wanted him to do.

I'm grateful to the Franklin Covey Company for helping me develop my values. While studying to become a certified time management facilitator through that company, their instructor directed all those being trained to write out our values. He told us there weren't a maximum or minimum number, and he encouraged us to write them in a positive style that related to the present ("I am"), and not the future ("I will"). Then he asked that we attempt to prioritize those values and from that point forward carry them with us for regular review and adjustment.

The company's objective was to allow us to see our values and allow them to better guide our decisions, decisions we would be making as leaders. In fact, they called these values our *governing* values, since they do, sometimes without realizing it, govern our life and decisions. I have to say that this has been a most rewarding experience. I now regularly work with other leaders and potential leaders to help them develop a set of values that will guide (or are guiding) their life and leadership.

I offer my own values as an example of how this can be done, not as a model list of values to be held. I developed mine by identifying my favorite passages from the Bible. I then did what Franklin Covey asked me to do: Put some narrative explanation to each value and prioritize them.

Developing values, however, isn't a science with rigid rules and procedures; rather it's an art. At the end of my list, I'll make some further recommendations of how to develop your list of governing values. Keep in mind that mine are based on a Christian life and worldview; they aren't offered with anything in mind except to give you a better understanding of my leadership style and what updated, prioritized governing values can look like.

GOVERNING VALUES – John W. Stanko
(Updated April 19, 2010)

1. I do the will of God.

I prayed one time that I would be like Timothy, not fully realizing what I was praying. I saw Timothy in a whole new light as I read Philippians 2:19-23:

> I hope in the Lord Jesus to send Timothy to you soon, that I also may be cheered when I receive news about you. I have no one else like him, who takes a genuine interest in your welfare. For everyone looks out for his own interests and not those of Jesus Christ. But you know that Timothy has proved himself, because as a son with his father he has served with me in the work of the gospel. I hope, therefore, to send him as soon as I see how things go with me.

The will of God, as I understand it, is to put other's interests before my own and to *serve* in furthering the gospel as the Holy Spirit and my oversight so direct. That also requires a vibrant and diligent prayer and study life that finds the will of God and does it.

2. I walk in faith.

The writer of Hebrews wrote, "Without faith it is impossible to please God." I please the Lord by exercising faith in Him concerning my purpose, family, finances, future, and relationships. The second part of that verse completes the thought when it says, "because anyone who comes to him must believe that he exists and that he rewards those who earnestly seek him" (Hebrews 11:6). God rewards me for my faith more than I deserve.

My faith has practical expression through my giving habits as I am generous with my time, knowledge, wisdom, and money.

3. I love my family.

The Lord has given me three wonderful gifts: Kathy, John, and Deborah. The Apostle Paul commanded husbands to love their wives just as Christ loved the church and gave himself for her to make her holy, cleansing her by the washing with water through the word, and to present her to himself as a radiant church, without stain or wrinkle or any other blemish, but holy and blameless. In the same way, husbands ought to love their wives as their own bodies (Ephesians 5:25-28).

I love my wife and release her to her purpose as a joint heir with me of the gracious gift of life (1 Peter 3:7).

He also told fathers not to "embitter your children, or they will become discouraged" (Colossians 3:21). I am a friend and encourager to my children and help release them to their God-given purpose.

4. I am a communicator.

Jesus was a great communicator. Mark reported that "the large crowd listened to him [Jesus] with delight" (Mark 12:37). That came from His insight into the Word, His love for people, and His effective speaking style. I follow in His footsteps. Jesus also said, "The Father who sent me commanded me what to say and how to say it" (John 12:49).

I have something to say and know how to present it with clarity, humor, and conviction, whether speaking, writing books and articles, or communicating through other media. (such as the Internet, radio and video). I study and effectively utilize humor to enhance my ability to communicate with others.

5. I am a servant-leader.

Because I am a man of purpose, I express my purpose by serving the world in many capacities. Since my childhood, I've also found myself in leadership positions. Thus I combine those two roles—servant and leader—to be a servant-leader from a biblical perspective. I lead and serve according to God's will and implement my decisions in the right spirit and attitude. Peter wrote,

> Be shepherds of God's flock that is under your care, serving as overseers – not because you must, but because you are willing, as God wants you to be; not greedy for money, but eager to serve; not lording it over those entrusted to you, but being examples to the flock (1 Peter 5:2-3).

I lead in the tradition of Jesus, Moses, Joseph, David, Solomon, and Daniel. I grow in my understanding of servant leadership, learning to listen well and to influence, not control others. I am also a leader of integrity and courage.

6. I am a team player.

I've been an avid sports fan since my youth. I now realize this was simply a love for the team concept so vital to, yet so absent from, much of management and ministry today. I help others identify their life's purpose and train and coach them to work with other people of purpose. I pursue the synergy that comes from teamwork when everyone has a chance to communicate and share their creativity in an open atmosphere as free from authoritarian techniques as possible.

The Apostle Paul almost always traveled in a team and was released into ministry from the context of "team" in Acts 13:1-3:

> In the church at Antioch there were prophets and teachers: Barnabas, Simeon called Niger, Lucius of Cyrene, Manaen (who had been brought up with Herod the tetrarch) and Saul. While they were worshiping the Lord and fasting, the Holy Spirit said, "Set apart for me Barnabas and Saul for the work to which I have called them." So after they had fasted and prayed, they placed their hands on them and sent them off.

7. I am a reconciler.

The gospel of Jesus Christ is the only answer to society's problems and that includes racism. I work with people of color and of various cultures to model relationships that will help reconcile people to God and then to one another. As Paul wrote in 2 Corinthians 5:18-20:

> All this is from God, who reconciled us to himself through Christ and gave us the ministry of reconciliation; that God was reconciling the world to himself in Christ, not counting men's sins against them. And he has committed to us the message of reconciliation. We are therefore Christ's ambassadors, as though God were making his appeal through us. We implore you on Christ's behalf: Be reconciled to God.

I mentor young men and women to equip them to be all that they can be in God and affirm their beauty and worth in God's eyes.

8. I am a learner.

Because the world is changing so rapidly, I can't afford to "crystallize" in my work habits or thinking. Paul wrote, "All Scripture is God-breathed and is useful for teaching, rebuking, correcting and training in righteousness, so that the man of God may be thoroughly equipped for every good work" (2 Timothy 3:16). That means I must continue to learn and grow in the knowledge of God (Colossians 1:10). My primary focus is the word of God and my prayer is "open my eyes that I may see wonderful things in your law" (Psalm 119:18).

I read, study, take classes, attend seminars, learn from role models, and master new techniques and technology that enable me to learn until my strength fails or I die.

9. I am energetic.

"I became a servant of this gospel by the gift of God's

grace given me through the working of his power" (Ephesians 3:7).

Paul accomplished his life purpose "through the working of his [God's] power." The Greek word for "working" is *energeo*. I apply this same *energeo* in my life and do not work in my own strength. I maintain this energy by staying focused on my purpose, eating healthy food, exercising, and getting appropriate rest. I use this energy to produce more than I consume and to engage in activities that brings increase and glory to God.

When I work, I work and walk in the truth of what Paul wrote to the Corinthians:

> But by the grace of God I am what I am, and His grace toward me did not prove vain; but I labored even more than all of them, yet not I, but the grace of God with me (1 Corinthians 15:10 NASU).

* *

I realize that stating these values in the "I am" style may seem a bit presumptuous or arrogant. I'm *not* everything that I've written above. But I'm striving to embody those values, and that keeps me humble and ever seeking, two traits often missing in some leaders. I can never say I've arrived; that could cause me to take shortcuts or expect certain privileges that could lead to defective leadership.

Now how about you? Are you ready to spell out your governing values? Here are some other sample values that I've borrowed from Franklin Covey to help you get started.

- I seek excellence.
- I am competent.
- I serve others.
- I am frugal.
- I am generous.
- I seek truth.
- I am self-sufficient.
- I am innovative.

The Leadership Walk

If you're ready, then follow these simple steps:

1. Set aside two hours.
2. Identify phrases that represent values that have directed your life up to this point.
3. Identify phrases that represent values you wish to incorporate in your life from this point forward.
4. Clarify those phrases and give them definition.
5. Are any of your values harmful to you or others? Do they represent selfish or selfless behavior? You may want to eliminate any that are inconsistent with a lifestyle of love and service (more on this later).
6. Set them in order of priority. Relax! There's no wrong way to do this.
7. Carry them with you. Review them every six months and change as needed.

John W. Stanko

APPENDIX THREE

Time Inventory Log Date _____

Begin Time	Activity	Category	Scheduled	Unscheduled	Was this an Interruption?	Total Minutes

Categories: Administration, Relationship-Building, Phone/E-Mail, Meeting, Planning, Reading/Personal Development

The Leadership Walk

1. Enter the approximate time you begin an activity.
2. Enter the name of the activity and its category.
3. Check whether this was a scheduled or an unscheduled activity and whether you consider it an interruption or not.
4. When you begin the next activity, enter the total number of minutes you spent on the previous activity.
5. At the end of the day or designated period of time, total the number of minutes over which you kept your log. Then add up the number of minutes in the various categories to get an overview of where your time is actually spent.

APPENDIX FOUR

Leadership Lessons from Egypt

I love to study leadership models in the Bible and I'm sure you do, too. It's a great way to garner valuable lessons from the case studies of people whom God used for His purposes. With that in mind, I want to present some lessons from a leader seldom studied: Pharaoh, the leader of Egypt.

When I mention Pharaoh, who comes to mind? It's probably the Pharaoh Moses encountered in the book of Exodus. That Pharaoh, however, isn't the one I want to focus on. There was more than one Pharaoh and, in this article, I want to look at the one who was Joseph's contemporary in Genesis 37-50. This Pharaoh was one of the best leaders in the Bible and has something to teach us! Here's why.

EGYPT IN JOSEPH'S TIMES

Egypt in Joseph's times was the most powerful nation in the world. Pharaoh had oversight over a large population and army. When Joseph first arrived, Egypt prospered and there was no end in sight.

Yet, God was doing something that would shape history for centuries to come. He wanted to move His people, Abraham's family, to Egypt from where they would make their exodus back to the Promised Land centuries later. To accomplish that purpose, God sent Joseph ahead of his family to Egypt on a mission.

While Egypt enjoyed their prosperity, Joseph was imprisoned – and then the drama played out that led to Pharaoh's famous doubleheader dreams. If you remember, Pharaoh had two dreams, one where seven gaunt cows devoured seven fat cows, the other where seven lean heads of grain consumed seven healthy heads. Joseph helped Pharaoh understand that these dreams indicated seven years of famine would follow seven years of plenty.

The Leadership Walk

The period leading up to the dream, the dream interpretation and dream application all give valuable lessons from Pharaoh's leadership we would do well to emulate.

PHARAOH'S LEADERSHIP LESSONS

Take the time to read Genesis 40:1-5, 20-23; 41:1-4, 33-57; 47:1-4. What can we learn about Pharaoh from these passages?

1. **Pharaoh wasn't afraid to lead his people.** When Pharaoh had his dreams, there were no problems in Egypt. There was plenty of food and he learned from Joseph and his dream that there would be seven more years of plenty. The famine wasn't even close to starting, but Pharaoh made firm decisions concerning the future. He began to prepare for the famine seven years in advance of its coming. What's your seven-year plan for your organization? Do you even have one?

2. **Pharaoh made quick decisions when he found the right person.** There was no procrastination when Pharaoh decided to act. Too often, leaders hesitate to gather more information. But Pharaoh knew he had found a "star" in Joseph and he acted quickly to secure his services and wisdom. Good people are hard to find. When you find them, hire them! You will still have to manage them or else you will eventually have a mess on your hands. Delegation doesn't mean abdication of responsibility. It means you hold your team accountable for results, but don't micromanage the process.

3. **Pharaoh understood personnel issues and effectively used probation, restoration and release.** In Genesis 40, Pharaoh was angry with his cupbearer and his baker. Rather than "fire" them immediately, however, he took time to reflect on the situation. Too often, leaders can let personality conflicts or

misunderstandings affect the relationships with the management team. Pharaoh could make quick decisions when needed, and I am sure he had a temper. In the case of these two "employees," however, he waited one year. In some sense, he put them on probation.

After a period of time, he "released" (all right, he executed) the baker and restored the cupbearer. Don't let your personal preferences regarding personnel issues rob your organization of its best talent. Learn to establish a "cooling off" period before making final decisions. Let the employees or team members know that they are on probation. Then when you've made your final decision about the future, don't linger any longer. Make it known to everyone.

It is significant that, using this process, Pharaoh made the best choice, for the restored cupbearer was the one who introduced Pharaoh to Joseph, the man with the plan.

4. **Pharaoh spent time with his team.** Pharaoh restored the cupbearer at his own birthday party that he held for his officials. The king of Egypt spent social time with his leadership team! It appears that they also talked some business while they met. It seems that Pharaoh never had his officials too far away from him at any point in time, so he could get their feedback and input. How close are you to your "team"? You don't have to be their friend, but you do need to be their partner and associate.

5. **Pharaoh partnered with his opposite.** Pharaoh didn't fill his staff with people like him. He brought in some "opposites." Pharaoh was obviously a visionary; he therefore hired a good operations man in Joseph to carry out the day-to-day plans of the kingdom. Partnering with your opposite can be difficult, for they see reality and life in contrast to

your viewpoint. They can, however, see what you can't (and vice versa), however, thus strengthening the team through diversity and friendly dissent.

Over the years, I have worked at not just tolerating people who aren't like me, but celebrating them! I need people who don't think or look like me to build an effective team (that means women and persons of color). How diverse is your team? If your family member fits this need and has the skills, employ them. If they don't, spare your organization the pain of a bad hire by not employing them.

6. **Pharaoh recognized talent, gifting and "special ability."** In Genesis 47, Joseph brought five of his brothers to meet Pharaoh. When Pharaoh asked them what they did, they responded that they were shepherds. Pharaoh then made a revealing statement: "If any of them have special ability, put them over my own flocks" (Genesis 47:6). He didn't give Joseph's brothers a job because they needed one or because they were Joseph's brothers. He only wanted those with "special ability" to serve on his leadership team. Pharaoh knew that world-class results come from employing world-class leaders and managers. Pharaoh had the good sense to hire Joseph but he also restored the right man in his cupbearer, for he was the one who eventually led Pharaoh to Joseph. Hopefully someone on your team can recognize talent. It doesn't have to be the lead person. When you find someone with that ability, listen to that person. They will save you much aggravation and the pain of a bad hire. And don't ever hire anyone only because they need a job or are related to you or someone already on staff.

7. **Pharaoh promoted youth.** Joseph was only 30

years old when he entered Pharaoh's court. Don't be prejudiced against youth. If you find someone who is talented, hire that person, regardless of their age. Youth can lack experience, but they do have energy and they don't know enough to prevent them from doing saying what everyone has said is impossible.

8. **Pharaoh hired someone with a shady past and no previous experience.** Up to this point, Joseph only had leadership experience in Potiphar's house and the prison. He also had an accusation of sexual harassment hanging over him from Potiphar. Pharaoh looked past that, however, to the needs that only Joseph could address. Almost anyone with talent will have some negatives; you can't find perfect hires. So stop trying and instead find and work with the best talent you can discover.

9. **Pharaoh gave authority and established boundaries.** Pharaoh put Joseph in charge of everything except "the throne." He put Joseph in charge of operations to store food for the famine and then to distribute food in the famine. Joseph's job description and expectations were clear; there was no ambiguity. While Joseph's hiring was a quick one, his job description was clear and well thought out.

10. **Pharaoh was secure in his leadership and had Joseph with him "in the chariot."** Pharaoh had Joseph ride in the chariot as "second-in-command." I have a picture in my mind that Pharaoh was in the same chariot or at least close by. When people honored Joseph, Pharaoh was secure enough that he wasn't threatened by Joseph's wisdom, power or position. Pharaoh was secure in his own leadership. He was taking a chance by putting this newcomer in

charge, but Pharaoh shared his power and prestige with this man recently released from prison.

11. **Pharaoh used his power to empower the right people.** All leaders have power. What distinguishes a good from a great or bad leader is how that power is used. Pharaoh used his power to empower Joseph to do the job that God had gifted him to do. Peter Drucker, father of modern management studies, stated that the job of management is to find out what management is are doing that prevents others from doing their job and then to stop doing it. Pharaoh used his power correctly; he used it to help his team get the job done.

12. **Pharaoh approved the plan and let Joseph carry it out.** Pharaoh listened to Joseph's strategy and then approved it. With his stamp of approval, he then let Joseph do it with a minimum of input or interference. Pharaoh did not micromanage or set up a bureaucracy that slowed things down.

13. **Pharaoh gave Joseph an unlimited travel budget.** The Bible states that Joseph traveled throughout Egypt; he had freedom of movement to get his job done (see Genesis 41:46). If you want to empower your team, let them travel. Give them freedom of movement to go see and learn what they need to get the job done. I am not referring to first class travel to exotic places, but instead trips with purpose to benchmark and observe best practices wherever they may be found. This may be onsite visits or conferences that feature world- class teaching and instruction. If you want the best, let them go and learn from the best.

14. **Pharaoh was concerned for Joseph's personal life.** Pharaoh found a wife for Joseph and then helped him take care of Jacob and his brothers when they came to Egypt. Pharaoh made sure that Joseph shared in the wealth and blessing that was within Pharaoh's power to bestow. Pharaoh made sure that Joseph had a life outside his work position and gave him land and money to go with it.

15. **Pharaoh stayed in touch with reality but let Joseph do his job.** When famine arrived, the people cried out to Pharaoh – but Pharaoh sent them to Joseph and told them to do whatever Joseph told. Wouldn't all like to have a boss or supervisor like that!

CONCLUSIONS

Pharaoh was rewarded well for his exceptional leadership skills. His country was saved from oblivion and suffering. He actually increased his power and position during the famine, because Joseph successfully leveraged their supply of food and seed for land and a future return on their investment. Pharaoh secured a place in history as a good leader, in contrast to his counterpart who wielded heavy-handed, authoritarian control during the time of Moses. Moses' Pharaoh was such a bad leader that he allowed his personal pride and blindness to ruin his country for many centuries to come.

What kind of leader do you want to be? I hope you want to be one like Joseph's Pharaoh. Take some time to reflect on your style as it relates to Pharaoh's and see where you need to improve. Then set about building a more effective team than you have now so that you and your organization can be the fullest, best expression of who it is that God intended for you to be.

APPENDIX FIVE

Servant Leaders

In Luke 22, I find a fascinating story about service. Jesus is gathered in the upper room with His disciples for what is now known as the Last Supper.

> Also a dispute arose among them as to which of them was considered to be greatest. Jesus said to them, "The kings of the Gentiles lord it over them, and those who exercise authority over them call themselves Benefactors. But you are not to be like that. Instead, the greatest among you should be like the youngest, and the one who rules like the one who serves. For who is greater, the one who is at the table or the one who serves? It is not the one who is at the table? But I am among you as one who serves" (Luke 22:24-27).

This isn't the first time that Jesus had this discussion about service with His followers. But even now, as He prepared for His death, He found it necessary to go over it one more time because they were arguing over who had the most significant ministry. He then went on to practice what He preached by giving His life for those same followers.

Service isn't easy, but it's what leaders must do if their leadership is to be complete. It requires humility and a firm grasp on purpose and values. Leaders who serve followers have found the way to prevent power from corrupting their leadership. They've also found a way to keep from manipulating and controlling followers. It's through the simple practice and mentality of service.

The major objection to leaders being servants is generally rooted in something that sounds like this: "I'm not working for people; they are working for me. I won't and can't have employees telling me (leadership) what to do." This reveals a faulty understanding of servant leadership and a bit of insecurity as well.

When I traveled with the Integrity Music worship team, I had numerous opportunities to put this into practice. I determined where we would go, picked the team members, worked out the budget, and made sure all the details were covered (I did this with the help and input of a lot of people). When we got to the concert site, I put on my servant's hat. I made airport runs, picked up the bottled water and air cargo, and did whatever needed to be done to make sure the event was a success.

On Saturday night, I personally handed out paychecks (I always had them ready beforehand) and said thanks for a job well done. I then took everybody to the airport to catch a plane home. I still try to take the same role in whatever project I find myself leading.

Are you a strong leader? If so, can you also be a strong servant? No matter how many mentors or role models you've had, Jesus is still the example that we must follow. And Luke 22:24-27 is Jesus' description of a servant leader. I urge you to follow in Jesus' footsteps by serving those around you while you lead them into the purpose of God for your company, church or ministry.

APPENDIX SIX

The answers to the three questions. "What are my strengths? How do I perform? What are my values?" should enable the individual, and especially the knowledge worker, to decide where he or she belongs. . . . But also knowing the answer to these three questions enables people to say to an opportunity, to an offer, to an assignment: "Yes, I'll do that. But this is the way *I* should be doing it. This is the way it should be structured. This is the way my relationships should be. These are the kind of results you should expect from me, and in this time frame, because *this is who I am*" – Peter F. Drucker, *Management Challenges for the 21st Century*.

APPENDIX SEVEN

Have you ever kept track of the money you spend so you can do a budget? Have you ever kept a record of how much time you were spending in a certain area so you could use your time more effectively? If you have, then you know that those simple steps can help you budget your time and money. Have you ever considered a similar inventory to help clarify your purpose? If not, then maybe this is the week for you to do so.

PAY ATTENTION

Joy is an indicator of what you should be doing, where you should be investing your time and energy. When I ask people what they enjoy doing, I get two responses. The first is, "I don't know." The second is, "I enjoy doing so many things that I'm not sure what *the* thing is that identifies my purpose." So what I am suggesting this week is to keep a record of what you enjoy doing. It's what I'm calling a joy inventory.

For you to do that, you must pay attention to your heart. You must not talk yourself out of how you feel or tell yourself that you should enjoy this or that. For example, here would be my joy inventory from this past week:
1. I didn't enjoy getting stuck in traffic this week to and from my church office.
2. I did not enjoy having a discussion with a staff member and friend about job performance.
3. I enjoyed sitting at the baseball game last Friday evening.
4. I enjoyed getting my desk organized for the first time this year. It's so clean and clutter free!

Here is my joy indicator for Sunday.
1. I enjoyed seeing my friends at church.
2. I did not enjoy listening to the same message in multiple services.

3. I enjoyed selling a few of my latest books to those who asked.
4. I enjoyed my conference call last evening to go over my next trip to Kenya.
5. I am blissful writing the Monday Memo to send to my readers.

So what does this inventory tell me?

THE RESULTS ARE IN

My inventory tells me that I love to write and get things done quickly. I enjoy small groups, but I don't enjoy larger settings where I cannot connect with the people. I like to connect in some small way with people who buy my books and could sign autographs all day! I am competitive and like games I can play against myself, but not against other people (I am not a good loser and never have been, which is why I agonize over the pitiful state of my local pro baseball team). When I read over this inventory, I am doing something unusual as I do. I am giving myself permission to be who I am, to enjoy what I enjoy and not to force trying to feel something that I don't.

I propose that you do one for every day this week. Keep a notebook nearby and write down what you do that gives you joy and what you do that doesn't all week. Then next Sunday, sit down to study the list. Are there any patterns that emerge? How can you do more of what you enjoy and less of what you don't? Is there enough of a pattern to clarify your purpose?

If there isn't, don't worry about it. The patterns you can identify will still help you. If the activities that give you joy are after work hours, why is your work so joy-less? If you aren't doing anything all week that gives you joy, what are you doing with your life? Why is there no joy? What can you do about that?

The objective of this exercise is to get you to pay

attention to your heart, for your heart matters where purpose is concerned. Your purpose doesn't have to make sense to you at first; you simply have to recognize it by the joy it generates. After you identify your purpose, God will show you ways to gain meaning from engaging in purposeful activities more often than you are now.

APPENDIX EIGHT

A Closer Look at What We Know About the Apostle Paul, a Man of Purpose

Paul made tents for a living, but he never saw himself as a "tent maker." What did he have to say about his purpose? In every epistle he wrote, he referred to what he had been born to do and *never* did he write that it was to make tents. He was clear enough to talk about his purpose every chance he had.

- Romans 1:5, 13, 16
- Romans 15:7-29
- 1 Corinthians 1:17, 24
- 1 Corinthians 3:5-15
- 2 Corinthians 5:16-21
- 2 Corinthians 10:12-18
- Galatians 1:15-16
- Galatians 2:2, 7-9
- Ephesians 3:1-10, 7-12
- Philippians 1:12-18
- Colossians 1:27-29
- 1 Thessalonians 1:4-5
- 1 Thessalonians 2:16
- 2 Thessalonians 3:1-4
- 1 Timothy 2:5-7
- 2 Timothy 4:17
- Titus 1:1-3

If you have some knowledge about the Bible, you'll say, "Hey, wait a minute! Paul wrote 13 epistles and only 12 are listed above. I thought you said he referred to his purpose in all 13?" I did say that, and it's true. While Paul did not specifically mention his purpose in his epistle to Philemon, he was writing about an escaped slave who was now a Christian. The whole letter addressed a problem unique to the Gentile world, which was Paul's sphere of ministry.

The book of Acts, which chronicles life and ministry in the early church, spends a great deal of time relating stories of Saul or Paul and his purpose.

- Acts 9:15
- Acts 13:1-4
- Acts 13:47
- Acts 14:27
- Acts 15:3,7
- Acts 21:11, 19-21
- Acts 20:24
- Acts 22:14-21
- Acts 26:16-19

On six separate occasions, Paul had a vision or supernatural visitation. It is of interest that on each occasion, the visitation was to reveal or encourage him in his purpose.

- Acts 9:1-9
- Acts 16:9-10
- Acts 18:9-11
- Acts 22:17
- Acts 23:11
- Acts 27:24

There was a seventh occasion Paul described in 2 Corinthians 12 when he was taken up into the third heaven.

APPENDIX NINE

If

By Rudyard Kipling

If you can keep your head when all about you
Are losing theirs and blaming it on you;
If you can trust yourself when all men doubt you,
But make allowance for their doubting too;
If you can wait and not be tired by waiting,
Or, being lied about, don't deal in lies,
Or, being hated, don't give way to hating,
And yet don't look too good, nor talk too wise;

If you can dream - and not make dreams your master;
If you can think - and not make thoughts your aim;
If you can meet with triumph and disaster
And treat those two imposters just the same;
If you can bear to hear the truth you've spoken
Twisted by knaves to make a trap for fools,
Or watch the things you gave your life to broken,
And stoop and build 'em up with wornout tools;

If you can make one heap of all your winnings
And risk it on one turn of pitch-and-toss,
And lose, and start again at your beginnings
And never breath a word about your loss;
If you can force your heart and nerve and sinew
To serve your turn long after they are gone,
And so hold on when there is nothing in you
Except the Will which says to them: "Hold on";

If you can talk with crowds and keep your virtue,
Or walk with kings - nor lose the common touch;
If neither foes nor loving friends can hurt you;
If all men count with you, but none too much;
If you can fill the unforgiving minute
With sixty seconds' worth of distance run -
Yours is the Earth and everything that's in it,
And - which is more - you'll be a Man my son!

APPENDIX TEN

Servant Leaders

In the last chapter, I outlined several key personal beliefs about leadership that have made their way into my leadership philosophy. They include
1. Leaders are born *and* made
2. Leadership requires a lot of hard work
3. Effective leaders, if they are truly effective, are surrounded by good people
4. Good leaders need to recognize and reward the good people around them
5. Leaders are servants.

Let's look more closely at the fifth one: servant leaders. A number of years ago I read Max DePree's book, *Leadership Is an Art*. It remains today one of my favorite books on leadership. In that book, DePree makes one simple statement about leadership that I have quoted and meditated on in many settings:

The first responsibility of a leader is to define reality. The last is to say thank you. In between the two, the leader must become a servant and a debtor.[1]

That summary is profound and I have found it to be true in my own leadership opportunities again and again.

On the front end, I must define the borders and parameters for those following me. That includes defining the job, its financial objectives, why it is being done, how it fits into the overall picture, and who will do it. At the end, I must say "thank you." And I try to say it with words *and* cash. But in between those two "bookends," I'm indebted to those who are doing the work and I must serve them in whatever way necessary so they can do their job. It's so simple, yet so hard to do!

I find the issue of service one of the hardest concepts

for leaders to grasp. Let's make it more personal—I find it the hardest! For help with this, I've turned to the Bible for both perspective and assistance.

As I do, let me say that I'm impressed with how many management and leadership experts quote from the Bible. Their search for wisdom always seems to lead them there. Yet when I go to conferences and ask them for their church affiliation, many want to let me know right away that they are not "church people." I find it sad that their search for wisdom has led them to the source of wisdom, yet has not affected their personal lives.

I have no such dilemma. I'm a "church people" through and through. For me, the Bible isn't *a* source of truth. It's *the* source of truth and I've found it always to be accurate, especially when it talks about humanity and the issues of life. Enough said. Now let's get back to the issue of service.

In Luke 22, I find a fascinating story about service. Jesus is gathered in the upper room with His disciples for what is now known as the Last Supper.

> Also a dispute arose among them as to which of them was considered to be greatest. Jesus said to them, "The kings of the Gentiles lord it over them' and those who exercise authority over them call themselves Benefactors. But you are not to be like that. Instead, the greatest among you should be like the youngest, and the one who rules like the one who serves. For who is greater, the one who is at the table or the one who serves? It is not the one who is at the table? But I am among you as one who serves" (Luke 22:24-27).

This isn't the first time that Jesus had this discussion about service with His followers. But even now, as He prepared for His death, He found it necessary to go over it one more time because they were arguing over who had the most significant ministry. He then went on to practice what He preached by giving His life for those same followers.

Service isn't easy, but it's what leaders must do if their leadership is to be complete. It requires humility and a firm grasp on purpose and values. Leaders who serve followers have found the way to prevent power from corrupting their leadership. They've also found a way to keep from manipulating and controlling followers. It's through the simple practice and mentality of service.

Robert Greenleaf wrote,

The servant-leader is servant first. It begins with the natural feeling that one wants to serve. Then conscious choice brings one to aspire to lead. The best test is: do those served grow as persons, do they, while being served, become healthier, wiser, freer, more autonomous, more likely themselves to become servants?[2]

The major objection to leaders being servants is generally rooted in something that sounds like this: "I'm not working for people; they are working for me. I won't and can't have employees telling me (leadership) what to do." This reveals a faulty understanding of servant leadership and a bit of insecurity as well.

To clarify this misconception, I turn to Ken Blanchard, the well-known author of One-Minute management fame. He explains traditional leadership,

Most organizations are typically pyramidal in nature. Who is at the top of the organization? The chief executive officer, the chairman, the board of directors. Who is at the bottom? All the employees—the people who do the work. . . . The paradox is that the pyramid needs to be right side up or upside down depending on the task or role.

It's absolutely essential that the pyramid stay upright when it comes to vision, mission, values, and setting major goals. Moses did not go up on the mountain with a committee. People look to leaders for direction, so the traditional hierarchy isn't bad for this aspect of leadership.

Most organizations and managers get in trouble in the implementation phase of the leadership process. The traditional pyramid is kept alive and well. When that happens, who do people think they work for? The person above them. The minute you think you work for the person above you for implementation, you are assuming that person—your boss—is *responsible* and your job is being *responsive* to that boss and to his or her whims or wishes. As a result, all the energy in the organization is moving up the hierarchy, away from customers and the frontline folks who are closest to the action[3]

Blanchard's remedy is to turn the pyramid upside down for the implementation. He further explains, "That creates a very different environment for implementation. If you work for your people, what is the purpose of being a manager? *To help them accomplish their goals.* Your job is to help them win."[4]

So leaders must serve the organization by setting the direction and then serve the employees and customers by equipping everyone that can help the organization accomplish its mission. This fits in perfectly with what Max DePree wrote. First, leaders define reality for the organization—that includes the vision, mission and goals. When it's all over, the leader says "Thank you," because the leader is the caretaker for the organization. In between, *everything* is service—making sure the staff, volunteers and customers have everything *they* need so the organization prospers.

When I traveled with the music team of Worship International, I had numerous opportunities to put this into practice. I determined where we would go, picked the team members, worked out the budget, and made sure all the details were covered (I did this with the help and input of a lot of people). When we got to the concert site, I put on my servant's hat. I made airport runs, picked up the bottled water and air cargo, and did whatever needed to be done to make sure the event was a success.

On Saturday night, I personally handed out the paychecks (I always had them ready beforehand) and said thank you for a job well done. I then took everybody back to the airport to catch a plane home. I still try to take the same role in whatever project I find myself leading.

If you want to do some more study and reading on servant-leaders, then I highly recommend any of Robert Greenleaf's works, specifically:

- *On Becoming a Servant Leader*
- *Seeker and Servant: Reflections on Religious Leadership*
- *The Power of Servant Leadership*
- *Insights on Leadership*

All of the above books are edited by Larry C. Spears, who serves as the director for

The Greenleaf Center for Servant-Leadership
921 E. 86th Street, Suite 200
Indianapolis, IN 46240
(317) 259-1241 (phone)
(317) 259-0560 (fax)
www.greenleaf.org

The Greenleaf Center has annual conferences and training seminars, a resource catalog that contains the books mentioned above, and other programs to help us all understand the implications and strategies of servant leaders.

ENDNOTES

1   Max DePree, *Leadership is an Art* (New York: Dell Publishing, 1989), page 11.
2   Robert K. Greenleaf, *Servant Leadership* (New York: Paulist Press, 1977), page 13.
3   Larry C. Spear, editor, *Insights on Leadership* (New York: John Wiley and Sons, Inc., 1998), page 23.
4   Ibid., page 25.

SCRIPTURE REFERENCES

GENESIS

1:28	February 15	Purpose
31:2	May 13	Emotional Intelligence
31:5	June 16	Emotional Intelligence
40:21-22	November 18	People Skills
41:39-40	June 1	Organization
41:41	October 23	Wisdom

EXODUS

5:7-9	October 27	Persuasion
16:26	February 11	Rest
16:29	February 18	Rest
18:14	June 21	Time Management
18:17-18	November 7	Time Management
18:21-22	October 3	Time Management
20:10-11	February 25	Rest
24:13	February 10	Team Building
31:2-3	June 7	Wisdom
31:3	February 22	Knowledge
35:2-3	August 23	Rest
35:34-35	June 17	Coaching
36:2	June 14	Collaboration

LEVITICUS

1:1-2	September 2	Communication
8:6	September 26	Relationships
10:8	August 11	Motivation
16:31	August 30	Rest
19:1-2	October 7	Communication
23:3	May 12	Rest
23:4	May 19	Rest
23:32	August 16	Rest
25:4	June 29	Rest
25:10	July 13	Rest
25:10-11	July 6	Rest
25:17	October 6	Decision Making
26:3-5	July 10	Knowledge
26:3-5	November 5	Productivity
26:9	October 1	Productivity

NUMBERS

10:6	February 17	Organization
27:18-21	July 22	Coaching

DEUTERONOMY

5:15	May 5	Rest
6:6	April 18	Spiritual Growth
8:17-18	August 28	Finances
17:19-20	June 23	Humility
31:19-20a	January 4	Spiritual Growth

JOSHUA

1:2	June 28	Team Building
1:6	August 1	Personal Development
1:7	November 12	Spiritual Growth
1:9	September 30	Attitude
1:10-11	July 30	Communication
2:8-9	August 15	Influence
2:17-19	September 7	Strategy
6:15-16	October 12	Strategy
6:25	August 4	Change
10:24	December 26	Coaching

JUDGES

5:2	December 15	Decision Making
6:14	December 24	Power
7:17	December 4	Collaboration
8:1-3	December 22	People Skills

RUTH

1:16-17	September 25	Collaboration
1:16-17	October 28	Values
1:18-19	October 30	Collaboration
2:20	October 26	Power
3:2-3	December 8	Coaching

1 SAMUEL

14:6-7	July 18	Collaboration
14:7	January 16	Motivation
14:13	January 26	Collaboration
16:23	May 1	Self-Awareness

1 SAMUEL (continued)

16:23	September 14	Service
17:25	October 16	Goals
17:37-38	September 11	Goals
20:16	July 19	Relationships
25:3	January 10	People Skills
25:10-11	February 14	People Skills
25:14	March 20	People Skills

2 SAMUEL

23:8	March 16	Team Building
23:15-16	March 2	Relationships

1 KINGS

1:11	July 21	Emotional Intelligence
3:9	November 19	Purpose
3:28	April 3	Values
4:29-30	July 11	Wisdom
4:29-30	August 14	Wisdom
6:38	March 22	Goals
7:1	November 20	Goals
10:4-5	November 21	Organization
10:11-12	September 12	Organization
17:4-6	September 6	Rest
17:14	September 13	Rest
19:15-16	March 9	Time Management
19:19	March 30	Influence

2 KINGS

3:11	February 19	Service
7:4	March 12	Decision Making
25:19	March 5	Coaching

1 CHRONICLES

11:6	July 4	Goals
14:15	January 8	Strategy
29:3	December 11	Finances

2 CHRONICLES

1:10	February 23	Wisdom

The Leadership Walk

EZRA

1:1-3	December 16	Communication
4:4	October 13	Change
5:17	August 8	Organization

NEHEMIAH

1:4	January 2	Decision Making
1:11	December 1	Persuasion
2:1-2	June 5	Self-Awareness
2:1-2	December 7	Emotional Intelligence
2:6	July 26	Time Management
6:3-4	March 13	Communication
6:11	March 4	Emotional Intelligence
8:10	July 20	Rest

ESTHER

3:5-6	March 26	Motivation

JOB

3:25-26	November 1	Rest
19:21	July 9	Self-Awareness
25:2	March 23	Organization
33:14-18	August 9	Rest
42:5-6	September 16	Self-Awareness

PSALMS

3:5	December 20	Rest
4:8	November 22	Rest
15:4	March 19	Change
16:7	March 27	Self-Awareness
16:9-10	November 8	Rest
33:11	April 25	Purpose
37:4	February 20	Motivation
55:6	November 15	Rest
62:1	September 20	Rest
63:6	October 18	Rest
75:6-7	August 31	Humility
91:1	September 27	Rest
116:7	October 4	Rest
119:66	March 28	Knowledge
139:1-6	November 26	Knowledge

PSALMS (continued)

139:14	October 9	Personal Development
144:1	December 18	Personal Development
145:3-5	April 26	Goals
146:3-5	December 9	Attitude

PROVERBS

1:5	January 19	Wisdom
1:7	February 29	Ethics
2:5	May 2	Knowledge
6:9-11	November 29	Rest
8:14	March 29	Wisdom
8:15	November 10	Decision Making
11:1	September 24	Ethics
12:10	May 11	Relationships
12:15	January 30	Coaching
13:10	April 9	Coaching
13:11	August 20	Ethics
14:4	July 24	Productivity
14:23	August 27	Productivity
14:28	October 17	Organization
15:14	January 18	Knowledge
15:22	March 18	Strategy
16:5	February 5	Humility
16:10 LB	April 1	Power
16:12	May 8	Values
16:23	May 7	Persuasion
18:9	August 7	Goals
18:12	March 11	Humility
19:20	May 14	Coaching
19:21	February 12	Strategy
19:23	December 6	Rest
20:8	June 12	Values
20:10	April 4	Ethics
20:18	April 22	Strategy
20:28	May 9	Ethics
22:26-27	October 25	Rest
22:29	February 9	Personal Development
25:2	March 14	Spiritual Growth
25:15	February 27	Persuasion

The Leadership Walk
PROVERBS (continued)

25:26	January 25	Ethics
27:9	April 6	Relationships
27:18	August 10	Service
28:15	September 9	People Skills
29:4	June 13	Ethics
29:12	October 29	Ethics
29:18	August 3	Strategy

ECCLESIASTES

2:23	October 11	Rest
3:1-3	July 1	Change
3:23	December 13	Rest
4:12	March 1	Collaboration
9:16	May 6	Wisdom
10:6	May 4	Power
12:9	January 13	Organization

SONG OF SOLOMON

3:7-8	November 30	Power

ISAIAH

45:1	March 21	Purpose
53:2	May 29	People Skills
56:2-3	April 28	Rest
58:13-14	April 21	Rest

JEREMIAH

1:5	September 10	Purpose
1:17	September 22	Persuasion
3:15	August 25	Coaching
17:22	July 27	Rest
27:2-3	September 19	Influence

LAMENTATIONS

3:58-60	September 3	Spiritual Growth

EZEKIEL

34:2	September 23	Values
36:26	February 13	Change

DANIEL

1:3-5	September 8	Change
1:5	April 19	Personal Development
4:18	September 29	Coaching
6:10	February 8	Spiritual Growth
6:18	December 27	Rest

HOSEA

3:4	November 4	Attitude
4:6	June 6	Knowledge
5:10	December 25	Ethics
10:4	November 16	Strategy
12:7-8	December 2	Values
14:9	September 18	Wisdom

JOEL

2:1-2	September 15	Motivation

AMOS

8:4-6	April 14	Rest

OBADIAH

1:15	December 23	Motivation

JONAH

3:6	May 23	Spiritual Growth

MICAH

2:1-2	December 3	Ethics
3:9-11	August 17	Power

NAHUM

3:16	August 21	Collaboration
3:16	August 22	Pow Relationships er

HABAKKUK

1:7	December 14	Humility
2:4-5	November 24	Motivation
3:17-18	December 17	Spirituality

ZEPHANIAH

2:15	October 20	Motivation
2:4-5	November 24	Motivation

HAGGAI

1:5-6	December 21	Strategy
1:13-15	December 19	Team Building

ZECHARIAH

7:8-10	November 13	Personal Development
10:2	November 23	Service

MALACHI

4:1-2	October 5	Humility

MATTHEW

1:19	April 16	Decision Making
2:16	July 14	Power
2:16	September 21	Power
6:24	March 8	Finances
7:3-5	October 10	Team Building
9:2	January 29	Emotional Intelligence
9:9	June 8	Influence
12:8	February 4	Rest
12:12	January 28	Rest
16:13	January 27	Relationships
19:13-14	August 5	People Skills
20:28	January 15	Service
21:46	September 1	Decision Making
23:4	May 10	Collaboration
23:5	July 16	Values
23:11-12	July 7	Service
23:12	April 15	Humility
26:35	January 17	Self-Awareness
26:35	October 21	Self-Awareness
27:19	November 25	Self-Awareness

MARK

2:27	January 7	Rest
3:4	January 14	Rest
3:20	December 12	Time Management
5:30-32	November 2	Emotional Intelligence
6:31	June 22	Rest
12:13-14	June 30	Strategy

LUKE

1:3-4	May 21	Decision Making
1:51-52	July 29	Decision Making
3:11	April 12	Finances
4:16	January 21	Rest
6:24	May 17	Finances
6:41	November 3	Coaching
6:45	February 7	Communication
7:38	April 24	People Skills
8:45	April 8	Emotional Intelligence
11:52	June 4	Motivation
11:52	October 22	Knowledge
13:15	March 3	Rest
14:28	February 6	Decision Making
16:10-12	July 17	Ethics
16:13	June 20	Finances
16:14	November 6	Finances
22:24-26a	March 25	Service
22:26-27	June 3	Service
23:12	June 15	Relationships
23:42-43	April 13	Time Management

JOHN

5:16	May 26	Rest
7:23-24	April 7	Rest
9:16	March 24	Rest
13:3-4	April 29	Service
13:3-5	July 2	People Skills
13:12-15	October 19	Service
13:17	May 18	Time Management
14:12	December 10	Productivity
15:4	April 11	Productivity

ACTS

2:7-8	June 25	Communication
4:32	May 3	Influence
6:3-4	April 27	Organization
7:22	May 24	Personal Development
7:23-26	June 27	Personal Development
7:25	January 11	Purpose

The Leadership Walk
ACTS (continued)

10:13-14	April 23	Change
11:2-3	May 28	Change
12:20-21	June 10	Power
13:1-3	January	Team Building
14:1	May 27	Strategy
16:10	June 24	Decision Making
17:2	February 28	Values
17:2	March 17	Rest
20:34	August 29	Time Management
26:13-14	July 3	Purpose
26:28-29	January 23	Persuasion
27:18	July 5	Organization

ROMANS

15:5	March 6	Attitude

1 CORINTHIANS

3:8-9	May 30	Purpose
9:17	July 23	Attitude
12:7	April 5	Collaboration
12:14	April 20	Team Building
12:14	October 15	Purpose
14:9	May 22	Communication
16:21	January 3	Communication

2 CORINTHIANS

10:8	January 22	Power

GALATIANS

2:7	August 6	Purpose
2:14	September 28	Emotional Intelligence
4:12	August 18	Persuasion
5:15	October 14	People Skills
5:22	May 16	Productivity
5:26	August 12	Self-Awareness
6:3	July 28	Humility
6:7	June 26	Spiritual Growth
6:9	July 31	Spiritual Growth

EPHESIANS

4:22-23	April 10	Attitude

PHILIPPIANS

2:5	January 31	Attitude
2:5-6	February 26	Power
2:19-23	January 1	Humility
3:8-11	August 19	Values
3:14	January 12	Goals
3:14	May 31	Goals

COLOSSIANS

1:10	February 1	Faithfulness
1:28-29	August 26	Attitude
2:16	March 10	Rest
3:23-24	April 30	Motivation
4:6	June 11	Persuasion
4:16	April 17	Communication

1 THESSALONIANS

2:9	January 24	Values

2 THESSALONIANS

3:7	November 28	Influence
3:9	October 24	Influence

1 TIMOTHY

1:15	February 21	Self-Awareness
3:1-2	July 12	Influence
4:15-16	March 7	Productivity
4:15-16	June 19	Productivity
6:10	July 25	Finances

2 TIMOTHY

3:15-16	August 13	Knowledge
4:13	September 17	Wisdom

TITUS

3:10	November 14	Team Building

PHILEMON

8	January 20	Influence
14	February 24	Influence

HEBREWS

1:9	March 15	Personal Development
1:9	July 8	Motivation
2:1	July 15	Persuasion
3:18	June 9	Rest
4:1	June 2	Rest
4:9-10	March 31	Rest
4:11	August 2	Rest
4:12	May 15	Attitude
11:6	October 8	Spiritual Growth
13:1	May 25	Team Building

JAMES

1:5-7	November 27	Wisdom
1:19	April 2	Persuasion

1 PETER

4:10	June 18	Attitude
5:2	February 2	Finances
5:6	May 20	Humility

2 PETER

1:5-8	January 5	Personal Development
3:8	February 3	Time Management

1 JOHN

1:8-10	August 24	Emotional Intelligence
2:16-17	November 9	Humility
3:17	October 2	Finances
4:7	September 5	Team Building

2 JOHN

1:5	October 31	Relationships
1:12	November 11	Communication

3 JOHN

1:2	September 4	Personal Development

JUDE

| 1:16 | December 5 | Relationships |

REVELATION

| 21:5 | January 9 | Change |
| 21:5 | November 17 | Change |

ABOUT THE AUTHOR

John Stanko was born in Pittsburgh, Pennsylvania. After graduating from St. Basil's Prep School in Stamford, Connecticut, he attended Duquesne University where he received his bachelor's and master's degrees in economics in 1972 and 1974 respectively.

Since then, John has served as an administrator, teacher, consultant, author, and pastor in his professional career. He holds a second master's degree in pastoral ministries, and earned his doctorate in pastoral ministries from Liberty Theological Seminary in Houston, Texas in 1995. He also completed a second doctor of ministry degree at Reformed Presbyterian Theological Seminary in Pittsburgh.

John has taught extensively on the topics of time management, life purpose and organization, and has conducted leadership and purpose training sessions throughout the United States and in 32 countries. He is also certified to administer the DISC and other related personality assessments as well as the Natural Church Development profile for churches. In 2006, he earned the privilege to facilitate for The Pacific Institute of Seattle, a leadership and personal development program, and for The Leadership Circle, a provider of cultural and executive 360-degree profiles. He has authored fifteen books and written for many publications around the world.

John founded a personal and leadership development company, called PurposeQuest, in 2001 and today travels the world to speak, consult and inspire leaders and people everywhere. From 2001-2008, he spent six months a year in Africa and still enjoys visiting and working on that continent, while teaching for Geneva College's Masters of Organizational Leadership and the Center for Urban Biblical Ministry in his hometown of Pittsburgh, Pennsylvania. John has been married for 38 years to Kathryn Scimone

Stanko, and they have two adult children. In 2009, John was appointed the administrative pastor for discipleship at Allegheny Center Alliance Church on the North Side of Pittsburgh where he served for five years. Most recently, John founded Urban Press, a publishing service designed to tell stories of the city, from the city and to the city.

You can stay in touch with John's world through the following sites and radio shows:
www.purposequest.com
www.johnstanko.us
www.stankobiblestudy.com
www.stankomondaymemo.com
www.blogtalkradio.com/acacthreads
www.blogtalkradio.com/genevacollegemsol

or via email at johnstanko@gmail.com

John also does extensive relief and community development work in Kenya. You can see some of his projects at:
www.purposequest.com/contributions

PurposeQuest International
PO Box 8882
Pittsburgh, PA 15221-0882

Additional Titles By John W. Stanko

A Daily Taste of Proverbs
A Daily Dose of Proverbs
What Would Jesus Ask You Today?
The Price of Leadership
Changing the Way We Do Church
Unlocking the Power of Your Purpose
Beyond Purpose
Life Is A Gold Mine: Can You Dig It?

www.ingramcontent.com/pod-product-compliance
Lightning Source LLC
LaVergne TN
LVHW052257070426
835507LV00036B/3102